TARGET TOKYO

The group commander began the briefing. By the time he had finished, one could have heard him breathe, so silent were the big briefing halls. The hundreds of fliers assembled before him were in deep shock.

They were to fly without guns, without ammunition. They were to attack at low altitude, which meant they would be sitting ducks for flak. They were to attack individually, which contradicted everything they had ever been taught about formation flying.

And their first target was Tokyo—the most heavily defended area in all Japan....

THE NIGHT TOKYO BURNED

HOITO EDOIN

ST. MARTIN'S PRESS / NEW YORK

THE NIGHT TOKYO BURNED

Copyright © 1987 by Hoito Edoin.

Library of Congress Catalog Card Number: 87-13978

ISBN: 0-312-91385-0 Can. ISBN: 0-312-91386-9

Printed in the United States of America

St. Martin's Press hardcover edition published 1987
First St. Martin's Press mass market edition/May 1989

10 9 8 7 6 5 4 3 2 1

Contents

Dedication/vii · 1. B-29s over Japan/1

2. The B-29s/10 · 3. Japan's Defenses/23

4. The Attack Plan/34 · 5. Mission No. 40/40

6. Tokyo, March 9, 1945/47

7. Bombs in the Night/58

8. The Long Night/77 · 9. Tokyo Aflame/95

10. Tokyo Aftermath/109 · 11. Nagoya/112

12. Results/119 · 13. Osaka/129

14. Kobe/150 · 15. Kobe Aftermath/164

Contents

16. Nagoya Revisited/172 · 17. Trouble Comes/182

18. Tokyo Again/191 · 19. Kobe Rerun/203

20. Refinements/215 · 21. Crescendo/226

Acknowledgments/240 · Bibliographical Note/242

Index/244

Dedication

This book is dedicated to the memory of all the people of Japan who were killed by the firebombings, and to all the Americans who were killed in killing them. Both sides were victims of the same malady: Man's inability to refrain from the mass murder called war.

If this book has any lasting value, it will be to remind its readers of the horrors that war in the twentieth century wreaks on civilian populations. The result of twentieth-century warfare is not likely to improve; rather, it will most certainly get worse, for, as the Marquis Kido said, the hundreds of B-29s with their firebombs were bad enough, but in August 1945, Japan learned that one B-29 with one bomb could do almost as much damage as three hundred planes had done in the past. Today it does not even take an airplane; it can all be done by pushing a button.

1
B-29s
OVER
JAPAN

WEDNESDAY, MARCH 7, 1945. ELEVEN B-29 BOMBERS HAD AP-
peared over Japan on Tuesday, the Japanese newspapers reported.
Only eleven. That was how it had been going for three days,
since the big raid of March 4, when about 150 B-29 "superfortresses" hit Tokyo.

"Blind bombing," Imperial General Headquarters called it. The
big silver planes had come in at high altitude at about eight-thirty
in the morning, and their bombs had started a number of fires in
the city. But the Tokyo fire department had extinguished them all
by ten-thirty. Life had returned to as near normal as it could in
this fourth year of the war. Tokyo had been hit before, most
recently on February 25 by B-29s and some 600 aircraft from the
American carrier task forces, which now dared come right into
Japanese home waters.

The Japanese air force rose to meet the invaders, of course, and
in the many battles that followed, one of those killed was Captain
Ryo Kurusu, son of Admiral Saburo Kurusu, one of the envoys
sent to America on the eve of the Pearl Harbor attack. Captain

Kurusu, American-born, was just then involved in serious engineering studies aiming at the development of a fighter plane designed specifically to combat the B-29 bombers.

The next bombing, that of March 4, had followed a familiar pattern: four sections of B-29s, coming in from different directions, dropped high explosive and incendiary bombs from high altitude. It was a typical stormy late-winter day in Tokyo; the cloud cover masked the city and the B-29s from the area's fighter fields. The bombing was not very effective, either by the reckoning of Imperial Headquarters authorities or by those of the U.S. XXI Bomber Command.

Thursday, March 8, 1945. In the center of the front page of every Japanese newspaper ran the Imperial Rescript proclaimed by Emperor Hirohito on December 8, 1941. The newspapers carried that two-column article on the eighth day of every month, as they had since the war began. Now it was headlined "Imperial Rescript Observance Day," and it had a new purpose: to fortify the spirit of the Japanese people and convince them that the lost war must go on.

That day the newspaper reported on the number of B-29 bombers that had been spotted over Japan on the previous day. One lone B-29 had flown over Hiroshima and Okayama and had dropped bombs near Okayama. Another single plane had bombed Shikoku. Another had raided Kochi City.

Far more interesting to residents of Tokyo was the coming of another single B-29, which had flown over the Kanto Plain, Honshu Island's primary industrial district, and over Tokyo, but had not dropped any bombs. The sirens had howled, of course, and the people had prepared for the worst.

Nearly every Tokyo family had dug a pit, either under the house or in the garden, and covered it over with boards. The children, the women, and sometimes the men rushed into these pits as the air-raid sirens moaned, and waited out the raids. The pits were no use against a direct hit, of course, but did protect against fragments and debris.

2

What seemed remarkable to the people of Tokyo was that so little bombing was being done. Eight B-29s appeared that day, just a handful when compared to previous raids, and most of the planes did not bomb at all.

Friday, March 9, 1945. Tokyo's newspapers reported that on Thursday five B-29s had carried out long reconnaissance flights over the Kanto Plain. Three of the bombers came in at about 9:30 A. M. The fourth arrived about a half-hour later and also flew over Nagoya. The fifth came at eleven.

Those who saw the planes wondered what they were doing, for they dropped no bombs, but lazed along at high altitude, circling.

The Japanese had by this time become accustomed to the shock of bombing. In the past three and a half months, various cities had been bombed twenty-two times by some 2,100 individual flights. The last bombing of any significance anywhere had been that March 4 attack on Tokyo. In these attacks, a large number of B-29s had been shot down or destroyed by suicide attacks, although not nearly so many as Imperial General Headquarters claimed. From the beginning of the war, the Japanese government had fallen into the trap of believing its own propaganda and concealing from the people the defeats that followed the surprising victories of the first days. The habit had persisted even after the war turned around in 1943 and Japan began her retreat, and the exaggerations and outright untruths became so prevalent that few civilians believed what their government was telling them, although they did believe in the necessity to continue fighting in the absence of a reasonable peace proposal.

The war was going very badly for Japan and her one remaining Axis ally, Nazi Germany. Benito Mussolini, the former dictator of Italy, had now fled to Brescia in northern Italy, where, protected by Field Marshal Kesselring's German troops, he issued a steady stream of propaganda, but even the propaganda indicated what was really happening to the Axis, which only two years earlier had seemed ready to swallow the world.

Italy's fate, said Il Duce, was irretrievably linked with Germany's. "We must remember that Germany and Italy are so closely related that they must live or die together. Germany is fighting for the very existence of the country and will not be defeated. Threatened with the complete destruction of the state, the German army as well as the people are maintaining a heroic stand in order to safeguard their Fatherland from destruction."

The threat was not confined to Europe; the Allied powers had made it clear that they would accept nothing less than "unconditional surrender" from Germany, what was left of Fascist Italy, and Japan. This was what Mussolini meant when he spoke of the threat of destruction of the state, and the men in power in Japan knew that it applied to them as well as to the Germans and Italians. Everywhere, the Axis powers were in deep trouble.

On the Eastern Front of the European war, the Soviets were pounding at Kuestrin Fortress, just a hundred miles from Berlin. On the Western Front, American troops penetrated into the center of Cologne, and Canadian tanks moved up on the eastern bank of the Rhine River.

On Iwo Jima, American marines were advancing against determined Japanese opposition. Casualties were high, but the American advance never faltered. In Burma, British forces crossed the Irrawaddy River at Nyaungu. In the Philippines, Americans continued to advance on Leyte Island. The Japanese, said Imperial General Headquarters, "are boxing carefully with the enemy with firm faith in final victory."

Each new defeat, each reversal, brought a new outpouring of rhetoric from Imperial General Headquarters. And yet, as far as the B-29s were concerned, IGHQ's claims were not as absurd as might be expected. The Japanese had destroyed 102 B-29s out of the total 2,100 sorties. That was about a 5 percent loss, and if it was acceptable to the American high authorities, it was not acceptable to the XXI Bomber Command, particularly because, as they and Imperial Headquarters both knew, the big bombers were not doing very much damage to the Japanese war effort.

B-29s over Japan

The attention of the people of Tokyo, however, was focused on the bombing raids that had grown ever more frequent since the American capture of the Mariana Islands and the reconstruction of Japanese airfields to accommodate the enormous B-29 bombers that had been built for the precise purpose of bombing Japan.

On the front pages of the newspapers of March 9, Emperor Hirohito called attention to the remarkable exploits of several Japanese fliers who had distinguished themselves by conducting ramming attacks against B-29 bombers in the Tokyo raids of February 10. One was Lieutenant Heikichi Yoshizawa.

> Lieutenant Yoshizawa, who shot down two B-29s and damaged four others in a series of B-29 raids on Tokyo, also damaged another enemy bomber over Shimodate when the B-29s attacked the Kanto district on February 10 this year. Although his plane was damaged by enemy gunfire he deliberately launched a ramming attack on another enemy plane and downed it, thereby meeting glorious death.

So went the Emperor's commendation, by far the highest praise that any loyal Japanese military man could expect. The Yoshizawa story was followed by that of Corporal Saburo Umehara. He had rammed the lead plane of the third section of B-29s, the Emperor said.

The stories were true enough. On that raid the Americans lost a dozen B-29s, several of them to the ramming attacks by Japanese pilots that seemed to be their most effective weapon against the big bombers. Ramming was necesary because to reach the high altitudes at which the B-29s flew, the Japanese fighters had to be stripped of all surplus weight, and that meant even the machine guns and cannon. For some inexplicable reason, although the Japanese had expected the B-29s for more than a year before they arrived, when they began bombing Japan proper

5

from the Marianas in November 1944, the homeland air defenses included neither antiaircraft guns capable of reaching 30,000 feet nor fighter planes that could climb that high and perform to specifications. It could have been done. In 1943 the Japanese knew very well what the Americans were doing. Reports from the Boeing aircraft factory in Seattle told of the production of a new "superbomber," and American air force generals revealed that it was being built exclusively for use against Japan. Enough of the performance capability was leaked through American media to neutral media in Buenos Aires, Lisbon, Zurich, and Stockholm so that the Japanese knew this plane would be far more formidable than the B-17s that were ravaging Germany. Japan had the engineering capability to produce fighters that could fly at 30,000 feet. The problem was a matter of priorities; if such fighter planes were to be produced, then something else would have to give, and no one in the Japanese military establishment had the imagination to project a future that included a sky over Tokyo filled with enormous enemy bombers. General Tojo had promised that Japan would never be bombed. The military was entrapped by its own propaganda. If there were men who could predict the future, they did not have the authority to do anything about it. So the production of the old-line fighters and bombers continued into the middle of 1944, although it was known that the Americans now possessed superior fighters in the highly developed Grumman, just going into the F6F phase, the P-38 interceptor fighter, and the P-51 Mustang fighter.

When, on November 24, 1944, the Mariana bases were ready and the first major strike against the Japanese Empire was carried out, the B-29s came in high and the Japanese antiaircraft guns popped away futilely, with their shells bursting 5,000 feet below the bombers. The fighters climbed desperately but could not pull up any closer than the antiaircraft guns.

It became apparent that emergency measures had to be taken, and as everywhere else on the fighting fronts in this fourth year of

the Pacific war, such measures meant suicide attacks, a simulta-
neous indicator of Japanese official desperation and the determination of the government not to surrender.

As a careful reader of the Japanese press would have learned on
Friday, March 9, 1945, there was a special reason for the attack
on Iwo Jima. Admiral Harry Yarnell, former commander of the
American Asiatic Fleet, had written an article for an American
magazine that had been picked up by the neutral press and appeared in *Yomiuri Shimbun* on March 9. The article stated that the
purpose of the attack on Iwo Jima was to secure a new airfield.
That meant an airfield for fighter planes, which would then begin
to accompany the B-29s all the way to Tokyo, making their
bombing missions that much more effective. The newspapers, on
this March morning, showed little indication of the desperate situation of Japan's war effort.

For months, since the fall of Saipan in July 1944, the vast majority of the Japanese people had known that the war was lost. A
constant reader of the Japanese press could sense the truth, no
matter what Imperial General Headquarters claimed. One by
one, the island bastions were falling. By the spring of 1945, the
Empire had contracted almost to its perimeters of the 1930s.
China, which had absorbed some 5 million troops, was not the
asset Japan had hoped for, but a continuing liability, where the
Japanese occupied the cities, but the Chinese held the countryside. The drain on Japanese resources was constant.

True, the Dutch East Indies were still largely in Japanese hands,
but shipping had been so badly reduced by the ravages of Admiral
Charles Lockwood's Pacific Fleet submarines that only a slender
trickle of oil was coming to the homeland. Indochina was Japan's
new rice barrel, but the rice rotted on the wharves because shipping was not available. In Japan, food was in desperately short
supply, and the main dietary item of Tokyo citizens was sweet
potatoes. Anything else was likely to be obtained only by a bar-
tering trip to the farmers in the countryside. Many of the chil-

dren of Tokyo had been sent to relatives in the country or in cities less likely to be the focus of air attacks. Others had gone to official camps across the country. On March 5 the Dai Nippon Mothers' Association announced a new plan to increase the number of women and children moved out of Tokyo to Yamanashi Prefecture, which had been chosen as the safest place. They would be housed in temples and other public buildings, accompanied by gynecologists, midwives, and pediatricians. Their moving expenses and food allowances would be guaranteed by the Tokyo civic authorities. Bedding and all other necessities would be provided. Mothers wishing to take advantage of the new offer were invited to apply to the Aliku Hospital in Moriokacho, Asaboku. The new evacuation would begin in the middle of March.

Anyone who had the resources to leave Tokyo was likely to have left by now. The people who remained were either too poor or had their work there, and a surprising amount of it was war work. Every sort of small factory had been turned to the production of ammunition and weapons. Hundreds of workers were even building parts of weapons at home or in community factories. In effect, Tokyo had become one huge arsenal.

The Americans had learned that the Japanese system consisted of the farming out of industrial production by central manufacturers, so that small home industries carried out a good deal of the manufacture of the components of defense products. Just now, in the Tokyo area, a number of factories around the Sumida River area were assigned production quotas for hand grenades, to be stockpiled for that day envisaged by Imperial Headquarters when every man, woman, and child in Japan would become a front-line soldier. Many households were making parts of grenades—firing pins, casings, and all but the explosive components—which were fitted together by experts at the bigger factories. On this day, March 9, the Americans had already decided that they would have to find some new technique to attack these "feeder industries." They had found the technique, and the respite of five days from the bombing in the industrial areas was being used by the 20th Air Force to prepare for a whole new method of attack. The Japanese, of course, did not know this, although they wondered why the B-29s had stopped coming over in force, and why so few of them dropped any bombs at all.

2
THE
B-29s

IN THE LATE WINTER OF 1945, THE AMERICANS OF THE 20TH AIR Force were still learning how to use that awesome weapon—the B-29 bomber—to strike the Japanese most effectively and destroy the enemy's war efforts.

The first efforts had come in 1944. At the Cairo Conference, late in November 1943, President Franklin Roosevelt, Winston Churchill, and Chiang Kai-shek had discussed the best methods of defeating the Japanese in the Pacific Theater. Roosevelt had announcd that the Americans had developed a new superbomber, which ought to be capable of reaching Japan from airfields in western China, and it was agreed that the new aircraft would be based in India and around Chengdu in Szechuan Province in China. But even before the B-29s reached India and China, it was apparent that the distances were too great for any really effective bombing campaign. The big bombers, called Superfortresses, required so much fuel to travel the thousands of miles that their payloads of bombs had to be minimal. Knowing this, the air force made strong representations to the Joint Chiefs of Staff about the need for capture of a base close to Japan. Thus, the capture of the Mariana Islands was decided upon in March 1944, and the planners at Pearl Harbor began their work.

On April 2, 1944, the first operational B-29 landed at the Chakulia air base in India. On April 24 the first B-29 to fly "the hump" landed at Kwanghan, China. Two days later a group of B-29s flying into China were intercepted by Japanese fighters, which made a few passes. The B-29s were hardly ready for a fight, since most of their machine guns were inoperable. Fortunately for the B-29s, the Japanese were so interested in observing these enormous new bombers that they did not make a serious effort to shoot them down, and there were no casualties on either side.

In India the B-29s began their missions. The first attack was made on the railroad shops at Bangkok. Ninety-eight B-29s set out, and seventy-seven of them bombed. Five planes were lost to accident. The attacks on Southeast Asian targets from the airfields near Calcutta were successful enough, but the damage had to be regarded as limited, not the sort of work that would seriously hinder the Japanese war effort.

At the China bases it was learned quickly enough that wind and weather conditions worked against the efficacy of long-distance attacks. The B-29s had to stage from their western China airfields to fields farther east. This increased the danger of attack from the Japanese air forces. On July 7, 1944, fourteen B-29s operating out of the Chengdu airfield headed for Japan. They bombed Sasebo, Omura, and Tobata on Kyushu Island. These cities represented the farthest point the B-29s could practically reach in Japan from Chengdu, and that was the far western sector of the home islands, not by any means the center of Japanese industrial capacity.

A few more raids were conducted on bases in Manchuria and Kyushu, but little was accomplished. Then in July the Americans captured Saipan Island and began the assault on Tinian. Before Tinian fell, the engineers were already hard at work on the Saipan airfields, lengthening the runways to handle the long-range bombers.

On August 20, 1944, B-29s from the Chengdu bases bombed the Imperial Iron and Steel Works at Yawata. It was an experiment. Sixty-one planes attacked in daylight and ten more came along at night. But the attrition rate was very high; fourteen bombers were lost, one to Japanese antiaircraft fire and four to Japanese fighters. That was the day the Japanese learned two techniques that were successful against the B-29s: one Japanese pilot bombed a B-29 from above, and destroyed it. Another rammed a bomber, killing himself, but bringing down the B-29.

All this was preliminary. On August 24, 1944, the first B-29s rolled down the long runway of the new field on Saipan. The ground support forces were on the water heading for the Marianas too, and would arrive in mid-September.

During this time, a number of command changes had jolted the 20th Air Force and its component forces. On August 28 Major General Lauris Norstad took command of the 20th Air Force. And on August 29, General Curtis LeMay became commander of the XX Bomber Command.

But operations were still centered in China. In September, Le May accompanied a mission that hit the Showa Steel Works at Anshan, Manchuria. He saw for himself the limitations of distance.

The Japanese responded to the Anshan raid. They sent fighters and bombers from Central China bases against the Chengdu fields, and damaged one B-29 at Hsinching (Xinching). They also bombed and strafed the headquarters area. The fact was made much of by Tokyo, where Imperial General Headquarters indicated that the Japanese had hit the major B-29 base. Let the B-29s come to Japan, they said. Immediately they would be destroyed.

The technicians in the Marianas worked at top speed, but still in October, the B-29s were flying from the Chengdu fields. The Japanese began bombing regularly. To relieve the pressure from Japanese fighters, P-61 night fighters were brought by the Americans to the Chengdu fields, but the effort was not very successful. What with a perennial shortage of fuel, all of which had to be flown in across the Himalayas, and a shortage of parts and even of technicians, China was not working out well as a base for the big bombers.

So it was with great relief that the XX Bomber Command learned on October 12 that the first B-29 had landed at Saipan and that the XXI Bomber Command was setting up there. The situation was not ideal; there was still no intermediate airfield between the Marianas and Japan from which fighters could be flown to escort the bombers to and from the target. But from Saipan and Tinian and even Guam, the B-29s would be able to carry significant bomb loads against the enemy.

On October 14 the B-29s from China undertook their most ambitious mission yet. One hundred and three bombers hit the aircraft plant at Okayama on Honshu Island. It was the deepest penetration of Japan yet. From this point on for two weeks they would fly against targets on Formosa to neutralize that island's air bases in preparation for the landings on Leyte in the Philippines.

The B-29s were operating every few days now from Chengdu. Then, on October 28, the XXI Bomber Command launched its first mission from the Marianas against the Japanese submarine base at Dublon in the Caroline Islands. It was not much of a raid. The pilots were green, and the planes were new and stiff. Only a third of the bombs fell in the general target area. The raid was so far from successful that General Haywood S. Hansell, commander of the XXI Bomber Command, who was along to observe, decided it had to be flown over again, and it was, on October 30. The results, unhappily, were not much better.

On November 5, 1944, came a raid in which the B-29 pilots really had their hearts. Twenty-four B-29s hit the airfields at Iwo Jima, in preparation for the coming invasion of that island. Iwo Jima was a solid piece of volcanic rock, worth virtually nothing except as a military base, but to the U.S. Army Air Force it was worth almost any price, because from here the fighters could be brought up, make the trip to Tokyo and back, and give that extra bit of protection to the bombers that were going to try to knock Japan out of the war.

On November 8 the bombers hit Iwo Jima again. But now they were encountering what they would so often find over Japan: very bad weather. Of seventeen planes, only six managed to bomb visually through a hole in the cloud cover over the island. The rest did not bomb at all. And the Japanese fighters were up in force. The new tactics, tried over Japan, had been brought to Iwo Jima, too. Several Japanese planes managed to get above the bombers and drop phosphorous bombs on them. One plane was damaged, and another was forced to ditch on the way home, the first bomber lost by the XXI Bomber Command. In the tents on the Mariana bases, there was a lot of talk about the need to go in at higher altitude to protect the bombers.

Early in November the B-29s hit Dublon base once more, and again with not very good results. This was the last of the training missions of the XXI Bomber Command. Soon the going would become much rougher; the next target was Tokyo.

On November 24 the XXI Bomber Command flew its first mission against Tokyo. One hundred and eleven silver aircraft took off under General Emmett O'Donnell, commander of the 73rd Bomb Wing, who was piloting *Dauntless Dotty*. The primary target was the Musashino aircraft factory, but only thirty-five B-29s managed to find that target. Fifty other bombers dropped their high explosives on docks, and just about anywhere in the urban area of Tokyo. Seventeen planes did not make the scene at all, aborting for one reason or another on the way to Japan. The rest—nine planes—just did not bomb, for one reason or another.

The B-29s arrived over Tokyo at noon, and the air-raid sirens, which had been screaming since the formations reached the coastal waters, kept up their wailing. Japanese stopped in the streets to watch the silvery formations above. It was Tokyo's first experience with an air raid since the Jimmy Doolittle "spectacular" of 1942, but since the fall of Saipan, everyone was expecting it to come. *B-san*, the wiseacres of Tokyo called the big bombers, but their name, half derogatory, half respectful, was not to last long. Too much was now at stake for joking.

From the air bases and air defense headquarters in Tokyo, the Japanese counted seventy planes over the Tokyo targets. Imperial General Headquarters claimed that the air defenses destroyed three B-29s, not far from the true figure of one rammed and one lost to fuel shortage, which might have been caused by damage to the fuel tanks.

The effectiveness of the bombing was marred seriously by the high altitude—30,000 feet—at which the planes came in. That meant there was not a great deal of contact with the enemy fighters, which came up in droves, but could not get within shooting distance of the bombers, since the effective ceiling of Japanese fighters was still 25,000 feet. Nor could the antiaircraft guns reach the invaders.

Finally, one stripped-down fighter did manage to get up high enough to ram a bomber, shearing off the right horizontal stabilizer. So the bomber went tumbling down into the sea off Honshu, the first XXI Bomber Command plane to be lost to enemy action. One other B-29 ditched when it ran out of fuel on the way home. The B-29 machine gunners claimed a total of seven Japanese fighters shot down.

The Japanese did not mention the lost fighters—they seldom did these days. But both sides agreed that the damage was very slight. It was, after all, the first B-29 raid on the capital, and everyone concerned was edgy. The bomb loads were not very heavy. The bombing from 30,000 feet was not very effective. The bombs started some fires, but did not destroy any Japanese factories. Within two hours the Tokyo fire department had put out the fires, and the damage-control parties were clearing away the debris from the bombs that fell on houses and in the streets.

Three days later the B-29s were over Tokyo again. This time

the eighty-one planes missed the targets completely: the Mus-ashino and Nakajima aircraft factories. Their bombs fell on the city and down by the docks, again doing very little damage.

"Blind bombing" was the derogatory term used by the Japanese to describe this high-altitude area bombing.

The concern of IGHQ about the B-29s was shown when Japanese air units were ordered to concentrate attacks on the airfields of Saipan and Tinian.

On November 29, twenty-two B-29s bombed Tokyo again and two others bombed Yokohama. On December 3, seventy bomb-ers attacked the Musashino Aircraft Factory again, but damage was negligible, and six planes were lost. The Japanese claimed to have shot down fifteen planes, but as was more and more often the case in these days of suicidal effort, the claims of survivor pilots in behalf of their fallen comrades were excessive. No one wanted to indicate that a pilot bent on ramming had been shot down before he could accomplish his mission, and that accounted for many of the excessive claims. A loss of six B-29s was bad enough news for the XXI Bomber Command. The Japanese were learning how to cope with the great planes: *taiatari*, the ramming attack. Two days after the raid, Imperial Headquarters increased its "score" to twenty-one B-29s shot down. Again, this change was the result of wild tales told by surviving pilots. "Wild eagles," Imperial Headquarters called the suicide pilots.

The seriousness of the raids over the Japanese homeland caused Imperial Headquarters to take special note. The reason for this new activity, said the generals, was the "unsatisfactory war developments on Leyte Island." The Americans had now begun "nerve warfare" against the Japanese homeland, designed to sap the people's will to fight.

IGHQ also announced the formation of a special air unit as-signed to ram the B-29s, the Shinten, or "heaven-shaking" unit, the name provided by Imperial Prince and General Naruhiko Higashikuni. "Thousands" of pilots were just awaiting their chance to get into the air and ram a B-29, said Imperial Headquarters.

Meanwhile, the XX Bomber Command was still functioning from Chengdu, now concentrating its efforts against Mukden's factories and the arsenal there. Eighty bombers hit Mukden on December 7.

As badly as the war was going in the Philippines and elsewhere, the Japanese were far from out of it, as they showed in the whole series of attacks against the American airfields on Saipan and Tinian islands. Most of the attacks originated on Iwo Jima and its surrounding islands. In half a dozen such attacks, eleven B-29s were destroyed and forty-three damaged. The most serious raid was made against Saipan's Aslito airfield on December 7. Bomber Command took enough notice to suspend air operations against the Tokyo area, and concentrate on Iwo Jima. A real campaign was launched in China and India as well, and several B-29s were damaged in a raid on the field west of Calcutta. Imperial Headquarters was well aware of the threat and hoped to keep the number of B-29s down, to minimize damage to the homeland.

But by December 13 the B-29s were back over Japan again. This time some seventy B-29s hit the Mitsubishi aircraft factory at Nagoya, in the most successful B-29 raid so far. Photos showed that a considerable portion of the factory had been destroyed. The big bombers were back over Nagoya again on December 18. Their claims this time were exaggerated.

The raids were not accomplishing what the Americans wanted to do. They certainly had not hurt the Japanese will to fight. The newspapers were filled with stories of heroism, and urgings to further effort by the people on the home front, and the people were responding.

In China, General LeMay had an idea that he thought would help bring Japan to her knees: firebombing against civilian populations. Of course, it was not put that way; a large portion of the American public would have objected if it had been. True, the

Japanese in China had pioneered the air attack against civilians as a form of total warfare. The Germans had done the same in the saturation bombing of London and other British cities, with no excuses about "military targets," and the Allies had responded with saturation bombing of Hamburg, Berlin, and other cities, and the Dresden raid that had killed an estimated 60,000 people in one night when the fires set by the incendiary bombs created a fire storm that engulfed the residential area of the city. But there were still men in the American air forces and elsewhere who believed that bombing of civilian populations was beyond the pale of civilized warfare, and attention had to be paid to that view, at least to euphemize the tactic. One way was to hold that any tactic that produced success would shorten the war, and thus save lives.

At Chengdu, General LeMay was one of the proponents of this theory. The way to get to the Japanese, he said, was to burn them out. And he proceeded to prove the efficacy of his theory in a fire raid against the dock area at Hankow, China. The raid, on December 18, was an enormous success. LeMay burned the entire dock area.

December, one might say, was "Mitsubishi month" for the B-29s. Time after time they raided Nagoya's Mitsubishi works, but the net results were really not too effective. After half a dozen raids, the Mitsubishi plant was still in operation, much of it underground. At Mukden, the Manchuria Airplane Manufacturing Company was still turning out planes, after a number of B-29 raids. In Washington the Joint Chiefs of Staff were showing their disappointment in the performance of the B-29s. The big super-bombers had been touted as "the solution"; too much had been expected of them because they carried a heavy payload for a long way. The fact was that though the B-29 bristled with machine guns, fore, aft, and top and belly, it was still just another airplane and not a superhuman weapon.

These December days, the newspapers of Tokyo and other cities were filled with stories of the heroism of the brave Wild Eagle defenders of the homeland, for example, the tale of Flight Warrant Officer Takashi Honda, who rammed a B-29 on December 20 over Nagoya. His plane was destroyed, along with the B-29, but Warrant Officer Honda parachuted to safety, and back at the base he insisted that he wanted to go up and do it again as soon as possible. Captain Junichi Ogata gave a clue to the new success of the Japanese airmen in opposing the B-29s. He was functioning as one of several *taiatari* attack directors, leading a flight of planes whose pilots were all bent on ramming the B-29s. His job was to direct each pilot in his attack.

> One enemy attacker, flying at an altitude of 9,500 meters (26,000 feet) was downed south of Nagoya. Detecting a formation of seven aircraft, I attacked the third one, which immediately opened fire. Flying to within 1,200 meters of the enemy, I directed the first attack and it was not long before the enemy plane began to emit white smoke and then it plunged into the sea. My plane was also hit and I had to make a forced landing.

The new year, 1945, opened with the B-29s still bombing the Mitsubishi factory at Nagoya, and still not destroying it. Washington was ever more displeased with the performance. Something had to be done. General LeMay was moved from China to Guam, to take command of the XXI Bomber Command.

The debate about use of the B-29s continued. From Pearl Harbor, Admiral Nimitz insisted that the proper use of the big bombers was to destroy aircraft factories and airfields, in support of the naval and military operations in the Philippines and elsewhere. The Japanese navy had been reduced in the battles off Leyte to an insignificant fleet force. The two major elements of the Japanese war machine remaining were the land army and the air forces of the navy and the army. If the Japanese aircraft production could be slashed, it would make the task of the Pacific Fleet so much easier. A great deal of the Japanese air effort was now devoted to suicide attacks, very costly to the fleet in terms of ship damage and lives lost. As they continued, Nimitz's concern about aircraft production increased.

On Guam, the new headquarters of the XXI Bomber Command, the debate went on, with General LeMay holding that his command should be concerned less with aircraft factories and airfields and more with strategic bombing, which meant to him the destruction of the Japanese people's will and ability to carry on the war.

At the moment, the Nimitz view was in ascendance. On January 21 the B-29s bombed Mena Airfield. On January 23 they hit the Mitsubishi plant again. That is, some of them hit it, but most of the bombs splattered around the city of Nagoya, doing serious damage to houses and businesses, but little to Mitsubishi. On January 24, twenty B-29s bombed airfields on Iwo Jima. On January 27, fifty-six bombers were sent to strike the Musashino and Nakajima aircraft plants near Tokyo, but most of them ended up bombing the urban population. On January 30, thirty B-29s bombed Iwo Jima again.

Japanese opposition was growing stiffer. In one raid over Nagoya, the attackers counted some 600 fighters. On February 4, attacking Kobe, the B-29s were met by 200 fighters. The fighters destroyed one B-29, but they damaged thirty-five others. Far worse was the raid of eighty-four B-29s on the Nakajima aircraft factory at Ota. Twelve bombers were lost that day, several of them to ramming attacks. The loss ratio was high enough to give General LeMay pause. But nothing could be done about it until the Iwo Jima operation produced airfields that could supply fighter protection to and from Japan. The invasion was scheduled to begin on February 19.

On February 15, the B-29s struck Nagoya again. Yes, the target once more was Mitsubishi.

General LeMay's arguments got some support on February 24

when 100 B-29s from the XX Bomber Command, now based completely in India, struck Singapore in an all-incendiary raid. They came back the next day to assess the damage, and put it at 40 percent of the warehouse district. Eminently satisfactory results.

Despite the attacks of the Japanese air forces on the various B-29 airfields, more and more B-29s were appearing in the Marianas. On February 25 the XXI Bomber Command staged its greatest raid yet, one in which 172 B-29s bombed Toyko. This time they were joined by planes from the U.S. carrier task force The Imperial Palace in Chiyoda district was supposed to be inviolate, but the high-level bombing was not very accurate, and some bombs fell on the Bureau of Imperial Mews of the Imperial Household. A guard's post at the gate of the palace was also bombed, obviously in error. A big raid, but once again, not very effective.

By March 4, there had come an important change in the war that was to affect the Japanese people deeply. Having landed on schedule on Iwo Jima, the Americans had made so much progress in clearing the island of the Japanese defenders that on that day the pilot of a crippled B-29 was able to land at Iwo Jima and thus save his aircraft and possibly his whole crew from destruction.

That day the B-29s were supposed to raid Musashino and the aircraft factory there, but heavy cloud cover prevented them from bombing. An assessment of the whole series of raids against the Japanese aircraft factories proved that the campaign had been a miserable failure. High-altitude "precision" bombing (which it was not) was not the way to destroy Japanese industry and force Japan out of the war. Between November 24, 1944, and March 4, 1945, the 20th Air Force had made twenty-two bombing raids on Japanese industry, and only one factory had been knocked out. To achieve that slight effect, 102 B-29s had been lost. Air intelligence indicated that the damage to the aircraft industry was really minimal. There had to be another way. And finally, everyone but Admiral Nimitz was convinced that this was so.

So, now, what was to be done?

General LeMay had an answer.

He suggested a series of low-level incendiary attacks on Japanese cities. As everyone knew, Japanese houses were built mostly of wood, with straw tatami mats on the floors, and the rooms were usually separated by paper screens. They should go blazing up like matches.

There was still some objection to launching raids directed specifically against civilian women and children, so the planners were at pains to deny that the purpose was to terrorize the civil population. According to a staff presentation of the XXI Bomber Command,

> These operations are not conducted as terror raids against the civilian population. The Japanese economy depends heavily on home industries carried on in its cities close to major factory areas. By destroying these feeder industries, the flow of vital parts could be curtailed and war production disorganized. A general conflagration in a city like Tokyo or Nagoya might have the further advantage of spreading to some of the priority targets located in the urban areas.

What was needed were plenty of incendiary bombs, and the XXI Bomber Command had them. For weeks the bombs had been coming in, and after high-altitude, high-explosive bombing was suspended on March 4 no further effort was made.

Also, to make an effective attack required hundreds of aircraft. The XXI Bomber Command had more than 300 B-29s, which should be plenty to test General LeMay's theory that the real strategic bombing of Japan meant destroying her cities, the homes of the people, and killing them by the hundreds of thousands.

3
JAPAN'S DEFENSES

WITH THE FALL OF SAIPAN TO THE AMERICANS IN THE SUMMER of 1944, the Tojo government lost public respect. More important, the army and the Privy Council decided that Tojo must go. Some of the Japanese intelligentsia, such as Marquis Kido, the Lord Keeper of the Privy Seal, had decided after the fall of Saipan that the war was lost, and wanted to get Japan out of it, but the militarists still maintained a tight grip, and not much could be done immediately. Over the past three years, Tojo had put many of his confidants in high places, sometimes to what the other generals considered to be the detriment of the war effort.

The movement to get rid of Tojo reached into high places. Admiral Okada, a former premier, and thus a member of the *jushin* (council of elder statesmen), suggested that Tojo lead an effort to recapture Saipan, so that the nation would learn how desperate its situation had grown. Tojo tried everything, including setting traps for his enemies and then having them arrested by the secret police. But after the fall of Saipan it did him no good. That event triggered a resolution of the ex-prime ministers of the *jushin*, stating that Tojo ought not to continue as premier. The resolution was passed to the Emperor, just at the time that Tojo was trying desperately to secure a royal audience and the expressed absolution of the Emperor for the fall of Saipan. The Cabinet began to fall apart with the resignation of Navy Minister Toshio Shimada, known previously in the navy as a Tojo toady. And so Tojo resigned, and as an indication of his complete fall from grace, he was immediately put on the army retired list. Although every prime minister before him had automatically been made a member of the *jushin*, Tojo was not invited. Thus he was reduced to the position of ordinary citizen on July 20, 1944, and thereafter he sat in his house in the Setagaya suburb of Tokyo and got his news from Radio Tokyo and the newspapers. On July 22, 1944, the Tojo government was replaced by that of General Kuniaki Koiso, with the understanding that the war must be carried on. In August, the Koiso government established the Supreme Council for the Direction of the War, which had unlimited powers. An emergency session of the Diet was called early in September to endorse the government's call for a total mobilization of the people of Japan. A "last line of defense" was established to run from the Kuril Islands to Western New Guinea, Java, Sumatra, the Andaman Islands, and Burma. Korea, Manchuria, and China were the strategic rear. By defending this line, the Japanese military believed, they could hold out and ultimately wear down the Allies until they offered a negotiated peace. But almost immediately the line had been breached, in Dutch New Guinea, and then in the Philippines. By the end of 1944 the Imperial Japanese Navy and Combined Fleet had ceased to exist. A handful of ships and air power were all that was left of the fleet. In January 1945, the Supreme Council for the Direction of the War decided on a detailed plan for the defense of the homeland, which would mean fighting on the beaches by women and children as well as the soldiers, and no surrender.

On January 1 the Emperor celebrated Shinohai, or Worship in

Four Directions, and offered prayers for Japan's prosperity and the welfare of its 100 million people. Prime Minister Koiso called on the people to perfect the air-raid defenses and "strengthen the national structure to prosecute the war," although he warned that it would bring new hardship on the people. "With the progress of the war, difficulties in the people's daily life will increase, and there is also the danger of air raids becoming more intensive."

That would just have to be borne, said the Prime Minister, but "this is the year when the dark cloud covering East Asia will be swept away."

On the positive side, said the government that month, the Americans had lost 550 B-29s and four thousand airmen to brave Japanese attackers. The figures, of course, were fabricated, but the fact that the government put these out indicated its feeling of the need to reassure the civil population that the B-29 was not a magic weapon.

Day after day the government put out its "Win" propaganda. Premier Koiso made a national radio broadcast on the subject early in January. Navy Minister Yonai made a similar speech.

As if to punctuate the speeches, the B-29s hit the Kanto Plain again on January 4. "A terrific battle," said Imperial General Headquarters, "but without much damage."

And two days later the government announced an increase in taxes to support the further defense effort, in which the personal income tax would go up from 15 percent to 18 percent; corporate taxes would go from 18 percent to 21 percent.

In January, every B-29 raid was noted by Imperial General Headquarters with heroic tales of the exploits of the brave Japanese defenders. Although the Japanese military tradition did not include special mention for valor, since valor was expected of every soldier, the awarding of special mentions and medals became quite usual. For example, the Abe Fighter Plane Unit, one of those six-man suicide squads, distinguished itself by being wiped out in the battle against the B-29s, Sergeant Masawi Samamoto was promoted two ranks posthumously and awarded the Fourth Class Order of the Golden Kite and the Sixth Class Order of the Single-Rayed Rising Sun.

The other members of the unit received similar recognition. To the public, the point was made: the brave soldiers and sailors of Japan are defending you.

The winter of 1945 in the homeland was devoted to strengthening air defenses against the bombing raids that everyone knew would be coming thick and fast as soon as the Americans moved adequate forces into the Marianas, and, as noted, they had begun to come.

Even then, the Japanese were slow to work on their air-raid defenses. Because of the structure of the army, which was responsible for the defense of the homeland, there was no central air defense command. Rather, each army unit in each prefecture had its own air force, and that air force's activity was confined to that particular prefecture. Thus, if an enormous raid was developing over Nagoya, the Tokyo-based air groups would not be involved in the slightest. Add to that the fact that, as the B-29 raids began, there were only about 500 operational fighters in Japan and only two groups of night fighters. Thus the air defenses were not nearly so powerful as had been those of the German cities at the outset of the Allied bombing campaign of the European war. General LeMay claimed that the reason for his request to conduct urban area attacks by firebombing was the power of the Japanese air defense. The statistics do not bear out that claim.

On the ground also, the Japanese were slow to act. By October 1944 they still had no provision for the clearing of streets and the disposition of rubble from bombing raids. Even then, there was no specific law to cover the allocation of funds, but the money was made available through the enormous powers of the Supreme Council for the Direction of the War.

The head of the Air Raid General Defense Headquarters in Japan was the Minister of Home Affairs. His agency, for all practical purposes, *was* the air-raid defense organization.

Greater Tokyo in the fall of 1944 was a city of 7 million people. The general civil defense was in the hands of the mayor and the 65,000 city employees. In each of the thirty-five wards of the city, the executive officer was the ward chief, appointed by the mayor. The ward chiefs issued information to the people of their wards about protective clothing and protective devices against the coming air raids, but again, such meager attention had been paid to the problem, even after the Doolittle raid of the spring of 1942, that very little was done until after the first October raids by the B-29s on Japan. Then the wards began organizing the people into *bogyodan* (ward defense group), *chokai* (neighborhood association), and *tonari gumi* (block organization).

Thus, in October, the city government of Tokyo was undertaking the improvement of air-raid defenses, the building of fireproof buildings, the stockpiling of supplies for firefighting, and other defense activity. Oddly enough, neither the metropolitan police, the prefecture government, or the Home Ministry had any part in this activity until the war went into its total defense period, and then the Home Ministry took control. Civil defense was split, and the governor general of the Tokyo Metropolitan District of the Home Ministry was made responsible for a number of activities. These included the fireproofing of buildings and the razing of selected blocks of buildings to provide "green spaces"—fire lanes—so that if fire broke out after bombing, it would not spread from rooftop to rooftop across the city, but would be stopped by the breaks. The Home Ministry was also responsible for firefighting, protection from gas attack, and the provision of gas masks for volunteer and paid firefighters. Camouflage of defense installations was also the governor general's province, and the building of air-raid shelters. The administration of the district associations and neighborhood groups, down to the block associations, was also the function to the governor general, and that agency supplied the people with firefighting equipment, such as protective hoods and flails (something like bamboo grass rakes), which were used to put out fires. The governor general was also responsible for rescue work and for medical treatment of survivors of air raids.

The district police governor had another area of responsibility. He was in charge of communications within the Tokyo district, of actual firefighting by paid and volunteer firemen, of the air-raid alarm system, of the control of blackout, and of the operation of the shelters built and maintained by the Home Ministry. The People's Vigilance Corps and the Special Self-Vigilance Corps were responsible to the police governor. The key to their activities lay in the *koban* (police boxes) out of which the uniformed police operated. Every little neighborhood had its own *koban*, and the police of the neighborhood were completely familiar with the neighbors and their habits. Licenses, information, and permissions of various sorts all emanated from the *koban*. It was, in effect, a little city hall where the people of Tokyo had their most intimate contact with government.

In the fall of 1944, metropolitan Tokyo was organized into 1,500,000 *katai boka gun* under the 120,000 *tonari gumi* or block associations. This was the basic neighborhood unit for air-raid protection, numbering about a dozen families, and its members patrolled their areas, passed along information, and made sure that all the people of the neighborhood knew their responsibilities and had the protective equipment supplied by the government.

By 1945, Tokyo was organized into several air-raid protective organizations. Primarily, the block association organization dealt with people in their homes. The Self-Vigilance Corps was concerned with people at their places of employment or study— banks, factories, schools. A third volunteer corps was made up of students who pledged to assist the police, the firemen, and the Self-Vigilance Corps.

To protect against air raids and fires, every household was required to keep a water supply of at least 100 liters for each 15 *tsubo* of area (50 square meters). Most householders build cisterns for the purpose, although some poorer families used tubs and buckets. Householders were also required to maintain at least 50 liters of earth or sand to be used to smother fires, straw mats for the same purpose, gas masks (if they were engaged in public defense), protective hoods, and long-sleeved clothing. All these requirements had been drilled into them through the neighborhood associations for many months. They had also been instructed that unless otherwise informed, when an air raid came, they should stay at home and await developments.

Each neighborhood association had a shelter of its own, where it kept a supply of water (1,000 liters at least) and a hand pump on a cart that could be moved around to fires in the neighborhood that threatened to get out of control, and ladders and shovels with which to fight fires.

In January 1944, the razing of buildings had begun, and by the late winter of 1945 about 150,000 buildings out of the city's 1,500,000 had been torn down to provide fire lanes. As the raids continued early in 1945, hundreds of thousands of schoolchildren, old people, and pregnant women were moved out of Tokyo to suburban relocation centers—sometimes whole schools of children—or were encouraged to go to relatives in other parts of the country where the danger of air raids did not seem so great. Before the war ended, the exodus from Tokyo would be enormous, with only about 2.5 million people remaining in the city.

But as for public shelters, there were practically none. The matter had not been given consideration in those early days of the war, when Japan seemed to be winning everywhere and war materials were in ample supply. By the fall of 1944, when the Japanese Cabinet considered the problem of air-raid shelters, knowing what had to be coming from the Marianas, it was too late. The materials were simply not available to do the job across Japan, and so the whole matter was dropped. They had the plans—the tunnel-type shelter was considered the best because of Japan's mountainous geography, but time had run out on them. It was another matter in which the enormous arrogance of the Japanese militarists had caused them to deny the possibility that Japan might be bombed.

The official air defense organizations were supplemented by one large private group, the Great Japan Air Defense Association (Dai Nippon Boku Kokai) which had forty-seven branches across the country. It was subsidized partly by the Home Ministry, but much of its money came from private contributions of industry. The real task of the association was raising funds for gas masks, protective hoods, and other firefighting equipment. The government could not seem to make up its collective mind as to whether or not the Americans would use gas against the civil population. General Ando, the Home Minister for a time, thought they would use gas, or any other weapon. But other officials did not think so. Therefore no cogent policy was developed. Ultimately, some civil defense workers were issued gas masks, but the general population was not (unlike Britain, where the government was so sure the Germans would use any weapon that gas masks were general public issue).

The association raised the money and put together the supplies: masks, helmets, buckets, hand pumps, and some ambulances, which were then turned over to the municipalities for issuance through the government civil defense organizations.

At first the association began sending out information to the public about the construction of home bomb shelters. In demonstration, three different types of shelter were erected on the grounds of the association's headquarters in Tokyo, and the managing director was seeking funds to help groups build shelters, but Prime Minister Tojo took exception to this activity and demanded that they stop it. There was no way the Americans were ever going to bomb Japan, he said, and the association was simply destroying public morale by such talk. So the association stopped mentioning bomb shelters, and most people forgot about building them.

This winter the army was devoting most of its training efforts to the production of suicide pilots. The regular pilot training program was moved almost entirely up to Manchuria, out of range of the American bombers. In the homeland, normal air force training had virtually ceased because of the shortage of fuel and the change in military policy so that army and navy both relied on the suicide weapon. Some 3,000 young men were undergoing suicide training. They were organized into six-man units, with twenty such units making up a squadron for administrative purposes. The two big training units were at Karashihara in Kyushu and Tsukuba in Honshu.

For the first month, the young men flew in gliders. This saved fuel, taught them the elements of aeronautics, and also prepared some of them for missions in the flying bombs that would be carried by bomber to a spot near their ultimate destination and then released.

The navy's role in antiaircraft defense was extremely limited, although under Vice-Admiral Matome Ugaki, the navy organized a large and effective force of *kamikaze* pilots. But their mission was to attack the enemy at sea and not to defend against B-29s; the latter responsibility belonged almost entirely to the army. Such ships as the Japanese did have at Kure, Yokosuka, and other bases retained their antiaircraft guns and were prepared to fight if attacked. But their power was being retained for that last great assault against the shores of Japan, where the Japanese still hoped to create so much devastation of the enemy landing force that ultimately the Allies would settle for a negotiated peace rather than continue the slaughter of Allied and Japanese fighters.

On January 9, when the B-29s attacked Tokyo, a military photographer managed to get a startling picture, taken just after a Japanese fighter had rammed a B-29. The photo, which appeared in all the Japanese newspapers, showed the B-29 going down trailing smoke, and the fighter plane going down beside it. "Victory Transcends Death," read the caption.

But there were many in Japan who did not like the concept of suicide flights, and for them, Imperial General Headquarters had another tale, the story of a brave fighter who rammed and lived. It was told the same day that the startling photo appeared.

Watching were thousands of Tokyo citizens. Goro Shimizu, vice-chief of the Seventh Civilian Defense Corps of Enmoto-Shindei, was interviewed by a reporter, and he told what he had seen when he and his firefighters approached the wreckage of the bomber.

> The parts of the B-29 were still burning when I came. When I first saw the B-29 it was already spitting fire in the air. It disintegrated in midair and then fell perpendicularly downward. I unconsciously clapped my hands. Upon ascertaining where the plane fell I immediately rushed to the spot with my men. We saw two charred bodies at one place where apparently the fuselage was burning. The gendarmerie soon arrived and started to clear the debris. I heard that the Japanese airman landed safely with a parachute and that he smiled as he walked off from the spot of the landing.

But the prevailing mood of Japan was apprehension. Lieutenant General Masaharu Homma, who had been quietly ousted from high command by Tojo after his victory in the Philippines in 1942, was asked to write an appraisal of the current fighting in the Philippines, and he used the occasion to warn the people of Japan that the real battle was yet to come; it would be the Battle of Mount Tenno (a medieval turning point in Japanese history), and it would be fought in Japan proper against the enemy. Homma noted that the enemy was conducting a constant campaign of bombing against Japan's aircraft industry, and he said that this bombing represented the greatest danger. What Homma did not know was that the industrial bombing campaign had come to an end on March 4, and that something far more frightening was about to happen to the people of Japan.

4
THE
ATTACK
PLAN

DESPITE GENERAL H. H. ARNOLD'S BELIEF IN PRECISION BOMBING as the proper method for destroying an enemy's industrial potential, by March 1, 1945, U.S. Army Air Forces Headquarters in Washington had to admit that the B-29s had so far failed to make a very impressive record in the war against Japan.

As noted, only one aircraft factory had been destroyed in all those high-altitude missions. Another very important one, Musashino, had suffered only 4-percent damage, by XXI Bomber Command's intelligence estimates, after 835 planes had dropped 2,300 tons of bombs aimed at the target.

General LeMay's response to criticism of his XXI Bomber Command was that weather and inferior pilot training had caused the problems. The good-weather months for the air forces were December, January, and February, but in those months 70 percent of the B-29s had bombed by radar. Only about 20 percent of the planes had managed to bomb the primary targets by visual means. There were only seven days of each month when visual bombing from high altitude was satisfactory.

One of the problems with the weather was that the Americans did not have a successful weather reporting system covering the mainland areas west and northwest of Japan. The Chinese Communists were to the west, but the Americans did not trust them enough to establish a weather reporting system in the Communist-held territory. To the north were the Russians, and they did not trust the Americans sufficiently to allow a reporting system; besides, the Soviets were still neutral in the war against Japan.

The high winds that coursed across Japan at high altitudes were a very serious weather factor. At 30,000 feet the winds often hit 135 miles per hour, and on one occasion the wind was clocked at 200 miles per hour. These fierce winds meant that the bombardiers of the B-29s faced extreme drift angles. The only successful approach was from the west, downwind, and this meant that sometimes the bombers were coming in at ground speeds of 500 miles per hour. The bombardiers were simply unable to cope, so there was virtually no precision to their bombing. Bombs tumbled down all over the place. Small wonder that the Japanese high command referred to the American efforts as "blind bombing."

If it sounds like an impossible situation, it was not. Some crews were able to make consistently good records. What it came down to was the inadequate training and insufficient ability of the crews of many of the lead planes. Learning this, XXI Bomber Command began a program of training lead crews, but by March 1945 the program had not been very successful.

In the very first attack from the Marianas, on November 24, the B-29s had dropped some incendiary bombs—about 65 tons, in fact. The results had not been very spectacular; about one-tenth of a square mile of urban Tokyo was burned out. But on February 25 the bombers had carried 411 tons of incendiaries over the target, and observation flights the next day showed that an entire square mile was burned out. In other words, the bombers had secured ten times the effect for about six times the increase in incendiary bombs. This was the clincher for General LeMay in his itch to try low-level area burnout as a new weapon against the Japanese. After the March 4 high-level, high-explosive bombing failure, Washington announced that he was to have his way.

A study of the effects of the February 25 raid showed that a successful incendiary attack depended on the ability to saturate the area with the incendiaries in the shortest possible time. To do this, all previous tactical orders were ignored. The bombers would come in at 5,000 to 7,800 feet. As close to 300 bombers as possible would be employed, although this was straining the XXI Bomber Command's resources.

The entire bomb load would be incendiaries, so as to overcome any attempts by the Japanese at firefighting.

Two types of incendiaries would be used. One was the M-47A2, a 100-pound napalm bomb. These bombs were to be carried by the three squadrons that would serve as "pathfinders." That is, these three squadrons would lead the attack, and their 100-pound bombs would start immediate fires no matter where they hit, and these fires would be large enough to mark aiming points for the next waves of bombers. Each bomber would carry 184 bombs, and they would be dropped at intervals of 100 feet.

The second type of bomb was the M-69 six-pound incendiary, also dropped in clusters, with fifty feet between each drop.

For five days after March 4, the bases in the Marianas were stimulated to furious activity.

The lead crews were selected. They were given the best-equipped and best-maintained aircraft. Each wing and each bomb group had its own distinctive markings. For example, the 58th Wing's distinctive marking was a triangle, painted in black on the vertical stabilizer and rudder; within that wing, the 40th Bombardment Group was further distinguished by an S. Others had circles, squares, arrowheads, and one a Z.

After the mission took off, the lead planes would take their bombers to the assembly area and here, before they approached the Japanese homeland, they would form up and straighten out all the kinks. For the 73rd Group, for example, the formation area was over the island Kito Io Jima. For the 315th, the assembly area was over Nishina Shima. The 58th Air Group's assembly point was over Iwo Jima.

Three wings would be employed, the 313th, the 73rd, both of which had flown many missions from the Marianas, and the two newly arrived groups of the 312th Wing, which had flown only one mission. General LeMay wanted to achieve the greatest possible concentration over the Tokyo area, and these three groups represented a startling figure of more than 300 aircraft.

Tokyo was to feel the incendiaries first, but the whole initial series of firebombing targets had already been selected: Tokyo, Nagoya, Osaka, and Kobe. Time was very important. March 24 was the date selected for the invasion of Okinawa, and the B-29s would have to be used around that date for attacks on the island and on airfields, and other installations to help with that important battle. So there were roughly two weeks in March in which to prove the effectiveness of the firebombing campaign.

The Tokyo attack was to be launched for a night arrival over the city, because the Americans knew that Japanese night fighter strength was very slight. Although the Seventh Fighter Group was now available to escort B-29s to Japan from Iwo Jima, the time over target of the fighters was only about ten minutes, and that, of course was limited to daylight hours. Thus the night attack, while not supported by fighters, was still decided to be preferable to the day attack, since the bombers would come in at low level. Also, because the XXI Bomber Command's tactical doctrine called for high-level bombing, this change should surprise the Japanese defenders and catch them napping.

Using so many aircraft and so many green crews, it was important to make takeoff and landing in the daylight hours, and attacking at night would make this possible. Further, it was believed that the weather over Tokyo would be better at night than in the daytime at this period of the year. So another reason for the night attack was added to the equation.

For the Tokyo raid, the takeoffs would be made between 5:30

P.M. and 8:10 P.M. on March 9. The mission would last about fifteen hours, and that meant the landings would begin at seven o'clock on the morning of March 10. The 73rd and 313th wings would take off simultaneously from their fields on Saipan and Tinian; the 314th Wing planes would leave from Guam. The whole force participating in the Tokyo raid would need two hours to get off the ground, even though at Aslito airfield they would be using two runways. On Tinian the 313th would have only one runway from which to operate. On Guam, the 314th Wing would have to allow forty minutes extra so that the three groupings of planes would all be airborne at about the same time and the further connections could be made.

On Iwo Jima, fighting was still going on, but the marines by this time controlled both airfields. That meant Iwo Jima would be available for emergency landings—a matter that relieved the minds of a good number of pilots, who did not relish the idea of ditching a damaged or fuel-short aircraft.

There were many advantages, the planners said, to the new plan for low-level attack: the bomb load could be increased, and bombing accuracy was expected to be much better than from high altitude. Of course, bombing accuracy was not very important, since the aim was to saturate a whole area of Tokyo with firebombs and create a fire storm. Each aircraft could carry forty clusters of firebombs; each cluster was designed to explode at 2,500 feet altitude, releasing about 40 firebombs, which would then fall in a random pattern over a quarter of a mile. Of course, the patterns would be mingled and overlapping, all of which would help create the effect of total penetration of an area. Nor would the green areas and fire lanes of Tokyo help much, because bombs would be dropped on both sides of the fire lanes.

The nature of the firebombs was such that they burned intensely and could hardly be extinguished before they had burned themselves out. This also would give a lasting effect to the bombing, unlike bombing with high explosives, which exploded and then were finished.

Three aiming points were chosen for the lead bombardiers, about 4,000 to 6,000 feet apart. The idea was that about half the bombs would fall within a 2,000-foot circle (diameter) around the aiming point; the rest would be short or long, but the general effect would be to reinforce the fires and create the general conflagration that was wanted.

Coming in at low altitudes, the planes would not face the extremely high winds that had bothered them at 30,000 feet, and that meant they could choose from several angles of attack. Nor was the likelihood of aborted missions or mechanical failure so great at lower altitudes.

Another factor was antiaircraft fire. At low altitude, the Japanese would have to rely on their medium antiaircraft guns and automatic weapons. The high-altitude antiaircraft guns were not effective below 10,000 feet, and the night attack was chosen partly to cut down on losses from antiaircraft guns.

Another important factor in the new sort of missions being planned was the "human element." The fact was that the long high-altitude missions without fighter cover and the relatively high losses the B-29 crews had been suffering in the recent months had sapped morale badly.

All of this was taken into consideration as the planners worked out the whole series of low-level incendiary missions designed to burn out the four major Japanese industrial cities. The results, they hoped, would be a distinct drop in Japanese industrial production and a serious blow against Japanese morale and the people's willingness to continue the war.

5
MISSION
NUMBER 40

ON MARCH 9, 1945, ALL THE PLANS WERE MADE FOR FOUR FIRE-bombing missions in quick succession, to take advantage of the element of surprise before the Japanese could respond with new defensive measures. The night of March 9–10, the target was to be Tokyo. Thereafter, it was planned that on alternate nights the bombers would hit Nagoya, Osaka, and Kobe, weather permitting.

On the morning of March 9, the aircrews assembled in the big tin huts with the barrel-vault roofs, and sat down on the long, backless benches. Most of the officers and men were wearing one-piece flying suits. The mission commanders took their seats in the front rows, and the intelligence officers handed out briefing folders with the latest word from the weathermen. On the wall were posted maps, charts, and other information assembled by the intelligence group for the briefing.

The group commander got up.

"I have an announcement," he said. "We are about to undertake a new type of mission. Here are the five points:

"1. We are going to make a series of night incendiary attacks on the major Japanese cities.

"2. Bombing will be carried out from 5,000 to 8,000 feet.

"3. No armament or ammunition will be carried, and the size of the crews will be reduced accordingly.

"4. Aircraft will attack individually.

"5. Tokyo will be the first target."

When the commander finished, one could have heard him breathe, so silent were the big briefing halls. The fliers were in deep shock. No guns, no ammunition, target Tokyo, the most heavily defended area in all Japan. Attack at low altitude, which meant they would be sitting ducks for flak. Individual attack, which contradicted everything they had ever been taught about formation flying and the need to keep a tight formation for mutual protection. "Tojo loves stragglers" had been the word. But that was no longer the word. Everybody was going to be a straggler.

The men on the benches tried to digest just what all this would mean as once again the briefing officers emphasized the purpose of the night's mission: to burn up a large section of Tokyo and thus damage Japanese ability to produce for the war, and hurt the Japanese home morale as much as possible.

Also, the point was made that this was the first mission of its sort, the first adventure in a whole new sort of war that ought to make the B-29 much more effective than it had been until this point. By lowering the altitude, the bomb load of each B-29 could be increased by 65 percent! By staging individual attacks, there would be no waiting and circling. The aircraft would go directly from base to target, and then bomb and return. By attacking from different angles, they would decrease their chances of being tracked by the enemy and fired upon. By reducing the size of the crews and eliminating machine guns and ammunition they could carry more bombs, six to eight tons of payload. By flying at lower altitude they would encounter better weather.

Many of the crews could appreciate this. The high-level missions had been growing tougher all the time, and the men of the 73rd Wing, who had carried much of the load, were getting tired.

Any sort of change was welcome. The best change, of course, was to go home on rotation. But any sort of change . . .

In each briefing hall, the group commander announced the target. The operations officer then told the men who was going, more than 300 planes from three wings, on Saipan, Tinian, and Guam. The intelligence officers then described the importance of the Tokyo industrial area they were going to strike, and explained that the system of cottage industry was enormously important to the Japanese war effort and that this night's raid would bring something new, a burnout of hundreds, perhaps thousands, of small industrial home factories.

Some of the fellows on the back benches began to squirm a little. All this big talk was not very meaningful. What happened up there in the air was what was going to count.

Another intelligence officer then described the route along the 3,000-mile journey they were making that night: the checkpoints, the assembly point, the aiming points, the flak situation to be expected on the target, and the number of fighters that might be met.

The weatherman got up and told them what the weather was going to be. They already knew: it was going to be lousy, because it was almost always lousy over Japan these days. But he also told them that the high winds they might encounter would do a great deal to help their military effort of this night. High winds should spread their fires and do part of their destructive job for them.

The operations officer spoke again, mentioning the assembly procedures, and the types of bombs they would be carrying. Then the briefing broke up into smaller sections for the aircraft commanders and the specialists—engineers, radio operators, navigators.

The men straggled back to their barracks, picked up their personal gear, and went to the latrine, or lay down on the bunks for a few minutes, or stood around, talking or just thinking and looking. They went to the mess hall for a meal, and then they piled into the trucks that came up, and began the dusty trip to the airfield. The closer they got to mission time, the less the talk. The sweating out of the mission had begun.

All the talk about the advantages of the low-level mission sounded good. But . . . no gunners, no guns? What if it didn't work?

The flight crews were not the only ones sweating out this mission. General LeMay had taken an enormous gamble, and his career was on the line. If he was wrong, and if the mission produced a disaster for the Americans, there most certainly would be a new commander of the XXI Bombing Command within a matter of days. And as for the staff—if anybody had screwed up in the detailed planning, his head was going to rest uneasy on his shoulders from then on.

So the tension rose.

At the fields, the planes were still undergoing the last labors of the mechanics. Some bombs were still being loaded from the dollies, the clusters lifted up by wire ropes into the yawning bomb bays of the Superfortresses.

The crews stowed their Mae Wests, canteens, parachutes, oxygen masks, and perhaps a paperback book aboard.

Here and there a crew was scratched from the night's mission: plane inoperable or in marginal condition, not worth taking the chance. One crew was displaced from its own plane because the B-29 was needed for a lead crew that would go in to drop marker bombs.

The aircrews now began to get down to business. The radar operator sat down at his scope. The radioman sat down at his table. Some of the men fumbled for the rabbit's foot or the lucky silver dollar or the rosary they carried with them. Some took out photographs of their girlfriends or wives and put them where they could see them.

No guns, no gunners. It became very apparent as the crew checked in over the intercom with the captain.

The captain started engines. As they roared into life, he watched the instrument panel and the copilot watched with him. Then came the order.

"Close bomb bay doors."

They were getting ready to go.

The flight engineer pressed a switch, and the four bomb bay doors swung up and joined in the outer belly of the Superfortress. It was now a self-contained unit, the airfield shut out, the men shut in. Just a few minutes now, and they would be on their way.

"Doors and hatches closed," the engineer reported through the intercom.

The pilot and copilot reached up and shut the side windows of the compartment. The noise level dropped, and the smell changed. Now the airfield smells of gasoline, dust, and exhaust fumes were replaced by the smell of an airplane.

The B-29s began taxiing toward the runway, bumping along, lurching a little, like prehistoric monsters out of their element. The lines of Superfortresses slowed, then speeded up again, and slowed again like an undulating snake.

Half an hour before takeoff, the B-29s were beginning to trundle out of their hardstands and move toward the strips for takeoff. There were two airstrips on Saipan, but one on Tinian; the second strip was not yet ready for operations. That meant the 313th would be moving late.

As more and more engines revved up, the din became deafening around the field. Dust kicked up and blew across the strip, as the big planes lumbered into position.

At the point of takeoff, the flagman motioned to the pilot to be ready. What came next, they all knew: the flagman raised his hand, which meant that in ten seconds the plane must begin to roll, and that in forty seconds it must be off the runway, so that the next B-29 could take off. The captain stood on the brake and pushed the throttles until the plane shuddered. The flagman's hand dropped. The captain gave the order.

"Cowl flaps closed."

The petal flaps around the four big engines closed up, and the engines were now streamlined. The pilot released the brake and shot the throttles all the way. The big plane gained full power and began lumbering down the runway, then picked up speed and the flow became smoother over the ground, smoother, faster, faster, faster. That trip along the runway took forty seconds, but to most of the crew it seemed longer, or they seemed just suspended in time. Then came the little bump that meant the wheels of the Superfortress had just left the ground, and the pilot gave the order:

"Gear up."

The copilot pressed the switch that activated the hydraulic system, and the landing gear folded up inside the shell of the aircraft. It was now an airplane, in its element. The eleven crewmen showed, each in his own way, the enormous relief that always accompanied a successful takeoff. Now all they had to do was fly to Japan, bomb Tokyo, evade the flak and the fighters, fly home again, and make that one last effort, the landing.

The pilot headed toward Iwo Jima, the point of assembly. The copilot slumped down in his seat a little. The navigator fiddled with his instruments. Others were not so relaxed. It was an entirely new sort of mission. What would the flak be like at 6,500 feet? Wouldn't the Jap fighters have a better chance at them this way? No one could answer these questions, but everyone could worry about them.

So the crew settled down to their own thoughts, the radarman and radioman alert, the bombardier resting his eyes, the copilot waiting, as always, and doing the chores that were his as the occupant of the right-hand seat.

The Superfortresses droned along over the sea for hours. As they approached the Japanese homeland, the weather began to worsen, heavy clouds (seven-tenths cover in some places) obscured the sea, and high winds buffeted the aircraft.

Not all the planes made Tokyo with their bomb loads. After landfall was made, some aircraft began dropping their bombs, either because of mechanical problems, fear, or misapprehension. Bombs fell that night on Choishi Point, Katsuura, Katsunigaura Airfield, Chichi Jima, Haha Jima, and Hachijo Jima; some fell in the countryside. But 285 B-29s made it all the way to Tokyo, coming in by waves, at from 5,000 to 9,000 feet. Behind them rose the fires set by the early droppers, and ahead were the fires set by the pathfinder aircraft to mark the drop zones.

One part of the Japanese defenses was alert enough. As the planes made their landfall they were picked up by Japanese searchlights, and as they flew inland the searchlights ahead kept picking them up, kept after them. Antiaircraft fire began, but it was not very accurate; as the planners had hoped, the surprise was so great that the Japanese gunners were confused. The high-level guns were not a problem. Automatic weapons and medium flak guns were the problem, and it had often been worse for the American pilots. The fighters appeared as almost always, but they had learned to treat the Superfortresses carefully, and for the most part they stayed out of the range of the gunners. A few tried to ram.

Then Tokyo was coming up. The pathfinders were out ahead, moving toward the aiming points. They reached the drop points and opened the bomb bay doors. The raid of the night of March 9 began.

6
TOKYO,
MARCH 9,
1945

FOR TWO YEARS THE PEOPLE OF TOKYO HAD GROWN EVER MORE anxious about the possibility of American air raids. That first small raid by Lieutenant Colonel James Doolitle's B-25s had been seen as a stunt and had nothing to do with the anxiety.

But when Guadalcanal fell and the Berlin correspondents of the Tokyo newspapers began reporting on the massive Allied air raids of German cities, it was a different story.

In December 1943, Lieutenant Colonel Kuni Akiyama predicted that the future of the war depended on air power. His article, published in most Japanese newspapers, was a call from the army for more effort to produce more aircraft to keep the Americans away from Japan.

Late in 1943, Major Jiro Chikushi published another article in the Japanese newspaper *Fuji*, predicting further advances in American air power. Early in 1944, a Chinese student who showed up in Chungking after an odyssey that included travel to Korea, Manchukuo, Outer Mongolia, and then back into China reported that Japanese "liberals" were fully expecting powerful air attacks on Japan to begin soon. Oddly enough, the American capture of Attu Island, which represented the end of a Japanese dream of attacking America proper, was an important morale factor in Japan. After the defeat in the Aleutians, many Japanese felt that it was only a matter of time before the Americans attacked the homeland.

When the talk about air-raid precautions began, and the government sternly urged the people to protect themselves, some began to ask why the government was not protecting them. Then the facts began to come out. From the neutral nations came the news that the people of London found protection in the London underground railway system. How about Tokyo? No, said the authorities, the Tokyo subway system was too shallow to afford protection against high-explosive bombs. Another dream demolished. Build shelters? The government had no resources for such a program. The Japanese people began to understand that their government had simply waited too long.

The newspapers, covering the heavy attacks on German cities, editorialized that the people must protect themselves. "All very well," said the public, "but if the government can do nothing for us, what can we do for ourselves?"

A wave of fatalism swept across Japan. "Our cities will be wiped out," was the reaction. But what was to be done?

Shikatta ganai. There was nothing to be done.

In the summer of 1944, the mood of fatalism grew stronger. Some mothers would not allow their children to go to play in the parks on sunny days, because they feared that an air raid might come.

As the summer continued, the public reaction grew stronger, although it was concealed. Censorship and the "thought-control" police prevented the public exchange of information, but in the wine shops around the universities and in the privacy of households, people talked about the coming air raids.

The Japanese government responded to the public's concerns

in an unprecedented manner. Promises were made to build air-raid shelters and to improve the defenses of the nation. Suddenly the militarists were conscious that the people were more concerned about events in the homeland than in the progress of the war abroad. So they responded with the promise that by September the Japanese air defenses would be impregnable, and that also by that date the Japanese forces abroad would have turned the war around. Morale began to rise.

Some thoughtful people looked around Tokyo and saw the congestion, the crowding of street upon street, of house upon house, so many little paper-and-wood boxes that would go up like kindling if fires ever got a good start. They saw what the Americans knew: that Japan's cities consisted largely of wooden houses, that only 10 percent of the structures were modern steel and concrete, that the modern factories were usually surrounded by wooden structures. The government's response, to pass out buckets and fire flails and shovels, was already seen as too little.

On paper, the civil defense authorities had a plan to spray the houses of Tokyo and the other cities with chemicals that should impregnate the wood and prevent fires from starting. What a fine plan! But where were the chemicals and where were the sprayers? They did not appear. The plan never got off paper. The chemicals were in short supply, and they were needed for the direct war effort. Stories about the plans and the wonderful methods appeared in the press, but that was all.

There was also talk of dispersing factories, and some new factories were being built outside the city complex of Tokyo. But the authorities complained of a shortage of cement and steel, and none of the old factories were torn down.

As for civil defense, that summer it began to become almost laughable. The authorities in Tokyo set up a block program, calling for women, children, and the old and the unemployed to train for civil defense every morning from 5:00 A.M. to 7:00 A.M. And what was the training? As one citizen put it, "They give prizes for those who can throw water highest in the air from a bucket."

And where were the fire lanes? It was not that the Tokyo authorities did not know what a fire lane was. The Chinese in Chungking had slashed fire lanes through their crowded city years before, when the Japanese bombers began appearing overhead. Why didn't Tokyo do the same? The reality was that although the people fully expected air raids, the government was trapped by its own refusal to admit that it was possible for the Allies to attack the Japanese homeland. General Tojo stood firmly on that policy. Therefore, it was officially impossible.

Then came the fall of Saipan and a new awareness by the Japanese government that the only reason the Americans would take so much trouble to capture the Mariana Islands was to use them as airfields from which to bomb Japan. As Admiral Nagano of the Japanese naval general staff put it, "Hell is upon us. This is terrible."

Prince Higashikuni, commander of Home Defense Headquarters, was privately convinced that the loss of Saipan meant the loss of the war, but of course he could say nothing like that in public, for fear of being clapped into jail even if he was a prince. But within his own organization he was open enough, and his attitude added to the general feeling of futility. "If we cannot stop the B-29s from coming over Japan, we can do nothing," he said. "We have nothing in Japan that we can use against such a weapon."

Even within the army, the feeling that the war was lost now began to emerge. Lieutenant General Kawabe, deputy chief of the Army General Staff, returned to Tokyo in August from a front-line inspection tour. Coming in fresh, he had the immediate sense that within the general staff a feeling of desperation and despair had been generated by the fall of Saipan.

The government's reaction to this was to begin a program designed to bring awareness of the danger to the people, and to increase the blustering claims that Japan was about to turn the war around. Air-raid drills were inaugurated in 1944 and held with increasing frequency as the year wore on. Corporate managers were informed by the Home Ministry that they were responsible for the safety of their workers and were encouraged to prepare air-raid shelters, although the government would not build shelters itself. Citizens were told that it was their responsibility to protect themselves, by building shelters either in the gardens of their houses or under the houses. Through the neighborhood associations, new communications about air raids were coming along all the time.

On March 1, 1945, *Mainichi Shimbun* devoted a column to the air defenses of Hammatsu, the "gateway" to the Kanto Plain for the B-29s. The purpose of the article was to provide a stirring example for the citizens of Tokyo.

Hammatsu was constantly getting bombed by B-29 pilots who for some reason did not make the primary targets. Since there were several munitions plants in the city, it was always a target. On virtually every raid, someone dropped some bombs on Hammatsu. But the residents of Hammatsu were not terrified. "The primary objective of these residents of Hammatsu is to do their part in beating and crushing the enemy," said *Mainichi*.

The city had been bombed on February 15, day and night. The next day some seventy carrier-borne planes had attacked Hammatsu again, sweeping the streets and houses with machine guns.

On the following day, another seventy planes had machine-gunned children in the streets as well as "other objects regardless of their character."

But, said *Mainichi*, "this ordeal intensified the determination of the residents, who have adapted their daily life to meet conditions necessary for victory in the war."

The people lived in their anti-air-raid uniforms, which meant long-sleeved shirts and the ubiquitous *monpei* (shapeless trousers) and protective hoods. They used small carts to move their belongings.

> They have already completed a perfect system of air-raid shelters located in holes dug horizontally in the earth. They are paying special attention to the prevention of fires. They are constructing water reservoirs on every available piece of land, using pieces of material from fences and other things which would hinder firefighting.

The motto of the area, said *Mainichi*, was to guard one's house by oneself. And the reporter told the story of Kiku Ishiuchi, a woman who singlehandedly pulled an incendiary bomb off the roof of her house on February 10, when the B-29s dropped firebombs on the city. Kiku Ishiuchi was eighty years old.

And here was the real point that the government wanted made:

> Each air raid brings about a noticeable increase in the ardor of the employees in the munitions industries. There are few munitions workers who would allow the damage caused by the enemy to their houses, even the death of members of their families, to interfere with performance of their factory work.

The Japanese had maintained all during the war that if the Americans ever did try to bomb Japan, the result would be the strengthening of the people's will to fight. That attitude had to be encouraged.

Yes, the people of Hammatsu were steadfast. Each time an air raid hit the city, said *Mainichi*, the residents increased their donations to the government to build more fighting planes to destroy the Americans. That was the spirit that was wanted everywhere in Japan.

By the first week in March 1945, the general public concern about the American air raids was increasing. One reason was that most of the recent raids had included increasing numbers of incendiaries. *Yomiuri Shimbun* discussed the matter.

"The enemy's air raids are becoming more systematic and larger in scale," said the newspaper. "A particular feature has been the recent indiscriminate bombing of shopping centers and residential areas. While this is, needless to say, indirectly aimed to destroy our fighting strength, there is a great deal of intentional scheming in it, too."

American planes, on their bombing raids in the western part of the Kanto area, scattered propaganda leaflets telling the Japanese that their government was doing badly in not protecting them.

"Their contents were absurd and only served to reveal the enemy's ignorance of the national characteristics of the Japanese." The Americans were trying to estrange the civilians and the military and thus stir up trouble. It was old stuff, said *Yomiuri*. American Ambassador Joseph Grew had spent ten years in Japan trying to stir up trouble before the war, and had failed. Did the Americans think that they would now be able to turn Japanese against Japanese?

That same day, *Tokyo Shimbun* called on the Japanese people for further effort in the total mobilization of the country against the enemy. The government had just changed the characters or ideographs used to describe the war. Since the battle of Leyte, the war had been referred to as *kessen*, or "decisive war." But hereafter it was to be referred to as *chinamagusai*—"bloody war" or "war to the death."

On March 8, the Tokyo newspapers announced that the National Labor Mobilization Ordinance would go into effect on March 10. This emergency law gave the government the power to transfer people from any industry to any other, depending on the needs as seen in Tokyo. It was a part of the stringent new regulations that constituted "total mobilization" for the war. Hereafter, no employee could leave his job without government permission, and no employer could fire an employee without permission. Men were to be transferred to the armed services, and women would take their posts in greatly increasing numbers. One of the most effective aspects of the new mobilization was supposed to be the increase in use of women in key roles.

Many industries would be closed down entirely if they were not deemed essential to the progress of the war, and the people employed in them would be transferred to essential industries.

In the railroads, there were to be new reductions in passenger travel, reserving more trains for the movement of goods and troops. All express train service was to be discontinued immediately.

In agriculture, more efforts were to be made to increase output. The standard now was a family of six cultivating five acres. More production was wanted.

Saturday, March 10, was to be Army Day, the fortieth celebration of the reorganization of Japan's modern war machine. It was the fourth Army Day to be celebrated in this war, the first having come just as the Japanese had occupied Manila. Major General Shutsu Matsumura, the chief of the army press section, was preparing a major radio address to the nation to be delivered on Friday evening. He was, in the roundabout way the Japanese now used to announce their defeats, going to tell the public that Iwo Jima was very nearly lost and would soon fall. After furious attacks that decimated the enemy, he would say, the fighting had now been centered on the northern half of the island (because the "decimated" Americans now had taken the southern half).

Increasingly, as the Japanese gave ground everywhere, official reports of fighting centered about the glorious heroic activities of Japanese fighting men, and Matsumura's address was no exception.

There was Captain Hayauchi, commander of a rapid-fire cannon unit, who personally operated a gun and when his gun was destroyed, carried dynamite and rammed himself against an enemy tank. There were the two heroes of Osakayama who felled more than twenty enemy troops by sharpshooting and who seized a machine gun from the enemy and fought with tremendous valor. And there was the Nagata Death Band, which hacked into the enemy hordes from the Tamanayama region to the foot of Suribachiyama, killing and wounding numerous enemy troops, and returned safely. The action of the Japanese defenders has been truly as to make the gods weep.

The Supreme Commander, Lieutenant General Kuribayashi, stands constantly at the head of his forces and exhorts them with the determination to remain in spirit even if the flesh be felled on the firing lines, to destroy the enemy. Recently the Supreme Commander, thinking of the contingency in which communications might be cut, sent this message:

"I greatly regret the fact that I was unable to carry out my heavy responsibilities. I will be reborn seven times to defend the Imperial Land."

So there it was, the sidelong announcement that Iwo Jima, too, was now lost, and that General Kuribayashi had sent his last message, in the same vein as had those defenders of Saipan, Tinian, Guam, the Marianas, the Marshalls, and the Solomons, on the eve of his "glorious death."

Matsumura would also tell the nation that the desperate fighting on Luzon Island was not going well.

Furious street fighting has been continuing more than a month since the invasion of Manila by the enemy, and now the center of fighting is about to shift to the mountainous area to the east. The Japanese forces, although fighting under enemy air control since the Lingayen landing, have struck out in shock attacks, and each man has been killing ten, nay a hundred, enemy troops.

The enemy, said the general, had suffered 70,000 casualties, while the Japanese forces were relatively intact.

Why, then, the listener might wonder, were the Americans winning everywhere? But it was all going to be turned around in the "full scale bleeding" to come. The Japanese would cause the enemy 200,000 casualties, and then inflict "a fatal blow on him."

The darkest hour, said the general, came just before the dawn, and he now promised a dawn. When? Soon.

Then, toward the end of the speech, would come the real warning:

> Since late last year the enemy air raids have become severe. I expect that the raids will be intensified more than ever as the war situation progresses. I cannot but be indignant over the enemy's blind bombings of harmless Japanese people. . . . Should the brutal Americans think that severe air raids would break the fighting spirit of the Japanese people, then this would be a fool's dream.

And here was the most serious warning yet:

> The war situation has developed so much that we may anticipate a decisive battle to be waged

upon the mainland of Japan. Should, however, the enemy invade the Japanese mainland, all the officers and men of the fighting forces will turn into a mass of bullets against the enemy attack and into a massive citadel of defense. The true value of the Imperial forces under the command of the great sovereign will then be displayed. The indignation of the 100 million people who firmly maintain the prestige of the fundamental character of the people of Japan is so great that we Japanese fully believe in victory.

We must make America realize that Japan cannot be invaded under any circumstances. However frequently the enemy may come to Japan, this country will smash the invader each time. We are determined to fight longer than the enemy. We fight on to the last. I believe the highest peak of war morale is to fight the enemy with the conviction of sure victory.

So there it was—a speech in sharp contrast to that of four years earlier, when Japanese forces were victorious everywhere, and the general needed do no more than count the victories. Now there were no victories. All he could promise the people of Japan was the opportunity to fight on the beaches and die gloriously for the Emperor. It was not much of a promise that the army was delivering on the night of March 9, 1945, in celebration of that Army Day.

7
BOMBS
IN THE
NIGHT

THE B-29S DRONED ON OVER THE PACIFIC, HEADING FOR Tokyo. There were 334 of them to start, but as the hours went by, here and there a plane slipped out of formation and headed back with mechanical difficulties.

As they neared the shores of Japan, they began bucking a stout north wind. Still, the increased range gained by flying at medium altitude would take care of the problem.

That evening of March 9, the air-raid defenses of the Kanto Plain were on the alert, but they were having difficulties of their own. There were a few night-fighter units in the Katsuura area. At 10:30 P.M. the squadrons were put on the alert, told to expect an air raid by B-29s. This was not an order to fly, but an order to be prepared to operate.

Over the Kanto Plain the sky was clear this night, but by ten o'clock high winds were sweeping the region, winds of sixty to eighty miles per hour. They played hob with the Japanese radar and radio reception, causing all sorts of distortions and actually breaking down many antennae. Consequently, although the picket boats out at sea were sending their frantic signals of warning to Japan, and the navy receivers on the shore were picking up the messages, the news did not reach the air defense command because it was an army command, and not hooked into the same system. Thus the major night-fighter unit in the Kanto area, Number 10 Squadron, did not get sent into the air to investigate.

At about midnight came a frantic call from the coastwatchers on Fushan Island. Noises that sounded like B-29 bombers could be heard passing over the west side of the island.

But again, communications were so poor that night that the full effort of air defense could not make itself felt.

In the Eastern Army Command operations room, this report arrived at 12:30 A.M. accompanied by one from Tokyo's Tsuki Island that big bombers were overhead and that in the neighborhood bombs had begun dropping. Then reports began coming in from other places, until it was obvious that the air attackers had arrived in strength. The army put out a general call to the country, announcing a major air raid on Tokyo.

What was most surprising about this attack was that it differed from all others in that the B-29s were coming in at low altitude to strike at this most important of all industrial districts.

Immediately it was apparent that the B-29s were concentrating on the Koto industrial area between the Sumida and Ara rivers, twenty-five square kilometers of mixed housing and industrial plants.

The first bombers arrived, and immediately fires sprang up. They were dropping incendiaries and nothing but incendiaries. At 12:08, the first bombs came down in large clusters and started very large fires in Kiba, on the Tokyo waterfront. These fires spread very quickly in the strong winds. Two minutes later the bombers dropped in the second and third spots, and the fires spread in areas where about 400,000 people lived. In fourteen minutes the hellfire began. The following formations then swarmed in, guided by the great fires, and as they dropped their bombs around all these fires, the stage was set for the final massacre.

Twenty-year-old Takeiro Ueba was inside his family house in downtown Tokyo that evening. He was studying the courses that would lead him later to become a teacher in the Tokyo public schools.

Also in the house that night were his father, Aichi, his mother, Umeko, his younger brother, Kenjiro, and his younger sister, Ueko. The father was employed by a fishing company as a manager. The radio announced that the planes were coming. Ueba's father was standing looking at the sky, but not yet seeing anything. Ueba went to an open space near the house. Ueba, as a member of the young volunteer fireman's organization, had duties as an air-raid warden. The remainder of the family went into the local park for safety. Fortunately they were safe; the house was on the edge of the burning district, but it was not burned, although the third and fourth houses down the street from it were burned.

Soon enough, Ueba was out in the streets trying to fight the fires with straw mats and sand. The water system had failed, and there was no chance of stopping a rain of firebombs with straw mats, about the only useful instrument the volunteers had. Chemical extinguishers, had there been any, might have stopped some houses from burning.

Miwa Koshiba was a pretty Tokyo housewife living in the industrial district—actually in Asakusa, near the temple. She came from a well-to-do family of very well-bred people who followed the old customs. Because she was the only child of her industrialist father, when she married, her husband changed his name, taking his wife's surname of Koshiba.

Dutiful to the government and responsive to the warnings of danger, Miwa Koshiba and her husband had sent three of their five children to stay with some of his relatives in Gifu, near

Nagoya—his relatives, because Miwa came from a whole line of Tokyoites and had no relatives anywhere else in Japan. She intended to keep only her new baby and her four-year-old daughter with her in Tokyo, because the little girls were too young for school.

Her six-year-old son, Aiyawa, was about ready to start elementary school, and Miwa wanted to make some new clothes for him, since buying anything decent was out of the question in these war days. So her husband went down to Gifu and fetched the boy home on March 8, 1945.

"Bitter memories! Bitter sadness, sharper than the unripe persimmon."

Miwa's mother, Yae, was ill and in bed in Miwa's house, and her father, Ichibei, who was ailing, was there too. Although she was used to servants, they had no servants; it would have been considered most unpatriotic in time of war, and only a few people in Japan did have servants these days. Miwa was wife, housekeeper, and nurse all in one.

So on the evening of March 9, 1945, the Koshiba household consisted of six people.

When the air-raid sirens began to howl, the Koshibas knew they must act swiftly. There was only one way to get the mother and father to safety, and that was for Miwa's husband to carry her mother on his back and for her to lead and support her father as they took them to the nearby school, which was the "safe place." But to do this, Miwa had first to take care of her children, so she put them down in the homemade air-raid shelter, the hole they had dug in the garden at the urging of the block committee. Then, mindless of the noise and the dreadful fires they could see rising in the distance, she and her husband took the old parents to the school.

Miwa hurried back to the house while her husband stayed with the old people, but she found there was no house, just ashes, embers, and rubbish where the house once had been. She ran around to the garden, and saw that the wooden cover of the air-

raid shelter was aflame. She grabbed the bucket the block committee had supplied, and going to the cistern they had built for
just such a purpose, she began dousing the shelter cover with
water. She put out the fire, tore away the cover, burning herself
through her *monpei*, and found her children inside, scared half to
death, disheveled and crying, but alive!

Aiyawa, the six-year-old boy, was badly burned about the face,
but he was alive.

Taking the children, Miwa began to walk. It was over half a
mile to the bridge across the Sumida River, but she hurried along,
carrying the baby, and urging the four-year-old and the six-year-
old.

The fire storm was raging on all sides, and the air was so hot
and full of debris that Miwa believed the Americans had dropped
not only firebombs but heavy oil on the region to make the fires
burn. (This effect might also have been achieved by the bursting
of the big napalm bombs used by the pathfinder planes.)

Finally, Miwa came to the bank of the Sumida River, which she
found almost completely ablaze, with people dropping all around
her. Frantically she searched for some shelter and discovered a
large sewer pipe that emptied into the river. Without a moment's
hesitation, she pushed the children into the sewer and followed
them. There she sat, all night long, bathing the children in sewer
water to protect them from the terrible heat. As it was, their
mouths, noses, and eyes were almost solidly caked with filth, and
the heat did not let up for hours. Three times that night the baby
stopped breathing, but each time Miwa brought her back to life.
How she did all this she did not know, for by the time she
reached the sewer, her eyes were caked shut and swollen so badly
from the heat that she could not see.

Thirty-two-year-old Satoko Sano lived in Takabashii on the banks
of the Sumida River with her forty-two-year-old husband and her
twin four-year-old daughters. Her husband was a factory worker,
his factory was very near the house.

At ten o'clock on the night of March 9, they heard the news reports about a coming bombing raid, but as always, no one could be sure that it would actually happen or that it would affect their area of Tokyo.

A few minutes later, however, she saw a B-29, flying much lower than any she had ever seen before.

Although the Sanos had an air-raid shelter in the garden, this attack came so suddenly that they did not even think of trying to go outside to use it.

When the bombing started, the news broadcasters warned everyone in the downtown Tokyo area to run away as quickly as possible. But the Sanos stayed in their house for a little while. Then they went to the Fukagawa Middle School grounds for shelter. But the school was filled with people and there was no room, so they went to a little park. Two or three hundred people were crowded into the park. They huddled there, the fire storm swirling around them, making the air so hot that it burned them through their monpei, and made the clothing stick to their skin. Sano's husband sugested that she and the children get into the Sumida River for shelter, but she refused. She was afraid, so she stayed in the park, the hot winds burning her and parching her throat. Satoko and her daughters all wore protective hoods, but all of them were burned off, and one of the children lost all her hair to the hot winds of the fire.

Nineteen-year-old Kimie Ono lived with his family in the Hamacho area of Nihonbashi District. At that time, because of damage from the earlier air raids, there were eight people living in his family's house. He had gone to bed early and was sound asleep when the air-raid siren suddenly began to scream. It was about midnight. Fuzzily, he got up. As always, he was wearing the monpei and long-sleeved shirt that were the night attire of virtually everyone in Tokyo. He knew it was something serious because the planes were so low that he believed they had awakened him. He went to the kitchen to put some food and other things into a rucksack. He sensed that if he was going to escape the house, he was going to have to do it in a hurry and that it was already very late. He went to the door and looked into the main street. Yes, it was late! The incendiaries were already falling all around his house and creating a sea of fire. It was midnight, but it seemed as bright as noon outside. Also, the wind was blowing furiously, and he could see the fires spreading. If he was going to escape before the house became an inferno, he had best be going. So he stepped out into the street and headed toward Ryogo-kubashi, following the electric train line.

The line was crowded with people carrying babies, packs, sleeping mats, and armloads of clothing, and pushing carts loaded high with household possessions. Shoving, shouting, shouldering others out of the way, they hurried along to escape the fire behind them. But the fires spread and soon were all around them. The heat grew more intense. People began to collapse on the roadway, but more waves of people came along, weeping, shouting, yelling, and trampling one another as they rushed toward the rivers. The wind was whistling with its waves of fiery death, at fifty miles an hour. People began dropping their possessions and staggering on. Carts were abandoned along the track. No one stopped to loot; to stop was to die. The fire wind swept lanes among the people, and families became hopelessly separated.

The horror was to grow worse. A mother and child were running ahead of Ono; suddenly the fire storm swept out a finger to lick at them, and in a second, before his eyes, the mother and child burst into flame. They were both burning everywhere. Their clothes afire, they staggered and fell to the ground. No one stopped to help them. Ono began shivering despite the heat as he ran on and on and on.

Ono felt that he and others should somehow stop to help, but how could they? He passed a burning temple ricefield, and saw nine roasted bodies lying there. He reached the Hisamatsu police station, and there asked an officer if it was possible to go to the Akira shrine for protection. It was impossible, said the policeman, the shrine was completely burned out.

A crowd had now assembled around the police station, and the fire was not far off. It was every man for himself, obviously, and everyone did what he thought he had to do. Ono and his eldest sister decided to escape the flames by diving into the Sumida River and remaining there until the fire storm passed.

But as they got to the bank they saw corpses of drowned people floating down the river. They turned back, even though they saw many people who were actually afire, jumping into the river. The scene was more horrible than ever.

They retraced their steps again and again. The fire had now left the temple ricefield, someone said, and they might go there.

It was about one o'clock in the morning, and the original ravaged area was beginning to quiet down as the fires spread to other areas. The fire had now spread into Yokoyama-cho.

Ono looked down at his *monpei* and saw that they were badly burned. He looked wildly about, and saw that a building on the riverbank had not collapsed, and they went there. But as they did, the building began emitting terrible noises and flames darted from it. It collapsed. What happened next he could not remember, but he found himself still alive, and dreadfully thirsty. He looked around for water, but found only mud.

Saki Hiratsuka lived in that same area through which Ono had run. On the evening of March 9 all was quiet, except for the strong winds that blew through the streets and shook the trees in the garden. At about 10:30 the air-raid siren began to give its eerie wail, but then it suddenly stopped. There was to be no air raid that night, it seemed. Even so, the siren itself had turned the whole night disagreeable.

Young Hiratsuka stayed up then for a while. After midnight, the air-raid siren suddenly began wailing again. Saki's mother and two sisters left the house, heading for the shelter area, which really meant one of the open spaces not far away. Hiratsuka and his father stayed on, for they had important affairs to take care of. They stuffed whatever valuables they thought they might salvage into rucksacks, and then piled on top the bedding that the family would need for the night in the open. Then they started out to join the women.

But by the time they got outside, the house was already on fire. They looked down the street. The fires were furious, and the wall of flame was advancing toward them, coming directly down the street they had expected to travel to join the others. There was no chance of that now. Indeed, they were threatened as the fire advanced, and the heat smashed at them. The fire was only fifty meters away. They turned to head back into the house, but there was no way back. The house was now fully engulfed. Fire and smoke and waves of heat threatened them on both sides.

Hiratsuka and his father dumped the rucksacks and the bedding and joined some people who were fleeing into the basement of a concrete building to the left of their house. It was the Yasuda Bank. About sixty people jammed into this building to seek shelter from the flames. Many of them had their belongings with them in packs or bedrolls. They pulled down the shutters and seemed to be safe. But in moments the heat became intense in the building, and people crowded into the middle room, where it seemed coolest.

Now the dilemma became worse, as the heat increased. The people inside knew that they could not stay, but outside the fires raged and they could not leave.

Hiratsuka had been crowded into a corner of the big room, and there he found water pipes. Quickly he turned the faucet open to the fullest, and by running water over himself he was able to bear the intense heat. All around, on other sides, people were beginning to collapse. One fell down, then another, and soon the bodies were covering the floor. Of the sixty people in that big room, half died.

* * *

Masuko Harino was a factory girl, living with others in a Volunteer Corps hostel in Nihonbashi. Every day after eating their breakfast in the hostel restaurant, they would go to Shinagawa to work in the Fukashi electrical machinery factory.

On March 9 their hostel was hit by firebombs. The bombs began falling all around the area, "like rain," the girls said. When the fires began to threaten the hostel, although it was not yet hit, the hostel manager said. "We will fight the fires to the last." He unfortunately did not survive the fires that night, and even his name has been lost.

As the danger grew, the hostel leader began giving more and more orders to the young men and women of the Volunteer Corps. Finally he saw that it was too late. The fires could not be put out. Here is Masuko Harino's account:

> As the worry grew over the fate of the hostel, one of the young people, Yoshikawa-san, and I went toward the factory, as we all fled. Somehow we two got separated from the others as we ran away fearing death.
>
> People's clothes were on fire, a fiery drama it had become. Some people were writhing about in torment and no one had time to help them. In front of me I saw the Meiji theater filled with people, so many we could not get inside. Intense heat was coming from the fire storm. My eyes seemed about to pop out. Yoshikawa-san cut her way through the mob and I followed along the road, seeking some respite from the blowing heat of the terrible fire. We ran. We saw fleeing shapes, but little else. A telephone pole collapsed, and twisted electric wires snaked out along the ground. The road on both sides was full of people's possessions, burning up.

My eyes hurt. Breathing was difficult and I felt
that life was escaping me. I found a broken
hydrant and soaked my *zukin* [air-raid turban] and
put it on my head, almost unconsciously. Finally
I fled as far as Kiyosu bridge. . . .

Seizo Hashimoto, although he was only thirteen years of age,
was an old hand at firefighting. His family had lived in Myoshiko
in the Fukagawa district until that area was attacked by bombing
and they were burned out. They had then moved into Koto.

Now that area was ablaze, and the family fled down Mitsubei
Avenue, facing the Omiya Bridge. Here, Hashimoto found the
fire both before and behind him. Both banks of the Sumida River
were ablaze, and the heat was almost unbearable. The fire seemed
to be everywhere. Hashimoto was terrified; it looked like a great
snake or dragon, its mouth belching fire. Heavy smoke was blowing everywhere in those high winds that swept the fire along. The
fire itself had not yet reached his area. He watched, terrified, his
whole body shaking. Then he saw a strange sight: a woman in a
gold-braid kimono with gold and silver threads and a one-piece
obi, shining in the bright light of the fire, a red lotus blossom in
her flying hair as she was whipped and twisted by the hot wind.
Suddenly her whole body burst into flame like a torch. Then an
unlined kimono came swirling out of the fire storm toward him
and dropped on the ground.

He saw two people emerge from the river, a father and child,
their clothes dripping wet, saved from the fire by the gods.

He approached the bridge, which was now swept by fire, except for a large central pillar that protected a small area, about
eighty centimeters high, from the wind and fire, and, alone, he
lay facedown there. . . .

Chiyoko Sakamoto, eight months pregnant, also lived in
Fukagawa district. She and her husband heard the air-raid siren as

soon as it began to wail, and rushed out of their house. But they were stopped by civil guards. They had started out toward the Sumida River, but there, as the guards said, they could see the flames shooting up, the wild flames of the fire storm.

They turned back, but the overheated wind was at them, and soon Chiyoko's eyes were closed tight from the grit and heat, and she could scarcely even think. She clutched at her husband, believing she could not go on. He encouraged her, and as in a dream, she fled the flames. In her advanced pregnancy, her belly was swollen to three times its normal size. Staggering, they moved through mounds of baggage and other people's burning possessions toward the Susaki red-light district, where they hoped to find refuge. They were stopped at a police box by an officer who said it would be impossible to go any farther into that area. The whole geisha district was burning. Ahead they could see the fires raging. What to do?

Masatake Obata was a small manufacturer in the Koto area. His factory was precisely one of the sort that General LeMay was interested in wiping out. Obata made component parts for aircraft, and some of his work was also farmed out to family industries in the area.

Obata was a retired soldier; he had spent his two years of compulsory service in the Japanese army, and had been released to join the reserve association. Of course, following the attack on Pearl Harbor, the current group of soldiers were kept on indefinitely, but those who had gotten out were for the most part left alone. Obata's service to Japan as a war materials manufacturer was much greater than it could have been as an ordinary soldier.

On March 9, 1945, there were eight people in the Obata household: Masatake himself, his wife and four chidren, and two sisters. His sisters actually lived up by Ueno Park, but as was the practice in these days of food shortages, they had undertaken a trip to the countryside and there had bargained with farmers to secure some food. Mostly what they got was sweet potatoes, but sweet potatoes were more than welcome in Tokyo in the spring of 1945.

The sisters had come to the Obata house during the afternoon, and what with gossiping with Mrs. Obata and eating dinner, they had stayed later than they had expected. Then at about eight o'clock came a preliminary report of an air raid, and Mrs. Obata suggested that since the ladies lived so far away—halfway across metropolitan Tokyo—they ought to stay the night with the Obatas and then go on home the next day.

When the actual air raid began at about midnight, Obata went outside. He soon saw that it was serious, and he hurried inside to change from his civilian clothes into his uniform. All retired soldiers had a special duty, and Obata's was as an air-raid warden. He had a specific area to patrol, and it was time for him to get to work.

He also told his wife and children to get dressed and prepare to go out of the house, since the firebombs were so dangerous. He took the family to Fuji Park, then went to a meeting of the neighborhood association to decide what course to follow. They decided in a hurry to evacuate the women and children from the fire area. They would, said the instructions, go to Sumida Park, one of the larger open spaces, and thus deemed relatively safe.

So Mrs. Obata and the children were instructed to go to Sumida Park and wait out the air raid there, and they left Fuji Park.

Obata moved out into the streets on patrol, wearing his helmet and uniform jacket. He began moving from door to door, checking to see that no one in his neighborhood had made the mistake of trying to wait out this air raid in the shelter hole in the garden or beneath the house. This raid, as the defense authorities could see from the beginning, was something new, and the very character of Japanese houses meant there would be a great deal of trouble.

He found a number of people inside the houses—some mothers tending babies, some older women, and some older men. He did not encounter any men of military age, nor did he expect to, since the vast majority of men were in the service. Obata told the people that they must leave their homes, and he helped them and waited while they got ready to go out. Then he went on to the next house. Everyone was sent to Sumida Park.

Warden Obata finished his work and then went into the main street again; this time heading for Sumida Park to meet his wife and children. He encountered many people who were complaining that the heat from the burning houses and the smoke were making it very hard to breathe. Even with their air-raid hoods, they were not very safe. Obata saw several of the hoods burning, and before the people could get them off their heads, they were injured. But when they got the hoods off it was worse, for in seconds their hair began to burn.

There was nothing Obata could do to help them. His own air-raid hood was afire, and he was trying to put it out by slapping at it.

Suddenly a whole cluster of six-pound incendiary bombs dropped not ten feet away. Before he could shout or move, the cluster exploded, sending the full impact of one bomb against his face. As a fire warden he was wearing one of the conical Japanese army helmets designed to protect soldiers from shellfire and bombs but not from bombs that burst and came up from below.

The steel helmet was more of a hindrance than a help in this case. The impact knocked him down, the steel helmet crashed against the hard roadbed, and Warden Obata fell unconscious.

He did not know how long he was unconscious, perhaps an hour or two. When he awakened, he discovered that his shoes had burned up and his toes had melted. His hands and arms were so badly burned that they were nearly black. Other bits of flame had burned him in many parts of his body, through the clothing.

When Warden Obata came to, still burning, he could not use his hands. He rolled on the ground to put out the fires. Then he got up and began trying to walk toward a trench built alongside the road to shelter the occupants of streetcars if they were caught in a raid. The planes were still coming over, still bombing.

His feet swelled up to three times their normal size, and as he walked to the trench he felt as if he were walking on tennis balls.

In the air-raid shelter he found seven other people. All were alive, but suffering from very severe burns. None of them knew how badly they were hurt, but each could see the burns of other people. Obata looked them over, and saw that all were badly injured. Some of them complained that they were very, very sleepy.

"Yes," said Warden Obata, "and if you sleep you will die. Wake up! Wake up!"

He instructed every person to wake up his neighbor if he saw him falling asleep. So they all shouted at each other. Then they began chanting Buddhist prayers together, to keep one another awake during this long night, while they waited for the dawn.

Tokyo's fire department was prepared to fight the fires this night, as they had done many times before. But suddenly the firemen found themselves facing totally new problems. The bombers came in low, and the bombs dropped like strings of firecrackers. With the first fires, the hose companies headed out, and almost immediately discovered that the fire storm had destroyed water mains and that the intense heat made it impossible to get to the center of the fires. The powerful winds picked up pieces of burning debris and carried them from block to block. After an hour, the firemen had to admit almost total defeat. Ninety-six fire engines were burned to ashes that night. Eighty-eight firemen lost their lives, and forty went missing, as did 500 civil guards who worked with the fire department.

Katsumoto Saotome was 12 years old. His family consisted of his mother, his father, an older brother who had been called into the navy, two older sisters, and himself. He was a student in a middle school in Tokyo.

Bombs in the Night

At eight o'clock in the evening the family heard the first sirens warning of an air raid, but the raid did not develop and the all-clear came soon, and then Tokyo Radio announced that there was no raid in sight.

That night the wind began to rise. It was cloudy, and occasionally a rain squall swept through the area. At midnight, the bombers came.

Kinosuke Wakabayashi was a commander in the civil guard, senior officer of Sumida district. Weeks earlier, he had responded to suggestions from higher authority that the best course was to move his family outside the Tokyo area, and he had sent his wife and children to the country to stay with relatives. On March 9, then, Wakabayashi and his teenaged daughter, who was still in middle school, were the only residents of the house in Sumida.

When the sirens began to sound, Commander Wakabayashi went from house to house in his district, making sure that all the people had left their houses. When every check had been made, and he saw that the fire storm had taken over the industrial section of the city, and that the firemen were unable to function, he also saw that there was nothing he and his men could do. The problem for every person was to save himself if he could. Commander Wakabayashi went to his own house, found it burning, picked up his teenaged daughter, and headed for the Asahi Brewery warehouse on the bank of the Sumida River. He went inside and found no one at all there. The roof was made of corrugated iron and the walls of concrete, and he decided he had found the place to ride out the storm.

They could not enter the locked and bolted doors of the warehouse, but the shelter of the concrete walls was enough to save them both. They had no food or water, but they were alive.

From their vantage point, Wakabayashi and his daughter could see the dreadful carnage that was occurring all around them.

When the fires became a fire storm, and the flames raged everywhere, many people of this area of Tokyo ran to find open spaces, parks, schoolyards—anywhere the fire might not lap at them. But the flames followed them, raging in those sixty-, seventy-, and eighty-mile-an-hour winds, and swept over whole wide spaces, carrying the fiery death. People were caught running in the street, their clothes would begin to burn, their hair would burn, and then they would fall and the hot winds and flames would pass over them until, mercifully, consciousness departed.

From their vantage point on the edge of the Sumida River, the Wakabayashis could see people running to the river, through the walls of flame, and jumping in to save themselves. But soon both banks of the river were clogged with people. The bridges were so hot that the concrete burned the feet of the runners, and any who touched a bit of iron or steel would be seared like a rasher of bacon on a skillet. The bridges, streets, and rail lines were scenes of death as people dropped from exhaustion, burns, and suffocation by the burning air.

After an hour, the Wakabayashis felt safe enough to look around the warehouse for an entry point. They came to a locked gate, and their presence attracted the watchman inside, who unlocked the gate and let them in. There they found Matsuo Hayashi, another resident of the area, who had also fled to the shelter of the warehouse. In spite of the terror around them, they felt safe here.

Kenji Moro lived in Koiwa, an area of Tokyo which was not hit that night. But from there, Moro could see that Kojima, where his factory was located, was nothing but a mass of flames and bombs, bombs, bombs. "The bombs," he said later, "were coming down like raindrops."

Kaneko Hideyoshi was a Buddhist priest who lived in Tokyo's Fukagawa district. When the bombs began to fall, Hideyoshi took his wife by the hand and, abandoning their burning house, they moved into the street. It was filled with smoke, so thick they could not see ten feet ahead. But for perhaps a foot above the ground level, there was no smoke. They dropped to the ground and crawled to the shelter of a large concrete building a block away. This was a cable manufacturing plant. There they found shelter in an enormous concrete pipe. Others kept coming, until there were perhaps twenty people crowded in the pipe for safety. They were safe from the flames, but not from the intense heat that swept through the entire area, heat so terrible that the bridges across the rivers were clogged with bodies. And in the Sumida River, where many had gone to escape the heat and the flames, the tide was changing. The swift current was beginning to move people out toward the sea.

Tatsu Sakai was at home alone when the bombs began to rain down on her house near the Sumida River. Her husband was at work. She heard the sirens and the bombers, and then began to see the flames. She ran out of her house into the shallow hole the Sakais had dug in response to the block committee's advice that every household was responsible for its own defenses. Down she went, taking with her the family pet, a cocker spaniel. She pulled the wooden cover over the hole from beneath, and crouched in the darkness, listening. The bombers came and the bombs rained down, and her house was destroyed. But, unlike many others who were burned to death in their holes by the fire storm, Tatsu Sakai was saved. The hot breath of death passed her by. In an hour she lifted the cover, saw the burning embers of her house and the other houses around it, picked up the dog, and set out to seek shelter. She walked for two hours, looking for a place of safety. Finally she saw a large group of people huddled under a bridge across the Sumida River, and she went down to join them. There, wonder of wonders, she found her husband!

Before the bombs began to fall on her block, Koiko Yoshie had time to put together her sleeping mat and quilts. Then, with her small son in hand she headed for Sumida Park, and for the pond near the Meiji theater. She stayed near the big stone memorial, put down her futon, and laid her small son on it. She was safe.

Nearby was the Ushijima Shrine, where many people huddled together and some more were saved. Others went to the grounds of Honju High School, where an unfinished construction project had left an enormous hole in the ground. The hole had filled with water, and it was another place of refuge from the fire. The school, like many others in Tokyo, was one of the places approved by the authorities for shelter from air raids.

Chiyoko Yokozawa was in the hospital, and on the evening of March 9 her second son was born. She was alone, in the sense that her husband Maasaki was in the service, and although he was stationed in Tokyo, he was on duty and had no chance to be with her.

Hardly had the baby been born when Chiyoko Yokozawa was evacuated from the burning hospital. Carrying her baby, she set out to save herself.

Still the B-29s continued to come in, and still the bombs kept falling down like rain.

8
THE
LONG
NIGHT

AFTER THE FIRST HOUR, THE TOKYO FIRE DEPARTMENT GAVE UP all attempts to control the fire storm. How could anything be done? In the affected industrial area the water mains were broken, and much of the firefighting equipment was lost. At one station, virtually all the firemen were killed as they tried to get their equipment out of the station. The fire storm swept over them and left behind a hill of corpses and a tangle of melted machinery.

The raid lasted for about two hours and forty minutes, not counting a handful of straggling bombers. For that period the B-29s raged ceaselessly over the eastern section of the Japanese capital city and brought widespread damage in the Koto section.

As noted, the relatively small fires in the central area spread very rapidly because of the high winds and became a fire storm that then swept northwest across the industrial district, and a general conflagration erupted, which then wiped out nearly every structure that would burn. Within the first hour, all of Tokyo's eastern section was in flames, or had burned out, leaving the ground exhausted and filled with roasted corpses.

Once the initial horror had passed, those who survived some-how managed to pull themselves together. Nearly all were alone or in small groups. Families that had been able to stick together were rare, and all too often they lost several members to the raging flames. Even men and women who seemed unhurt would still bear the scars of this night: a most common one was a darkening of the skin that lasted for days, weeks, months, and sometimes forever because of the intensity of the heat.

Takeiro Ueba, who had found sanctuary relatively easily, roused himself the next morning and went to have a look at his family's house. It was unhurt, which was a miracle, for in the night 261,000 houses had burned, and a million people had been made homeless. All this had been accomplished by fewer than 300 American bombers, using conventional weapons—if a firebomb can be called a conventional weapon—within a few hours.

To Ueba, the full impact of the disaster was some time in strik-ing, since his own family was not directly affected, no member of the family had been lost, no one was injured, and their house remained, just on the edge of the drop zone. A few houses nearby were burned by early drops, but the damage there was scattered.

After the bombing ended, Ueba went out to survey the dis-trict, and to see a good friend. He did not find the friend that day because his house had burned down. Where to look? Ueba went to the Asakusa Shrine, but found it burned down. He was shocked to see the hundreds of dead people and horses on the side of the road and on the Nobashi, a bridge over the Sumida. He had no way of knowing that the death toll had already passed the 100,000 mark.

In a few days, Ueba went back to school, but soon he was called up to the army in Kumamoto. He was assigned to a ma-chine-gun squad, but the weapons shortage was such that Ueba got very little training. Then, almost before he knew it, the war ended, and he returned to battered Tokyo and his studies. He graduated and went into teaching, and retired finally in the early

1980s, to become an editorial consultant to a large Tokyo publishing house with offices in New York as well as Tokyo.

But what about the others whose stories have so far been followed?

Miwa Koshiba somehow got through the night in her stinking sewer on the bank of the Sumida River. She saved her baby daughter from death three times that night. She devoted as much of her attention as she could to her six-year-old son, for she could sense that he was growing sicker by the hour. Time after time she wrung out a rag in the filthy sewer water, to cool the boy's fevered brow.

Morning came, but dawn brought little relief for Miwa and her children. She sat in the sewer, still blinded, her eyes sealed shut by the hot winds, which had carried a sort of gluey grit. Finally, late in the morning she was discovered by some kindly people who took her by the hand and led her out of the sewer, to a place where someone had brought water and some cooked rice. She was able to wash her face then, and to unglue her eyes.

Later in the day she decided to take the children back to the school where her husband had remained with her mother and father. But when she tried to cross the Sumida River, she saw that it was impossible. The bridges were piled high with the bodies of people who were trapped there and then kissed by the devilish fire storm, the dying bearing down the living and then helping to suffocate them.

Kotatori Bridge was the worst, the one where most of the people fleeing from the fire had fallen and died. Miwa decided to go upstream and cross on Hajima Bridge, and later in the day, with her three children, she made her lonely way to the bridge and found that she was able to cross. No one paid her any attention as she struggled along, carrying the baby and sometimes the boy, who was now more than half delirious with fever. Everyone in downtown Tokyo seemed to have his own tragedy to occupy him that day; there was little concern for strangers.

Somehow, during the night, Miwa had lost her shoes, and now, walking along the streets, she felt the retained heat and her feet grew very sore. When she reached Hajima Bridge, this became a real problem; the bridge was still so hot that she could not cross in her bare feet. She went back and wandered around until she found the body of a woman who wore shoes that would fit her. Then this elegant, wealthy, cultured young woman took the shoes of a corpse and put them on without a whimper, to make her way across the bridge and to the school where she hoped her husband and parents were safe.

As she went, she inquired of all who would listen, "Where can I get some medical help for my son?"

No one seemed to know, so she went on, back to the school, for she knew that if the school was standing and the authorities were still there, they would help her.

It took her three days to reach the school. Each day she found food and water for her children. Each day she saw her six-year-old son growing worse. She did find an aid station, and there the brusque doctor in charge told her it appeared that her son had contracted typhus.

"What is to be done?" she asked.

"Nothing," he said.

Was there not a vaccination against typhus?

Yes, but all the vaccine was reserved for the army troops.

And so Miwa, the native Tokyoite, knew that if she wanted help for her son she would have to seek it outside the city.

Finally she did reach the school, and found to her relief that her husband, father, and mother were all alive and safe. The flames had not come this way, and the bombers had missed this target.

Now the problem was to get to Gifu, to the hot springs that would help them all, and to find medicine and medical help for her son. The family started out for the main railroad station of Tokyo, to take the Tokkaido line to Gifu. They had a long wait to get aboard a train, for half of Tokyo, it seemed, had the same idea. But finally they squeezed aboard a train (there was no such thing as an express after the March 9 bombings), and the cars inched their way from station to station, heading west. But on the train, Miwa's mother suddenly had a heart attack and died. And before they reached Gifu, little Aiyawa died in his mother's arms.

Miwa survived to prosper, and in the 1980s, after her husband died, she was the head of two large manufacturing companies, a handsome woman of seventy-five whose expensive clothing concealed the external scars of the terrible fire storm of March 10, 1945. But the internal scars remain. Miwa still talks about the terror of that night. What frightened her most, she said, was not the bombing or the fire storm, but the sight of the American bombers coming down to machine-gun the Japanese civilians as they ran.

The fact is that there was no machine-gunning. As mentioned previously, by General LeMay's order the bombers carried no machine-gun ammunition or gunners. But Miwa did not believe this when told by the author during an interview in Tokyo, and never will. What happened to her in those terrible early-morning hours of March 10 is seared into her soul; she can talk about her own tragedy quite dispassionately, but when she thinks of that machine-gunning . . .

Satoko Sano and her children remained in the improvised shelter near the school until the all-clear sounded in the morning. As for Satoko's husband, had he lived in Hammatsu, according to *Mainichi Shimbun*, he would have trudged off through the fire storm to the munitions factory near his house, to put in his hours and give more to the defense effort in spite of the threat to his family. But in truth, Sano did not even think about the factory. In the confusion of the fire storm, he had become separated from his family, and he spent the night looking for them. He found them that next morning at the little park where they had taken refuge, one small daughter with her hair burned off, all three with many burns. They had been lying on the ground with many other wounded, and when Sano came up to them, he thought at first that they were all dead. But now there was a joyful reunion. *Mainichi Shimbun*'s propaganda about Hammatsu did not hold for Tokyo. Even after being reunited with his family, Sano did not think of going to see what had happened to the munitions factory where he worked.

That morning the Sanos began to think about their burns. All of them had been burned to some extent. Satoko had burns on her arms and back, where flying embers had hit and stuck. She knew what to do. She and the family headed for Nanamo, her hometown, which was famous for its hot springs. They had a difficult time getting there. All the ships on the Sumida River had burned; all the trains in the entire district were destroyed; all the buses, streetcars, trucks, and automobiles were gone. There was only one way to get there. She walked the entire twenty kilometers, as did all the rest of the family, in *tabi* and *geta*, the wooden sandals that nearly everyone wore.

They stayed with Satoko's relatives for some time, and every day they bathed in the hot springs. The warm soothing waters cured all their burns, and the little girl's hair came back.

Kimie Ono, having rejected the muddy water beside the road, felt as if he were dying of thirst, but what was to be done? They came to the Hisamatsu Akira police station but there was no help there; the building was too small to hold any more people. Nearby was the Meiji theater, a great ferroconcrete building that looked very promising. Ono and his elder sister headed there, but when they got to the entrance and were swept inside by the enormous milling crowd, they discovered that the building was completely jammed. With great difficulty they pushed their way to an exit and got out of that place, fearful that they would be suffocated inside.

Now, looking for a place to hide from the fire, they found the basement of a building. From the depths they heard the groans of someone who was dying. Mixed with the groans came words in a ghastly voice. It was uncanny and horrible to hear, but they went down into the depths, because Ono and his sister were exhausted and could go no further, and the fire was right behind them, pressing onward with its hateful, heated breath. Holding hands, they climbed down into the basement room. There they saw a sight terrible to both of them. The person who was dying was someone they knew, a girl named Hayama, about the same age as Ono's elder sister, whose house near their uncle's house they had visited many times. The two families were so close that their mother called the girl *kimichan*, or "baby." As they came to Hayama-san and hugged her, she died, and Ono and his elder sister broke out crying.

Behind them the fire storm was still raging, coming toward their hiding place. More and more people came into the basement, people with skin burned from their arms, their faces ruined, vomiting, retching, dying. Ono had never seen so much suffering. And as the fire came, so did the smoke and the heat, and soon he found that he could scarcely breathe. A greasy sweat enveloped his entire body, and he felt that his chest was bursting. Then he lost consciousness.

He saw both his parents, in his wild dream, and they were happy and smiling. His mother was wearing kimono and *geta*. It all seemed very real, and even at the time he realized he must have been very near death at that moment. It seemed sad that his life would be snuffed out when he had not yet reached his twentieth year.

Death was actually just a few steps away. For as he lay there, an enormous booming sound came from the theater building. Inside, the people were being baked as if in a casserole. The terrible Meiji tragedy had begun. The roof, not air-raid-proof, was caving in. The people were crowded in so tightly that there was no chance of escape. All the exit and entry doors were jammed by bodies. Inside, hundreds were being trampled to death underfoot as they roasted.

Suddenly Ono awoke, and felt the strength returning to his

legs and his spirit coming back to him. He moved. As he watched, there came a crunching sound from the Meiji theater, and the whole building began to burn up. Inside and out, a mountain of corpses smoldered in the heat. And to think of it, Ono had been just one step away from joining in that death march. . . .

Kimie Ono survived the bombing and the fire, and lived to return to that scene twenty-six years later, to recall the terrible tragedy of that dreadful night.

The water kept rising in the basement of the building where Saki Hiratsuka and his father had taken refuge. It was the Yasuda Bank building. The heat was dreadful. Saki found his strength going. By this time the heat and the rising level of water in the basement of the building had taken their toll; of the sixty people who had taken refuge here, only about a half-dozen people were still alive, including Saki and his father.

The water level kept rising. To the right and left, bodies floated to the surface. Saki and his father were growing weaker, and death was very near. So they decided that Saki must make the ultimate effort to break their way out of the basement. The metal door was very hot, and when he climbed up to it, the heat radiated at him. He summoned all his strength and made one enormous lunge to try to push the door open. He could feel the heat burning him, but the door did not budge. He had failed. Death was now inevitable.

But just then, the civil guards opened the door from the outside.

Saki Hiratsuka and his father went out, along with the pitiful handful of other survivors among the sixty people who had chosen this basement as their place of refuge from the fire storm. The storm had passed, leaving smoking embers and the stink of holocaust. But they had survived.

When Masuko Harino reached the Kiyosu Bridge to cross the Sumida River, the fire was bouncing along like volleyballs. Looking toward the Honjo and Fukagawa districts, she saw nothing but walls of flame, a virtual sea of fire. Her eyes smarted and soon hurt so badly that she could not open them. She dropped down by the side of the road, and there found an abandoned seat cushion. She wiped her hands and face on it, and somehow found that it eased the pain of the terrible heat.

When they had left the hostel, some seventeen or eighteen people were together, but now she found that only she and her friend Yoshikawa were left of the whole group. She saw people jumping into the Sumida River to save themselves from the fire, and she heard their voices, but she could not make out what they were saying. All around her were unconscious bodies covered with ashes. She lay there beside the road all through the long, long night, waiting for the dawn.

Finally the first rays of dawn broke through the smoke and dust. She found some water and swabbed her face again and again. She looked around her at the living. Every person's face was black from heat and grime. With dawn came a renewed spirit, and after that, barefoot, she headed back toward the hostel, treading carefully to avoid the fallen electric power lines, broken glass, and bits of wood, lumber, and nails that littered the ground now. She went back past the Meiji theater—or where it had been the night before. Now all that remained was an enormous mound of human bodies, a black mountain of the dead, a dreadful sight, a reminder of calamity. Every person who had been there was dead of suffocation.

All around the area, twisted bodies lay like enormous ginseng roots; it was impossible to tell which of these bodies had been men and which had been women; they were distended, swollen masses of burned, tortured flesh, turned so dark that no one would have recognized them as human, had it not been for the caricatures of shape left by the fire.

To Masuko it was clear that the Imperial Capital of Japan had been destroyed that night.

She came to an aid station, where she was offered water and

rice. A sip of water. A bite of food. She could take no more. Finally she found her way back to the ruins of the hostel, where she met the other survivors. There were two of them.

Seizo Hashimoto had found his shelter behind the pillar of the big Sumida River bridge, and he huddled there, his face close to the ground, to avoid the fire and smoke that surged all around him. The angry river hurled up wet spray, which was a blessing. But time went on and the fire and heat continued, and Hashimoto began to despair of rescue. Then, as dawn broke, the fire lessened, the heat began to die down, and he felt once again that he might live. Just after dawn he looked up above the river at the four-story building of the Tokyo Department of Sanitation, a big concrete structure with iron bars on the windows. Several hundred people had taken refuge in this building during the night. As Hashimoto watched in horror, he saw great gouts of black smoke come spouting from the windows. And then he saw the flames inside. . . .

After the police stopped Chiyoku Sakamoto and her husband from going into the Susaki red-light district of Chiba, they did not know what to do. (The police were certainly right; that night the entire Susaki district was completely burned, and Tokyo lost most of its famous geisha houses and, with them, its most famous geishas.)

They followed along the Jikan River, traveling eastward. As they moved along the road, they saw atrocious sights: people with skin hanging down from their arms, people overcome by burns, writhing in pain, screaming, and with no one to pay attention to their terror and their torture. It was a world gone mad.

The Sakamotos came to the bus company's high wall. It seemed that they were stymied and now must die, if the fire storm continued to blow their way. And the fire storm was coming.

Chiyoku lost confidence completely and was prepared to die. Her husband shouted at her, took her by the arm, and told her that she must summon all her endurance. He grasped her hand, just as the fire and smoke engulfed them.

She went into a dream as the smoke curled around her. She no longer felt any pain; she knew she was going to die, and even felt happy.

They walked on through the smoke. She had been carrying their child on her back, but her husband now took the child. She did not care. She was past caring.

Finally they came to the Nanshucho Railroad Company's property. The gate had been demolished by the fire, and they entered. Was it shelter? The fire was still pressing toward them. But here were concrete walls to hide behind, to get out of the reach of the fire dragon.

Chiyoku's husband suddenly saw a seat cushion that was soaked in river water. He picked it up and, by keeping it wet, managed to protect his wife and the child from the furious effects of the fiery wind.

The air was completely filled with smoke, but finally, as the rays of dawn crept across the night sky, the terrible fire and wind slackened. The Sakamotos now decided it was time to return to see what had happened to their own house.

On the way, they passed hundreds of corpses. They went by what had been Ki Bridge, a big bridge. It was entirely burned, and they saw bodies floating in the river, bodies that had obviously been jammed on that bridge as it burned.

Finally they reached their home—or its ruins. They looked across the Nihonbashi district. As far as they could see, it was a burned empty prairie where, a few hours before, thousands of houses had stood.

They learned the story of the family next door. As they fled the fire, the wife went into labor. Halfway through the birthing process, she began to die. She was terribly burned and crying out in a loud delirious voice before she died. The child was born, filthy and burned in the face, but alive. The father swept it up in an overcoat, clutched it to him, and saved the baby.

The Sakamotos lived on through the war, and at the end had many tales to tell, and an abiding interest in the circumstances under which the Americans had brought this ravaging fire storm to their city. They never forgot the name of Brigadier General Thomas Powers, the American officer who had led the XXI Bomber Command's Mission Number 40, the firebombing of Tokyo.

Masatake Obata, the fire warden, was the most knowledgeable of the people in the shelter that night. The other seven had not been trained in civil defense. All of them were very badly burned, they could tell by looking at one another, not by how they felt, for actually at this point all of them were numb from their burns. Obata's hands and feet were so swollen that he had to sit with his legs akimbo, his arms held out in front of them.

Others began murmuring about being sleepy, and Obata came alert.

"Don't sleep," he said. "Don't go to sleep. If you go to sleep, you die."

And he urged them to shout at anyone who appeared to be nodding off.

Dutifully they repeated Buddhist prayers in unison, in voices as loud as they could muster.

Finally, the last American aircraft left the scene. Then came the dawn, and the eight people in the shelter got up to go their own ways and try to resume some sort of life.

Obata knew he was so badly hurt that he must seek immediate medical attention. He remembered that Sensoji Hospital was nearby, behind Akasaka Shrine, so he decided to go there.

With his hands stretched out before him, walking as though on rollers on his battered, swollen feet, he staggered to the hospital. When he got there, he asked for medical treatment. A doctor looked him over and checked his pulse. The nurse brought burn medicine.

They removed all his burned clothing and gave him a hospital gown. They treated his burns with medicine, and bandaged them. When they were finished, he was a mummy, bandages covering almost all his body except his eyes, and his eyes were swollen almost shut, so that he could barely see.

"Where shall I take this gentleman?" a nurse asked a doctor. "Which ward?"

The doctor considered this, then said, "It's not necessary to take him to any ward. Take him downstairs to the morgue in the basement. Let him join the other dead. There is no hope."

So the nurse helped Obata walk downstairs to the basement. There was nothing in the basement but the morgue, and some old straw mats. There he was left to die without food or water. His jaw was so badly damaged that he could not speak. He was so terribly injured that he did not realize the passage of time. So he lay there. Once in a while he would rouse enough to hear something upstairs. His eyes swelled shut and remained shut. The doctor's prediction seemed near to fulfillment.

The only thing that kept Obata alive through this dreadful period was his will to live. Over the past few years he had amassed considerable property, but it was scattered and no one knew the details except himself. He had no will. If he died now, the property, which included his munitions factory, would undoubtedly be confiscated by the government. So he must live to dispose of his affairs and be sure that his children got their inheritance.

March 10 crawled off the calendar. No one came to help him.

March 11 passed, and he remained in the cellar of the hospital without food, without water, without any attention.

March 12 came.

Obata's brothers came to the area, looking for him and his family. They found nothing but a burned house.

His mother, who lived near Ueno Park, had a feeling that Obata was still living. She came down to the area and went searching for him. She came to the hospital to check the names of the patients inside, but Obata did not appear on the regular list of patients. He was indeed listed as an almost certain fatality, but when the doctor asked his name, Obata had been barely able to speak, and he could not see. The doctor had written down the wrong characters for Obata.

Even so, Mrs. Obata had a feeling that her son was somewhere in that hospital, and she went around the building calling his name. Finally she came to the basement.

Obata could hear her, and he tried to answer. But his damaged jaw would not permit speech. He could simply make a noise like an animal.

His mother heard the noise.

"There's somebody downstairs," she told the doctor. "I want to go look."

"There's nothing down there but dead bodies," said the doctor.

"Not all of them. There's somebody down there. I want to look."

So a nurse took Mrs. Obata down into the dank basement. She walked around, calling Obata's name. He tried to answer. Finally she found him, and she knew, despite the bandages, despite his inability to speak coherently, that this was her son.

Mrs. Obata went back upstairs and asked the doctor to treat her son one more time. She would then take him home to Kojima-cho, where she lived. So the doctor did treat him, and he was moved on a bicycle cart to his mother's house, by the employees of his factory.

When Obata arrived at his mother's house, she called a private doctor. He came, took one look at Obata, and said he could do nothing for him. Obata was beyond his powers, he said.

Obata's brothers then remembered a sergeant in the army whom they had befriended, and decided that Obata should go to a military hospital and ask for treatment there. They took him down to the Central Tokyo railroad station. He came into the station on a stretcher, bandaged from head to toe. The national railway officials refused to let him aboard a train, saying, "We don't carry dead people."

Obata's brothers then called the military ordnance officer in charge of the district, and reported that Obata needed help. The officer came down to the Tokyo railroad station and told the railway officials that Obata was engaged in important war work and that they should let him board a train to get to a military hospital.

Obata was moved to a hospital outside Murawa. The hospital authorities were very leery about taking him in. They looked at his jaw and came to the same conclusion that the Tokyo doctor had reached: this one was for the morgue. His brother called an oral surgeon. The doctor was sent over, but he again refused to accept Obata as a patient because he was sure he was going to die. The brothers then said they expected that Obata might die, and they did not intend to hold the hospital or the doctor responsible for Obata's death, but that they must take him.

But the hospital did not have the medicines to treat Obata, said the doctor.

Then they would get them, said the Obata brothers. They called the army ordnance offices again. An army medical officer appeared at the Murawa hospital and told a doctor to give him a list of the medicines needed. The doctor made the list and gave it to the medical officer, who took the list to the National Hospital in Tokyo and secured all the medicines. The Murawa hospital accepted Obata. He then spent four months in the hospital.

Obata expected that his wife, children, and sisters would be safe, since they had left the house for Sumida Park long before he had. But they never reached the park. The whole group from his neighborhood simply disappeared. His wife, four children, and sisters were all eaten by the fire dragon that roamed the streets of Tokyo on the night of March 9–10, 1945.

The noise of the B-29s overhead woke twelve-year-old Katsumoto Saotome out of the sound sleep he had fallen into when the first air-raid warning was canceled. He looked out his window and thought it was bright day, the light from the fire was so intense.

As he watched, fireballs seemed to run along the skyline and into the road. Tiles from other houses were blowing off the roofs.

Saotome got up and put on his protective long-sleeved clothing and fire hood.

What was to be done next?

Under Japan's air defense law, every family was responsible for the defense of its own house, and there were penalties for anyone who ran away and failed to do his civic duty.

But yet, as anyone in the streets could see, what possible use could it be to try to fight such a fire as this? The incendiary bombs were water-resistant, even if there had been a way to get water on the fires. And almost immediately the roads in the affected districts of Tokyo were jammed with people, handcarts, and animals, so that even those fire engines that could be manned could not get through the mobs. Thus by the time any of them reached their destinations, the fire dragons had taken control.

Katsumoto, being 12 years old, did not have to worry about the problem. All he had to do was go someplace to survive, as his family and the authorities said, and fortunately he did.

But whatever remained of this boy's belief in his government was destroyed that terrible night. That faith had not been very great even before March 9. At school, the teachers put up big war situation maps in the classrooms and discussed the war every day. But by March, young Katsumoto recognized that it was all propaganda. Every day the propaganda came in three parts: a discussion of the stability of the territory controlled by the Empire of the Rising Sun (the Greater East Asia Co-Prosperity Sphere), a discussion of the enemy bombing attacks and the valorous acts of the brave Japanese fliers, and a discussion of the number of enemy ships that had been sunk.

And yet, by this time Katsumoto and his two best friends at school, Mida and Harida, knew very well, in the way that children know about such things, that the number of Japanese warships had been greatly diminished and that the Americans had almost all of them targeted.

They no longer believed that Japan was going to win the war.

Kinosuke Wakabayashi and his daughter remained in the Asahi Beer Company warehouse on the bank of the Sumida River until the fire storm ended. They felt the heat, but they were in no danger. On the morning of March 10 they decided they would go back to their house and see what had happened. They picked their way back through gruesome scenery—destroyed vehicles, burned-out buildings, and acres of rubble where once Japanese houses had stood. Along the roadsides the twisted, blackened bodies lay, already beginning to bloat.

Wakabayashi and his daughter finally came to the block where their house had stood. It was a mass of rubble. But he began picking through it. He had an idea. He would build from the wreckage of the houses in the area a new house to last until something real could be established. His family would all stay in the country, but he had work to do in Tokyo. There would be more air raids in the future. He had a responsible job as civil defense commander of Sumida Prefecture. So Wakabayashi began that very day to start life anew. A beam here, some unbroken tiles there, a shoji screen, some lengths of pipe . . .

From the distance of Koiwa, Kenji Moro watched his factory in Kojima burn. Next morning he came to Kojima to see what had happened. He made his way through the bodies, across the vast wasteland of the Sumida River area, until he came to the place. There was nothing left but twisted wreckage. He was ruined. He had no factory and no way to make money. Now he would have to start all over.

Kaneko Hideyoshi, the Buddhist priest, survived the air raid, and so did his wife. After they crawled along the ground to the cable factory and hid in the big pipe, they were sheltered from the fire, although the hot winds searched for them. Next morning they went out to try to find the other members of the family. They found Hideyoshi's wife's mother and sister, alive and well in one of the shelter places. But search as they did for days, they never found any sign of Hideyoshi's father-in-law. He had, like many others, simply gone up in smoke.

Hideyoshi and his wife then went across Tokyo to stay with a friend near Tokyo University. There, those who had not participated in the dance of the fire dragon showed that they could never appreciate the terrors of that night. They joked with Hideyoshi about his experiences. "Your wife is a Negro," they said. "She is so black."

And of course she was, blackened far more than he by the hot breath of the dragon. The effect lasted for many months.

A few weeks after the firebombing, Hideyoshi was called up by the army and sent to the Nagoya area, where he served until the end of the war.

Tatsu Sakai, her daughter, her cocker spaniel, and her husband huddled under the pier of the Sumida River bridge with scores of other refugees all night long, praying for the bombers to leave and the dawn to come.

Their clothes were burned, their faces were blackened by the breath of the fire dragon, but they survived.

Koiko Yoshie and her son remained near the big pond on the grounds of the Meiji theater through the night. All the water was evaporated from the big pond by the heat, but she and her son were protected from the fire and embers by their futons. Next morning they felt blessed; they too had survived.

9
TOKYO
AFLAME

FROM HIS ROOM IN THE TALL BUILDING ON THE MEIJI DORI BOU-
levard in downtown Tokyo that housed the Imperial Japanese
Army Medical School, Captain Shigenori Kubota had a magnifi-
cent view of Tokyo, and particularly of the harbor district around
the Koto section of the city. On the evening of March 9 he was in
his room, on call for duty, and he looked out over the city as the
sun went down. What a marvelous view it was.

Captain Kubota was a teacher in the college, and also chief of
the Army Medical School's Number One rescue detachment. Under him were nine different groups that were prepared to go out
into the city in time of trouble and help the public. The rescue
organization was divided into two parts, nine groups for the public and five groups that were responsible for the Imperial Palace.
The difference, of course, was a vital element of Japanese society.

On the evening of March 9, Captain Kubota was in his room
considering a research program in which he was engaged, when
at 10:30 he heard the air-raid sirens.

He was not worried. Recently, day after day a few planes had flown over in the evenings—obviously observation planes, since they had not dropped any bombs. Like everyone else in Tokyo, Captain Kubota had gotten used to them.

Even so, when the sirens sounded, it was the call to duty. The rescue squads must now be prepared to watch and wait. So Captain Kubota went to his command post in the building and made sure that all the units were alert and prepared to act. Then, like the others, he watched and waited.

An hour went by, and then it was midnight. Captain Kubota heard the sound of airplanes, and went to look out the window at the Koto section of Tokyo.

Suddenly, he realized, everything had changed. As he watched, he saw the eastern area of Tokyo begin to take on a reddish glow. It was not a bright red, but a rusty yellow-red, an eerie color that he soon saw meant disaster. For it was fire and smoke together, and it was spreading like water across his city. The topography of Tokyo was such that the fire could spread fast; also, houses were built on lots with twenty-five-foot fronts, and sometimes three deep back from the street, which aided the swift proliferation of the fire. And then, of course, there was the wind. Captain Kubota did not have an anemometer handy, but he could sense that the wind was whipping that fire into a frenzy. Below him, he watched as the sea of fire boiled and then boiled over, and spread, and spread.

There was no point in the rescue units starting out until they knew where they were supposed to go. Slowly, steadily, the airplanes bombed, and from the Army Medical School building the sound was that of distant thunder. He watched from his window as the planes kept coming in, and the fires continued to spread across the southeastern section of the city.

At 3:40 A.M., the Tokyo area army commander sent official word that Captain Kubota was to command the Number One Rescue Unit. A staff officer arrived to report on the current situation. There was going to be some difficulty, he said. For four days, supplies of medicines and other goods that would be needed for just such an emergency had been waiting to be shipped to Tokyo.

What was the problem? There were not enough trucks, and too few drivers. Only now were the drivers being sent down to pick up the trucks at the manufacturers' establishments.

It was a measure of the growing national crisis that when the army talked about medical supplies for the civil population, it had to talk about faraway places. The army's slender supply of medicines and first-aid equipment had to be kept on hand for the "final battle" that everyone knew would be waged on the shores of Honshu and Kyushu. Thus Tokyo, in its hour of need, must be dependent on supplies from all over the country. But the great rub was that food, medical supplies, and all else were stacked up, awaiting the arrival of aircraft and other transport to carry them to the capital. The fighting in the Philippines, in Burma, and on Iwo Jima had so decimated the army's supply of air transport that there were going to be inevitable delays.

"*Shikatta ganai*," said the staff officer—"It can't be helped." They would just have to make do with what they had at hand.

At 3:50 A.M., Captain Kubota and his command staff left the hospital entrance and got into their command vehicle. They drove slowly through the deserted Tokyo streets. Everyone was tense as they went from one district to another. Off to the side and in front they could see the bursting flames of the fire storm, moving fast, throwing fireballs as though they were fireworks for some monstrous celebration.

They climbed Yanagicho Hill, and Kagura Hill, then hastened across Iida Bridge. Until tonight, this entire area had been virtually undamaged, hit once or twice by stray bombs but not really hurt. But tonight the bombers had done their job, they had totally wrecked the area.

Captain Kubota drove through smoldering ruins until he reached the Kudanshita army command post, and there he stopped. All around him were smoldering fires, still smoking, still bearing hot embers that burned anything they touched. The smoke from the fires had spread everywhere and lingered above the ground. The Miya mansion of Kaya, of all things, was completely burned out. This once-resplendent building, with its tall columns and ornate woodwork, now looked like a charcoal drawing, blackened pillars with smoking ruins collapsed around them, standing lonely in a sea of burning rubble.

All around this neighborhood, Captain Kubota saw the women and even children of the Volunteer Corps, who were scurrying about in *monpei* and canvas shoes, trying to find survivors and help them to the aid station. Where the fires were not burning, the wind was cold, and the women were shivering as they worked.

From Kudanshita they followed a ditch for 3,000 meters, and saw the fire advancing on their left. Finally they reached Itsu Bridge, where the last army post was located. They drove up and waited. From the building came a single staff officer, who had been designated to give Captain Kubota his orders.

The Army Hospital Number One Rescue Unit was ordered to go into Honjo in east Tokyo and rescue injured people. Captain Kubota would be responsible for the entire operation, although, of course, he was to work closely with the Honjo civil defense chief.

It was, of course, laughable that twenty-four men in half a dozen vehicles could be responsible for the evacuation and treatment of perhaps a hundred thousand people over twenty-five square miles. But it was no laughing matter at all. The army was completely serious. Its officers knew what they had to work with, and they were making their assignments accordingly.

The staff officer spoke of "private doctors and medical facilities." But the fact was that nearly all the private doctors in Tokyo had already been enlisted in the military medical service, and most of the private medical facilities had closed down or been scattered to the four winds.

Captain Kubota and his men said nothing about all this. It would have done them no good. Orders were orders. They tightened their helmets and prepared to go on.

At 4:50 A.M., they pulled up the ambulance at the army head-quarters of Honjo. No one was there. They drove on, through the sections of Ogawa and Suda and Iwamoto, looking in shock at the scenes of utter devastation that greeted them. They drove straight on eastward, watching carefully the fire that continued to advance to the east.

The devastation was more than ghastly. Asakusa Bridge was still standing at the moment, but it was covered with smoke and fire and was beginning to collapse. All around, the electric and telephone poles had burned up or fallen down. Live electric lines lay in tangles across the streets and had to be avoided. The electric train overhead wires had also collapsed, creating more danger for the injured and the refugees and for their rescuers. The trains stood on the lines, gutted. Here and there a "charcoal car" remained; if it were not so hot, a push with a finger would have made it disintegrate. All along the streets lay the remains of push-carts, large wagons, and bicycle wagons. Some were even intact, mute evidence of the haste with which their owners had abandoned everything in the frantic rush to escape from the fire storm. The twisted bodies all along the streets and in the fields of rubble that had once been houses and gardens showed how few had managed to escape. The streets were no longer streets, but thoroughfares of rubble and destruction, littered with glass and scraps of iron that could slash a tire and stop them once and for all, as well as boards, nails, clothing, pots, pans, futons, mountains of plaster, and all the other debris of a city destroyed. The wind had picked up whole piles of trash and scattered them everywhere.

Captain Kubota drove as far as he could. But then the debris became so thick that he found it impossible to go on. Bodies and wreckage were everywhere.

The immediate problem was that a water main had burst and flooded the road, and the sides of the road were so thickly covered with corpses and debris that the vehicle could not move out around the mess. The crew piled out and cleared the passage through the wreckage with their hands, and then went on.

As they proceeded, the long, panic-stricken night began to end and streaks of light showed through the smoke and haze above the eastern section of Tokyo.

They drove to Ryogoku Bridge, and there they were stunned by the sight of the countless dead bodies that lay everywhere around. They were in a forest of corpses, in every direction, bodies were crumpled so closely together that they must have been touching when they died. They lay there now, mute evidence of the fury of the American attack on Tokyo's civil population.

The captain looked out over the Ichido River, and shook his head. What a pitiful situation it was, so appalling that it exceeded the imagination's ability to deal with it. What could rescuers do in a situation like this? There was no one to rescue. Touch one of the roasted bodies, and the flesh would crumble in the hand. Humanity reduced to the essential, turned into carbon.

They moved to the Sumida River, and here found the scene even more horrifying. The entire river surface was black as far as the eye could see, black with burned corpses, logs, and who knew what else, but uniformly black from the immense heat that had seared its way through the area as the fire dragon passed. It was impossible to tell the bodies from the logs at a distance. The bodies were all nude, the clothes had been burned away, and there was a dreadful sameness about them, no telling men from women or even children. All that remained were pieces of charred meat. Bodies and parts of bodies were carbonized and absolutely black. The whole area was still covered with smoke, the smoke that had asphyxiated these people even as they leaped into the water to save themselves from the fire storm.

Captain Kubota's eyes roved the area, and came to rest on one river bank. Both banks were being beaten by angry waves from the wind that was still blowing in fitful gusts. The waves subsided for a moment, and there on the left bank he saw a terrible sight. Stacked in neat precision, as though by some machine, lay row upon row of corpses. The instrument was the tide, which had come and gone since the fire storm passed by, leaving the rows of bodies like so much cordwood cast up on the beach. The river told its own story. When the heat had become deadly, the mob, for it was no more than that, had rushed like lemmings to the water's edge and leaped in, to be suffocated by the smoke, or drowned. How many bodies had washed out to sea was impossible to tell, but they must have been in the thousands, for there were tens of thousands in the river.

And there was more evidence of tragedy. On the right side of the bridge, the waves lapped against the National Sports Center building, a huge structure that stood enveloped in smoke. The captain knew what they would find inside: more mountains of corpses roasted like so much *yakiniku*, meat on a spit.

There it stood, this enormous building, a lone monument standing in a field of death, a tribute to some construction engineer, but now a skeleton, wrecked inside by the scouring fire.

In Midori, next on the captain's list, he gazed in anguish at one entire block, a crowded block the day before, where perhaps a hundred houses had stood. Ten houses now dotted that open field. On the left side of the block was a busy road that ran under an overpass 1,100 meters long. The overpass had collapsed, and now the only way to get through was to crawl.

In the heart of Honjo stood a large government office building, which miraculously had escaped the flames. Captain Kubota stood looking up at the building, with many sad thoughts racing through his heart. How miraculous it was. How strange were the ways of fate. For the fire storm had passed by here, leaving that great building, and yet all around it was the rubble of the city, and beneath the rubble, and lying twisted atop it, were the seared corpses of the unlucky people of Tokyo who had been in the wrong place.

The damage was staggering. Captain Kubota drove back to the center of the city and found that serious damage had also been inflicted on the Asakusa, Honjo, Fukagawa, Kito, and Mukaijima wards in the center of town. Asakusa, the amusement center of Tokyo, with its restaurants, geisha houses, and houses of prostitution, was virtually destroyed. In all these wards, 99 percent of the rooms in even the houses that were standing had been gutted by fire or destroyed by heat. Water pipes all over the city had burst, adding to the damage, so that even houses that looked whole were no longer habitable. In some areas, burst mains were spewing water like mountain streams. In other places it was impossible to get a trickle out of the taps. In all these areas, most of the telephone and power poles had burned down, creating dangerous situations. And where the poles were standing, in the midst of the great new wilderness of rubble, they were like dead sentinel trees. From the center of the city, Captain Kubota saw that as far as his eyes could measure, Tokyo was sorely hurt. Even the houses and buildings that stood seemed somehow changed by the fire. The enemy had indeed struck a powerful blow at Japan's major industrial center, and had, in effect, reduced it enormously.

Captain Kubota, like many another Tokyo resident, had long been told that the city would never be bombed, *could* never be bombed, and he had believed it. Now he had the evidence before his eyes. Not only had Tokyo been bombed, but the city had suffered enormous damage.

On he went in his truck, to the city offices in Honjo. He stopped at the district office for a moment, to see the overworked officials handing out food and blankets and all the necessities of life for the homeless refugees.

At 6:00 A.M., Captain Kubota was back on the road again, heading westward into Kamezawa. Here, through the haze and smoke, appeared another manifestation of the carnage. All along the roadside lay blackened corpses, and the captain could tell by the way they were bunched together that they had been the victims of asphyxiation. There was no mistaking that reddening of the faces.

So numerous were the dead, so many the obstacles in the road, that the truck could move only at a snail's pace. He watched absently out the window as they drove. On the left, by the weak light of the growing day, he saw another mountain of corpses. Then the smoke closed in again, and the gruesome truth was hidden from his eyes. But he knew now that it was the same everywhere in the bombed area. The Americans had set out to destroy the industrial potential of Japan's capital, and to Captain Kubota it looked as though they might have succeeded.

There was really no point in going farther. Nothing could be done for the dead; the living were Captain Kubota's affair. So he headed back to the Honjo district office building. There he learned that the National People's School, near the Nishiukushu railroad station, by the Taiyoko River, had been designated as the site for his operations. It was an old building, made of concrete, and seemed admirable for the emergency task.

He and his crew got out of the truck and went into the big lecture hall on the ground floor. It was overflowing with refugees. The medical crew selected a corner of the building and set up a desk and lines of chairs, and in a few minutes they were ready to begin work.

The captain noted the great similarity among the faces he saw, all lighted with relief at finally getting to a place where their afflictions could be treated after the long, terrible night in the open, with the fire everywhere around them.

Many of these people had lost flesh, some had lost their eyesight, some had horrible wounds. The ones who worried Captain Kubota most were the smoke victims. Many of these people would succumb in days to follow because of the damage done to their lungs. But there was no point in philosophizing about the medical problems to be faced. It was time to get down to work.

When the people awaiting medical treatment lined up, the hall began to look like a maze. There was every sort of injury and disorder. Almost uniformly, the people suffered from conjunctivitis caused by the smoke and hot winds. All he could do for them was wash out their eyes with salt water. They were lucky to be in the rescue center at all, for most of them told how they had been caught in the smoke, had lain down to avoid it, and had gone to sleep. Some, who managed to wake up, made it to the rescue center. The others had the long, long sleep, and their corpses were lying along the roads and in piles in the open spaces, roasted.

Captain Kubota saw pain this morning as he had never seen it before. And as he worked, he questioned his patients. What had happened to them?

Toraji Ono told how she and her children had been fleeing on the Sumida River bridge when suddenly the bridge folded up beneath them. She and the children leaped into the water, grabbed onto a log, and rested there. Fortunately the water of the river put out the fires that were burning through their protective clothing, and none of them was seriously injured. They were wise enough to keep their eyes closed to protect them from the smoke and heat.

But Toyo Tsumano, another Tokyo housewife, had spent the whole night with her children in a hiding place, stamping out the flames in their clothing and protecting them as best she could. Her eyes were so tightly sealed with soot and grime that at first Captain Kubota thought she was dying. What a pitiful figure she made in the rescue center. She had also burned her hands severely and was in great pain. The captain treated her as best he could with the limited medical supplies available, and then went on to the next patient.

She was Katsuko Yamamoto, and when he first looked at her he thought she was blind. Mrs. Yamamoto lived in what was by Tokyo standards a very old house, dating back to the Meiji period—seventy years old. The whole clan lived in the large house, sixteen people in all, and downstairs they ran a clock and watch business. Mrs. Yamamoto's personal family consisted of nine people, herself and eight children. The oldest, but by Japanese standards still the man of the house, was her nineteen-year-old son.

On the evening of March 9, when the first air-raid alarm came, the rest of the clan went to the shelter designated for their area.

Mrs. Yamamoto and her children remained behind, but when the bombs began to fall, they started to leave. She thought she saw everyone go out, and she was to be the last to leave. But before she knew it, the strong winds had sent the flames swirling around their block, and she found herself trapped by the fire. Then the dirt and dust and smoke got into her eyes and soon she found that they were sealed shut and she could not see. She felt no pain, but she could not open her eyes. Then she felt the heat and she knew she was going to drown in that sea of fire.

She decided that whether she could see or not, she would fling herself through the wall of flame and hope to survive. Just as she was moving, there came a flurry of the wind, and sparks and flames flew everywhere. Now she was certain that if there was anyone left in her house they were dead, and that she would soon be, too. She began to feel her way, toward the door. Just then her eldest son advanced, and handed her a rope. He led her out of the burning building. She was reborn, she felt, on that night of March 9–10, no matter what happened to her eyes.

Outside, she found that all her family had survived, and they made their way slowly, block by block, behind the fire storm, to some place of shelter. Finally, the next morning they arrived at the emergency center at the school, and now she was waiting to be treated, to save her sight if possible. Dr. Kubota found that the eyes and lids were damaged, mostly by the heat and dirt. He operated, and saved her vision.

Thus it went all that day and the next. Not all cases ended as happily as Mrs. Yamamoto's, by far. Many of the people who had survived the fire storm died of shock and injuries and of infections that could not be controlled with the meager medicines available to the civil population.

As the civil defense workers labored hour upon hour, it became apparent that Tokyo had suffered the worst disaster of its history, not excepting the great earthquake and fire of 1923.

To begin, the bombers wiped out the Number Two ward of

Kiba district. Never had anyone in Japan seen an area so totally covered by firebombs as this was.

In Fukagawa, half a dozen wards were wiped out, and at the end only 500 buildings were standing. Twenty-five square kilometers were burned out in the Tokugawa area, but in all of Tokyo the Japanese figures showed forty-two square kilometers of land destroyed, with 261,000 houses burned, and estimated 80,000 people killed, and a million left homeless. Those were the best figures the Japanese authorities could come up with, but they were not very meaningful as far as people were concerned, because so much had happened recently in Tokyo that there was no way the government could know how many were in the city that night, and how many were killed. Many thousands turned up missing, but who was to be told? The Tokyo authorities had all they could do to try to hold the city together. Later estimates put the number killed at over 100,000, and even that may be low, for thousands of bodies were swept out to sea from the tidal rivers that flow through the city, and none of them could be counted. For weeks afterward, the public workers of Japan were busy burying the charred remains of thousands of their citizens in mass graves.

For a week, all of Tokyo was disrupted. On the day after the bombing, virtually nothing operated. Every available person was working to try to undo some part of the damage. Power supplies failed through much of the city, thus newspapers were not published, and it was only with difficulty that Radio Tokyo remained on the air to communicate with the public.

By Sunday, March 11, communications and transportation had been restored enough that the Diet was able to hold a session. Nothing that was said in that session—nothing that was said anywhere about the appalling disaster of the American attack—was printed in the newspapers or broadcast. The horror was kept as secret as possible from the country and from the world at large. Of course, there was really no question of keeping the secret, for on the morning of March 10, American B-29s flew over Tokyo and photographed the results of their raid the night before. But the rest of Japan knew virtually nothing immediately. After a few hours the grapevine began to operate, and it was not long before all Japan knew of the tragedy, and knew that the bombing of Japan had only just begun.

The Diet that day heard Prime Minister Koniaki Koiso pledge the country's utmost efforts to the winning of the war. That speech, to both houses, was followed by one given by War Minister Field Marshal Sugiyama, and the representatives of the Imperial Rule Assistance Association, which had replaced political parties as the spokesman for the people, pledged popular support. There were many now who believed the war was lost, but their voices were not heard.

At the Imperial Palace in Chiyoda, in the middle of Tokyo, the Emperor began hearing dreadful rumors about what had happened in his Imperial Capital. Chiyoda was not bombed that night, and although the fire and flames had been horrible, not much was seen from the sprawling palace behind a deep moat across from the Yasukuni Shrine. Still, the Emperor's emotions were so much aroused that he began talking about going out into Tokyo to see for himself what had occurred. The ministers of the Imperial Household were aghast. The Emperor should not see what had happened, it was too dreadful, and they tried their best to persuade him to give up his plan. But Hirohito would not give it up, and when he set his mind to something, he would have his way. So a few days after the tragedy, an Imperial caravan drove across the moat from the palace and out into the city. The emperor wanted to go to the bank of the Sumida River, where, he had heard, the worst of the damage had been centered. He did go there, and he got out of the car and looked at the dreadful scene of destruction along the riverbank. He saw a camp of pitiful refugees in tents and shacks in an open spot, and to the awe of the people, the Emperor stopped for a moment to talk. There was really nothing to be said. He looked at the people in their rags, with the scorch of fire storm still upon them. He got back into his limousine in his general's uniform and riding boots. He stopped one more time for a few words with other survivors, and then went back to the palace. He said nothing, and no one really knew his innermost thoughts. But for the first time it came home to him that Japan had lost the war. There was no possibility even of working out an arranged peace—not when the enemy had power like that which the Americans had shown on the night of March 9. And so, in addition to all else that the firebombing of Tokyo did, it put into the Emperor's mind the necessity of finding some way to get out of the war. It would not be easy. The entire ambience—the polity—of the militarists who still controlled the country was designed to fight until the end if necessary. But the Emperor could now see just what that might mean: the destruction of the entire country and the massacre of the Japanese people. It was something for him to think about.

10
TOKYO
AFTERMATH

WHEN THE RESULTS WERE IN, GENERAL LEMAY WAS INFORMED that fourteen B-29s had been lost that night of March 9–10, 1945. It was not a low figure, even by previous mission standards.

One plane of the 73rd Wing was shot down over Tokyo.

The 313th Wing lost three aircraft that night, damaged but not shot down. The crews ditched them on the way home.

The 314th Wing's planes took the heaviest blows. They were last over the target, and by the time they got there, the Japanese air defenses were recovering from the surprise engendered by the new American bombing technique. Forty-nine of the fifty-four planes that had set out reached Tokyo, but eight of them did not return to base. One ditched, and seven were missing.

By the time the 314th Wing got to Tokyo, the city was a hell of fire. The winds of forty knots and more had fanned the blazes set by the earlier planes, just as intelligence and operations had hoped and the pilots saw the streaking flames covering whole sections of the city. The thermals caused by the heat tossed one plane 2,000 feet higher in the air in a matter of seconds.

On the morning of March 10, the camera planes were over Tokyo, and even the most hardened pilots were impressed with the damage they saw below them. The fires were still smoking. They could not see the piles of bodies from their altitude: they would not have recognized them as bodies anyhow, for even on the ground it was hard to equate those masses of charred flesh with human beings.

The observation planes returned to the Marianas with their pictures, and when they were developed they were taken to the desk of General LeMay. He took one look and was exultant.

"We've got them," he said.

The mission had been so great a success, so far beyond the general's dreams, that he felt a new weapon had been forged.

The photos showed that nearly all the buildings in the target area had been destroyed, and much more. The total area covered by the fire storm was 15.8 square miles of Tokyo. This area included twenty-three Army Air Corps military targets. The area affected included 11.3 square miles of Tokyo's industrial section, too. A photo interpreter's view of the photos showed the destruction of thousands of vehicles, and the apparent gutting of steel and concrete buildings. The bombers had flown over a city and had left a wasteland.

There had been many questions about the new technique of fire bombing, but now in General LeMay's mind they were nearly all answered. The use of 100-pound M-47 napalm bombs by pathfinder aircraft to start marker fires had been proved out, as had the use of the thousands of the six-pound M-69 incendiaries in delayed-opening clusters. The saturation of at least 250 tons of bombs per square mile had been shown to be effective. Effective was not the word. It had been devastating.

The Japanese had been caught totally by surprise. Their night fighters had not even gotten into the air. Their antiaircraft had proved mostly ineffectual at this altitude. They could be expected to improve, but Iwo Jima was now an added asset to the XXI Bomber Command. Iwo Jima meant fighter support over the Japanese targets, and a halfway landing field for crippled B-29s. On the evening of March 10, 1945, the future seemed clear. Three more incendiary missions were scheduled in quick succession, to burn up as much of Japan's major industrial sites as possible. The missions would go on. The plans would be unchanged.

11
NAGOYA

THE BIG INDUSTRIAL CITY OF NAGOYA HAD BEEN BOMBED MANY times. The major attraction to the American air force was the Mitsubishi aircraft engine plant, but there were many subsidiaries and many other factories involved in Japan's war production.

The first bombing of Nagoya had been by Lieutenant Colonel James Doolittle's B-25s on the celebrated raid of April 1942, from one of Admiral Halsey's aircraft carriers. As a raid it had been of no significance, but as a warning it had brought sober thoughts to some Japanese.

The warning was amplified by the coming of the B-29s, which first hit Nagoya's industrial plants on November 5, 1944. The bombing was done from high altitude and was not very accurate, which meant that the aircraft industry plants, which were the targets, were not much hurt, but many buildings and houses were destroyed by high-explosive bombs.

Expecting further raids, Nagoya undertook what, for Japan, was a highly enlightened program of civil defense, building fire lanes throughout the city. There was, of course, the problem of

Japanese houses, and there was nothing that could be done about that. As in Tokyo, the city was divided for civil defense purposes into wards and ultimately into block associations. The citizens were provided with buckets, warned to maintain supplies of water in cisterns and even in tubs and bottles, and given flails and mats to put out the fires.

Shortly before the firebombing, the chief of firefighting in Japan's police department suggested in a newspaper interview that the effects of bombing could be overestimated.

> It is doubtless true that our houses of wood and paper, as foreigners term them, are at a disadvantage in air raids, but with training and courage why should they be feared? Fire, wherever it originates, will always run up the paper walls to the ceiling. Provided it is then prevented from going higher by a partition of earth, tin, or even wood above the ceiling, it can be checked there with water. If, however, it brings the ceiling down and gets onto the roof, it will at once spread everywhere and the whole building will be enveloped in flames.

What the citizen must do, said the authorities, was to remove from the house all flammable objects before the bombing. When the air-raid sirens began to sound, that was the time to take down the shoji, the screens that provided partitions between the rooms, and clear the cupboards. If there was no time for such action, then the screens should be smashed so that they would not provide fuel for the fires from bombing.

The best way to put out a fire immediately was to stamp it out with mats—smother it, in other words. But if the fire had progressed too far for that, then was the time to use those buckets of water. This was where the next-door neighbors came in: every householder was responsible for defense of his own house *and* to help the neighbors on either side if their houses got into trouble. The efforts of three families with water buckets should be enough to control the fire until the fire engine could arrive. This theory, of course, suggested that only one house in three would be affected. The other two would have no troubles of their own while their occupants were helping out the family in the house that was afire.

In the summer of 1944, the Mitsubishi factories had been taken over by the Munitions Ministry, and thereafter the work force had changed significantly. Most of the men who had worked in the aircraft industry in the past were now drafted into the armed services, and so most of the 15,000 workers in this plant were women of the Volunteer Corps who had been called up for this duty. By the end of 1944, Japan was truly fully mobilized, and in the normal sense there were no more civilians in Japan. The government considered the civilian population to be just as much an element in the prosecution of the war as the soldiers at the front. Total mobilization was what they called it, and it was the justification for the American approach to the bombing of Japanese cities and industry as an essential part of the war effort. There was no way by 1944 that civilians could be separated from the military in Japan.

On December 13, the B-29s had come to bomb Mitsubishi's Number Four engine factory.

In the raid of December 13, not much damage was done to Mitsubishi Factory Number Four, but 300 workers were killed. Five days later came another raid, doing abut the same minimal damage, but killing another 300 workers.

Four more raids were made on Factory Number Four with similar discouraging results. The high-altitude "precision bombing" was not precision bombing, but as usual bombs spattered all over Nagoya.

By December 13, 1944, Factory Number Four had been bombed seven times, and the death toll was 2,800 people. On

January 3, 1945, the bombers came again with a combination of high-explosive and incendiary bombs. This time they killed only seventy people, but burned out 3,500 houses.

Then came the new policy of firebombing. On March 11, 1945, at 7:30 P.M., from the three Mariana Islands, 307 B-29 Superfortresses took off, loaded with thousands of incendiary bombs. Their destination was Nagoya, and their aim was to try to do with the firebombs what the high-altitude campaign against the Mitsubishi factory complex had failed to do.

The 73rd Wing supplied 134 planes, the 313th provided 111, and the 314th Wing contributed 42. Into the night the big planes pointed northwest and droned on hour after hour. Eighteen planes were forced to abort the mission because of mechanical difficulties, but the rest continued on, to arrive over Nagoya beginning at 12:20 on the morning of March 12.

Nagoya had been chosen by the planners largely because of the presence there of that Mitsubishi Aircraft Engine Factory Number Four. Mitsubishi manufactured fourteen different types of military aircraft for the army and navy, including several new types of planes, and was then managing 40 percent of Japan's total aircraft engine production.

The bomb load for the Nagoya mission was the same as that used in the Tokyo attack, the combination of 100-pound napalm bombs for the pathfinder planes, and the small cluster bombs for the rest of the B-29s. In examining the results of the Tokyo raid, the planners had grown greedy. They decided that in the Tokyo attack, bombs had been wasted on areas already burning fiercely, so they increased the intervalometer setting for the small cluster bombs from 50 to 100 feet.

The planes took off from their Marianas fields. To avoid airspace problems, the planes of the three bombardment groups flew at different altitudes, one group at 4,000 to 4,500 feet, the next at 5,000 to 5,500 feet, and the third at 7,000 feet.

They headed first for Iwo Jima, and made their landfalls there, as a checkpoint for radar and radio. Then they headed straight for Nagoya Bay, the most direct route to the target. Each plane was on its own as far as flight and bombing were concerned.

Down below, although the pilots and crews could not see them, were submarines, destroyers, and destroyer escorts, ready to move in to pick up crews from ditching aircraft. It was a comforting thought.

Shortly before midnight on March 12, the air-raid sirens of Nagoya began to blow. The bombers were on their way, said Radio Tokyo.

The crews of the 200 heavy antiaircraft guns in the Nagoya area were alerted, as were the fighter bases and the crews of the fifty searchlight installations in the area. The army was also trying an experiment with half a dozen barrage balloons, which were raised to various heights in an attempt to ward off the bombers by presenting the danger of collision with a balloon cable.

The bombers came in over the Shima peninsula, beginning at twenty minutes after midnight. The first of them arrived, at about 6,000 feet. They came in small groups or singly and, as planned, they varied their approaches so that the searchlights and the antiaircraft guns could not get a bead on a formation.

The attack was conducted in much the same way as that on Tokyo two nights earlier. The Japanese aircraft defense was very limited, and only a few attacks were made. Some planes did try to ram the B-29s.

The Japanese defenders, of course, made extravagant claims about their effectiveness. They had destroyed twenty-two B-29s, said Imperial General Headquarters in a communiqué the next day, and had damaged sixty more. It was, of course, nothing like the truth.

Several of the bombers missed the main target area and bombed the Kii Peninsula, or the Shikoku area. But most of them were on target. They burned 25,000 houses that night. *Chunichi Shimbun*, the big Nagoya newspaper, referred to the bombing as "burning hell," but the fact was that as a military operation that first Nagoya fire raid was a failure. This time there were no high winds, and thus no fire storm to help the bombers along.

There was another reason for the failure. The Nagoya city government had been far more provident than that of Tokyo. Many more fire lanes had been prepared in the industrial district of the city. Besides that, the shape of Nagoya city was quite different from that of Tokyo—it was no great, sprawling metropolis on the Kanto Plain, but a tightly centered industrial area, most of whose factory buildings had some degree of protection against fire.

Still, from the standpoint of the civilian population of Nagoya, the firebombing was terrorizing. Two thousand seven hundred people were killed, most of them burned to death in their houses or in trying to escape or fight the flames. The vast majority of these were women and children—not workers in the Mitsubishi factory, but housewives and schoolchildren. As Tokyo had discovered two days earlier, there were no more noncombatants in the air war over Japan.

The raid on Nagoya aroused the Japanese government information bureau—the controller of all government information except the communiqués from Imperial Headquarters—and the chief propaganda and censorship agency rolled into one—to new fury against the American firebombing.

The national press now compared the firebombing of Tokyo to the burning of Rome by Nero.

There was good cause for the government's worry, as the employment records of Mitsubishi Factory Number Four began to show. During the high-altitude, high-explosive bombings of Nagoya, absenteeism in the factory had been minimal, but after the first fire raid on the civil population, the figures shot up, until they reached 40 percent. The government could say all it wanted about the fury to which the firebombing aroused the people of Japan, but the fact was, as the chief editorial writer of the *Nippon Times* put it, that the people of Japan were deeply impressed by the B-29 raids, and all the more so by the fire raid on Tokyo, whose results were beginning to trickle across Japan as the civil population was evacuated from the Japanese capital.

The Tokyo raid had showed the futility of civil defense efforts as they were currently employed by the Japanese. Even as the bombers struck at Nagoya, the civil defense workers of the Home Ministry in Tokyo were burning the midnight oil, handing out supplies still, trying to find emergency housing where there was none, trying to help the victims of the worst disaster Tokyo had ever suffered. One of the odd side effects of the Tokyo bombing was the placement of some refugees in housing in the better districts of Tokyo, which had not yet been hit by the bombings. Instead of arousing gratitude, the encounter left the people of the industrial sections—slums, as it were—with a feeling of great bitterness. They found that the middle classes of the better Tokyo districts were not suffering nearly so much from the shortages of everything as the residents of Kiba and Koto.

Now criticisms of the military began. Why couldn't the army break up the B-29 raids before they began? Why couldn't the government provide decent air-raid shelters for the people?

These questions were asked, but not answered. And by the end of the first week after the beginning of the great fire raids, the people had even stopped asking them. They were beginning to feel that the B-29s were a power over which there was no possible control.

The government had gambled, and had lost. The major reason for not building air-raid shelters, now forgotten in the passing of the Tojo Cabinet, was the unreasoning arrogance of the Prime Minister, and the feeling that to admit that Japan was vulnerable to air raids would be to encourage absenteeism and cut production. Now that policy of forgetfulness was coming home to roost, and the effect on Japanese morale was quick and lasting. Many people, outside of the fanatic circle of militarists, now believed there was no chance at all of winning the war, and that there was a very good chance that Japan would be destroyed.

12
RESULTS

ONE OF THE REMARKABLE RESULTS OF THE GIANT FIRE RAID ON
Tokyo was quite unexpected. General LeMay had inadvertently,
if welcomely, created a schism among the Japanese people for the
first time.

When the authorities sought assistance from the general public
of Tokyo to house the 800,000 homeless refugees, they called
upon such areas as Chiyoda, the center of government and corporate business, or, one might say, the Manhattan or West End of
Tokyo; here the middle-class people responded with a great will,
taking in whole families as nonpaying guests. But the result was
not quite what the government had expected. These people from
Kiba and Koto were largely slum dwellers, and suddenly they
were brought into houses of opulence such as they had not
known even before the war. The general feeling on the part of the
slum dwellers was resentment against the well-to-do, and the immediate result was a series of lootings and riots that created great
problems for the police. New orders were issued by the Home
Ministry, to the effect that in the future no evacuation to private

homes would be permitted. All evacuees would go to schools, temples, and public buildings.

Of course, none of this activity reached the press; the media were too tightly controlled for that. Yet, despite the tight restrictions on news of the damage done in the Tokyo and Nagoya raids, even the government had to yield to public pressure enough to allow press comment on the fire raids.

America has revealed her barbaric character before in the terror bombings of civilian populations in Hamburg, Berlin, and other German cities, in her destruction of priceless cultural monuments in various parts of Europe, in her sinking of innumerable hospital ships, and in countless other acts of savagery beyond mention. But the raids on Tokyo and Nagoya within the last few days have demonstrated more spectacularly than ever the fiendish character of the American enemy.

For these recent raids have been the most unquestionable examples of calculated terror bombing. Raining flaming incendiaries over a vast area of civilian dwellings, the raiders can make no excuse of having aimed at military or industrial installations.

It was an attempt at mass murder of women and children who had no connection with war production or any activity directly connected with the war. There can be no other result than to strengthen the conviction of every Japanese that there can be no slackening of the war effort. . . .

The action of the Americans is all the more despicable because of the noisy pretensions they constantly make about their humanity and

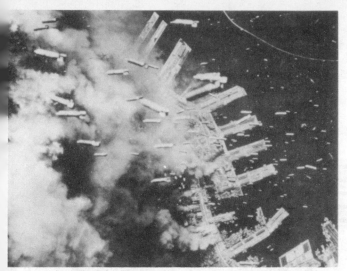

On March 17, 1945, 300 B-29s raided Kobe with fire bombs. Except for the Tokyo raids this was the worst. 8841 people died.

In three great fire raids the B-29s destroyed 75 percent of downtown Osaka, as shown. The raids were on March 14, June 1, and August 14.

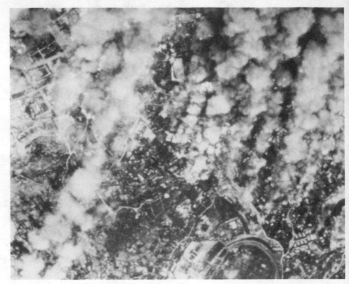

Yokohama was also the target of fire bombs. On May 29 it was hit by 517 B-29s plus 100 P-51 fighter planes as escort. The raid began about 9 A.M.

Fire victims try to escape along the Kyohama National rail line on the morning after the great Tokyo air raid.

Civil defense workers hand out food and blankets from a truck in the Kanagaua area.

After the fire storm the banks of Tokyo's Sumida River were lined with more thousands of corpses, people who drowned while trying to escape the heat.

Corpses of the people killed in the American fire raid of May 27, 1945.

Bomb-leveled areas in Tokyo, Japan. The imperial palace in ruins.
(National Archives)

Low-flying planes
photographed these
sections of ruin and
destruction in
Tokyo.
(National Archives)

Aerial views of ruins
in the Tokyo area;
taken by plane from
the USS *Essex*.
(National Archives)

Kobe, Japan. Taken
by plane from the
USS *California*.
(National Archives)

Presentation of the Distinguished Service Cross to Brig. Gen. Curtis E. LeMay, right, of the U.S. Army 8th Air Force Bomber Command, by Gen. Henry H. Arnold, Commanding General, U.S. Air Forces, for extraordinary heroism displayed in action against the enemy during the raid on Schweinfurt and Regensburg, August 17, 1943.

Five Star General Henry Arnold, commanding U.S. Army Air Forces, got his first look at the American air base nearest Japanese home islands when his plane landed at Yontan airfield, Okinawa. Looking pleased and confident, he is shown here talking to the commander of the Tenth Army Tactical Air Force on Okinawa, Marine Major General Louis E. Woods, Commanding General, Second Marine Aircraft Wing.
(National Archives)

Japanese people readjusting themselves to life in Tokyo after the end of war.

A Japanese woman gathers kindling from ruins.
(National Archives)

Japanese mother and children trudging down rubble-strewn street.
(National Archives)

The great mushroom cloud of the A-bomb blast at Hiroshima on August 6, 1945. According to Japanese records 118,661 people died in that raid, and 73,774 people died in the Nagasaki A-bomb raid of August 9. But far more persons, perhaps 300,000 or more, were killed in the firebombing of Japan.

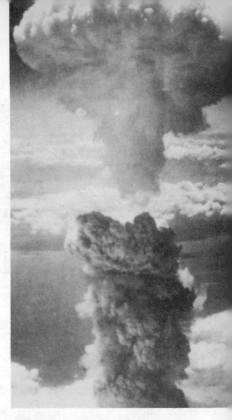

American Avenger bombers over the Japanese coast on a raid from a carrier. These air strikes augmented the B-29 fire raids.

idealism. They are the first to accuse others of atrocities, raising loud protests over claims of alleged Japanese mistreatment of prisoners of war [the Bataan Death March] and alleged Japanese destruction in the zones of hostility [the Rape of Nanking]. But even the most extravagant of the false American charges against the Japanese pale into insignificance beside the actual acts of deliberate American terror aganst civilian populations. No one expects war to be anything but a brutal business, but it remains for the Americans to make it systematically and unnecessarily a wholesale horror for innocent civilians.

On March 15 the Cabinet met in emergency session and ordered the immediate dispersal of all civilians from the Tokyo-Yokohama, Osaka-Kobe, and Nagoya areas. The fire raids had convinced the government that the Americans were out to destroy all of Japan's cities and civilian population. Only essential workers would remain in the cities. All others would move out to the countryside to stay until the danger was past.

Radio Tokyo felt it necessary to make a statement clarifying the problem. General LeMay was the immediate target.

The man who invented and carried out the big raids on Hamburg now directs the attacks on Japan from the Marianas. A few nights ago he repeated here in Tokyo what he had learned in Germany. Owing to unfortunate circumstances, the storm of fire caused by incendiaries swept whole districts, which were burned to the ground, only here and there were blackened walls of the rare stone buildings left standing.

Having admitted this much, Radio Tokyo then felt impelled to deny that the bombing had any effect other than to add a new surge to the determination of the Japanese to fight harder and longer.

"This is a sacred war against the diabolical Americans," said Radio Tokyo. "Once a house has been set on fire, it cannot be fired a second time."

This strength-through-joy adjuration was not recognized by Radio Tokyo as ironic; it was said quite seriously. "Now we can fight with complete freedom, since a heavy toll has been levied on us," went the logic. In other words, the more Japanese were killed, the harder the survivors would fight.

> Enemy aircraft will set many Japanese towns on fire, but underneath the fires will be the indomitable flame of the just anger of 100 million Japanese. This is the source of our war strength. Our fighting spirit, which is already of steel, will become harder, stronger, and more acute through this baptism of fire.

The government officials of Japan really believed this was true, or, rather, the militarists believed they had convinced everyone it was true. They had adapted an old Japanese belief that right made might; they were right, they said, and therefore all the modern machinery of the Americans would be as chaff before the sweeping winds of the Japanese spirit. No matter that the kamikazes were falling like cherry blossoms. The Japanese people knew it, and they accepted it, just as they accepted the suzerainty of B-san over Japanese skies. There was nothing to be done.

The chief of the Tokyo fire department had to contend with the facts. The first bombs had fallen on his city at fifteen minutes after midnight on March 10. He sent two of his assistants up to the roof of city hall to observe the air raids. They came down all too soon, to report that the situation was getting out of hand. Within three hours the flames were totally out of control, he had lost all the fire equipment in the affected areas of East Tokyo, and too many firemen. The blaze had become an inferno with such speed that there was nothing the firemen could do to contain it. They could not put out individual fires because by 3:00 A.M. there were none; it was a fire dragon, weaving its way across the city, and it was a juggernaut, unstoppable. The firemen from that point on joined with the volunteers and the police in trying to save as many people as they could.

The fire chief could tell the governor of Tokyo, which he did, that if the wind had not been blowing that night, the damage done would have been about one-third of what it was. But what good did that do?

From the provinces to Tokyo came demands for more air-raid defense equipment and fire engines. From the fringes of the burned-out areas, where the equipment was undamaged but the surrounding area was razed, the Home Ministry culled the available fire equipment and began shipping it to other cities.

Despair and resignation were the growing reality in Japan. The publicity director of the Japanese Foreign Office, although constrained to follow the official line, had some private thoughts about it. He knew that Japan's morale had taken a nosedive with that first shocking fire raid. He knew that the policy of dispersing Japanese industry to the countryside was going to fail. Japan's industry was centralized around the power grids of the big cities; there was no way that in a short time the whole system could be rearranged.

This official also knew what General LeMay knew, that the destruction of the home industries that supplied components to the factories a few blocks away would put an enormous crimp in the Japanese war effort.

He also knew that "the morale of the people themselves, their will and capacity to continue to fight, would certainly not increase after a series of fire raids. They were about to find out all about the 'total war' which their groggy Axis partner had invented."

As for the Tokyo raid itself, say what he might to the public, the official knew the truth:

> That bright stark night will remain in the memory of all who witnessed it. After the first incendiary bombs fell, clouds formed and were lit up from below with a pink light. From them emerged Superfortresses flying uncannily low above the centers of conflagration, which gradually spread. A B-29 exploded before our eyes like a magnesium tracer bullet, almost over the center of the city. The fire clouds kept creeping higher and the tower of the Diet building stood out black against the red sky. The city was as bright as at sunrise, clouds of smoke, soot, even sparks driven by the storm were flying over it. That night we thought the whole of Tokyo had been reduced to ashes.

Despite the government's claims of solidarity, it was quite apparent that the fire raids had shocked the Japanese people into recognition that the war was going even more badly than most of them had believed.

The Home Ministry was responsible for citizen morale, which it bolstered through the use of such agencies as the "thought control police," whose task it was to search out rebels and dissidents and entrap them into disloyal remarks, then arrest them as horrible examples to the rest of the population. At this time the thought police began operating on high levels, within the Cabinet agencies of the government. Even Cabinet members were cognizant of being watched, and very careful of their statements even to associates.

And yet the chief of the police bureau of the Home Ministry had this to say about what was really going on:

Results

Morale change was chiefly due to a loss of certainty of victory, which grew through successive defeats into a loss of faith in government news, and then in government's ability to safeguard civilians, and finally into a loss of faith in the military. Control measures within the purview of the police largely had to do with the control of rumors: police visits and lecturing and "converting" persons to whom rumors were traceable, with fines and imprisonment in a few cases.

For months the Americans had been dropping propaganda leaflets, but just now, with the fire raids, the success of this program became visible. People has always turned the leaflets in to the police, many times refusing to read them. Now people stopped turning the leaflets in.

Starting in Tokyo and spreading across the country was a wave of criticism of the air-raid-defense program, so broad and so deep that the Home Ministry knew it could not be combated by arresting a few people.

On March 14, *Mainichi Shimbun* made it a point to call on the public for endurance. "The victims of the recent air raid are now experiencing hardship beyond words," said *Mainichi*. The paper was referring to the 200,000 injured people in Tokyo who found it almost impossible to get any medical attention, and to the 800,000 people left suddenly homeless in what was still a winter month, with inadequate food, water, and sanitary facilities. The people must have courage and trust in the authorities, said *Mainichi*. But the people were no longer so trustful as they had once been.

Special efforts were made to restore that confidence. The Emperor's doings were almost never reported to the public except on national holidays and state occasions. But now the press was told that the Emperor was taking special interest in the plight of Tokyo following the firebombing, and that he had dispatched two court chamberlains, Torahiko Nagazumi and Prince Sansatsu Tokudaiji to investigate the activities of the authorities and report directly back to the emperor. Also, General Toshizo Nishio, the governor of Tokyo, put out a statement intended to reassure the people. But all the people had to do was look about them at the dreadful destruction. The scene spoke for itself.

The policy of official encouragement parted the curtain of secrecy a very little. The people were told that the Emperor had ordered Prime Minister Koiso to meet with the officers of Imperial General Headquarters, inform himself fully concerning their activities, and report back to the Emperor.

A few days after the Tokyo fire raid, the American planes had come back over Tokyo and the other cities, but this time to drop leaflets telling the Japanese that it was time to end the war, although, as noted above, such propaganda had been tried before, but without visible effect. The government had taken no official notice of the effort. But now the Home Ministry was seriously concerned about the morale of the nation. The government reacted as one might expect of a military dictatorship: a new ordinance was issued demanding that anyone finding a leaflet turn it in to the authorities, and severe penalties, including imprisonment, were ordered for those caught disobeying. So it was apparent that all was not well with the Japanese civilian morale, no matter what the newspapers claimed.

In the wake of the firebombing, Tokyo was pulling itself back together. A number of refugee centers were established in parks and other open spaces. The people were given tents, blankets, and supplies of food for five days at a time: rice, sweet potatoes, millet *mochi* (sweetened grain), miso, and pickled radishes. For infants, there was powdered or condensed milk.

Candles, towels, matches, toilet paper, soap, shoes, and clothing were distributed to the refugees. The magnitude of the task was staggering. Suddenly a million people had lost everything they owned, and the government had to provide for them, or watch them die and take the consequences.

Results

The Emperor had made his visit outside the Imperial Palace, to satisfy himself that the government was doing what it could for the bombed-out million of the capital city. The media responded by publicizing the matter to the hilt. No stone was to be left unturned in trying to stem the wave of bad feeling that was sweeping the country.

A whole new set of directives were issued by the Home Ministry regarding air-raid precautions. The block wardens looked at them and saw that nothing had changed. The problem, of course, was that deep shelters were needed for the public, and deep shelters did not exist, nor was there any indication that the government was going to initiate a crash program to build them.

Instead of taking action, the government contented itself with words. On orders, the newspapers now began to indulge in what one cynical journalist called "mathematical hocus-pocus" to try to convince the Japanese people that the B-29 threat was only temporary. Here was the logic:

The best estimate was that 135 B-29s were manufactured each month at the Boeing plant in Seattle. Assuming that thirty of these were lost through wear and tear and accident on their way to the Marianas, that reduced the number delivered to 105 per month. Another 10 percent, just over ten planes, were put out of action by Japanese bombing raids on the Marianas. The number, by Japanese official calculation, has now been reduced to ninety planes per month. Assuming that the B-29s raided Japan six times per month, and that the Japanese shot down fifteen planes on each raid, that meant the Americans lost ninety planes a month, so the losses of the Americans would equal the production rate. With this logic, it was easy to see that the Americans would soon run out of B-29s.

And there was more:

Up to 14 January 1945, 1,350 enemy B-29s have raided Japan. Of this total, our forces have either shot down or damaged 424 Superfortresses. In Manchuria thirty-one enemy Superfortresses and in Shonan twenty more were similarly accounted for by our forces. The enemy has therefore lost 475 Superfortresses shot down or damaged. Assuming that some fifty bombers either met with accidents or otherwise broke down on their flights to Japan and that 181 more were damaged or destroyed by our raids on the Marianas, the grand total of enemy Superfort losses is 706. In personnel, the enemy has lost 5,775 airmen.

Since a single Superfortress costs $750,000, the enemy's total loss is $529,500,000. In working hours the enemy has suffered a setback of a month and a half's continuous work by ten factories with 10,000 workers sweating on ten-hour shifts.

Thus the Japanese government propagandists could "prove" that the Superfortress threat was nearly ended.

But the fact was that General LeMay had 300 Superfortresses in the Marianas, and more on the way. His triumphant report on the burning of Tokyo had reached Washington and impressed the Joint Chiefs of Staff. The raid on Tokyo had been an enormous success. The failure of the Nagoya raid was not yet fully appreciated. There was a reason. General LeMay was in a hurry to hit two other cities and then present Washington with the results. The bombers were making ready just now for the raid on Osaka.

13
OSAKA

BEFORE THE WAR BEGAN, OSAKA WAS THE CENTER OF JAPAN'S foreign trade. One of her largest cities, it was growing by leaps and bounds, almost as fast as Tokyo. Its combination of heavy and light industry and its position as a great port made it doubly important.

Before the war, Osaka had been a crowded city, and when the war began in the Pacific its population density was the highest in Japan. Also, it was seen as the easiest city in Japan to burn, because of the many old buildings crowded together.

Osaka had first been bombed, more or less, by the Doolittle raiders in 1942. The real effect of the Doolittle raid here, as in Tokyo, was to force the authorities of the Central District of the Japanese army and the army air force authorities in Tokyo to re-think their air defense policies. Osaka, at the time of the Doolittle raid, had virtually no air defenses, since the possibility of Japan's being bombed had never entered anyone's head until that time, even after the beginning of the Pacific war. After the Doolittle raid, the Imperial General Staff had decided that air defense must get a new high priority. It was, however, an army priority, which meant that the air defense would consist of anti-aircraft guns to be placed in the areas where military production was important.

Thus the Eastern Area Army (Tokyo) got 108 new high-powered antiaircraft guns, the Central Army (Nagoya, Osaka, Kobe) got 110 new guns, the Western Army (Kyushu) got eighteen guns, the Northern Army (Hokkaido) got eight guns, and the Korean Army got another eight guns. Manchuria, which was now Manchukuo, was not included in the list, since the Japanese always maintained that Manchukuo was independent, and thus the Kwantung Army, which guarded Manchuria, drew its support from the Manchurian economy, and continued to be virtually independent of Tokyo.

The defense plans of the army, of course, made no provision for the civilian population. If that seems odd to Americans in the 1980s, it was totally expected by the Japanese people of the 1940s. The responsibility for civil defense in Japan always rested with the Home Ministry. The Home Minister, in fact, was a general, but that did not mean the army as such was involved.

On March 4, a solitary B-29 flew over north Osaka and dropped leaflets. These were about twenty centimeters long and ten wide, printed on black paper in red ink. They carried on their faces illustrations of firebombs. The message was very clear.

The firebombs were waiting, said the leaflets. The bombs would be dropped on industry, railroad installations, port facilities, army military installations, and the munitions industry. The public was warned by all means to keep away from any sort of military installations.

A few hours later, another B-29 came over and dropped more leaflets. These were thirteen by eighteen centimeters and printed on red paper. This leaflet again warned the Japanese people that Osaka's industry, army installations, powerhouses, railroad yards, and railway stations were to be targets of the bombing to come.

The Americans meant the Japanese people no harm, said the leaflet. However, it said, the Japanese Army clique was absolutely evil. It had used its evil power to build up the munitions industry in Osaka, and this must be destroyed. It *would* be destroyed, without question.

The Japanese army clique had begun this war, and had carried it on for years, the leaflet said. It included other statements about the war, and called on the Japanese people to remember that the United States was going to end what the Japanese army clique had begun.

This was the second warning, given out of the kindness of the Americans' hearts, said the leaflet, just to be sure that innocent people were warned of the bombings to come.

On the face of the leaflet, four steps were marked off, and on each step were shown some of the installations to be bombed:

> Industry
> Trains
> Car barns
> Cargo piers
> Antiaircraft gun installations

On each step these were shown as destroyed.

Below them was the expression *ABUNAI!* [Danger!] followed by the admonition, WARNING! STAY AWAY FROM JAPANESE ARMY INSTALLATIONS!

An hour after the leaflets were dropped, urgent orders went out to the urban police stations, instructing the police to begin collecting the leaflets and holding them so they would not infect the populace. The police picked up 82,592 leaflets, but obviously thousands were not picked up and the warning got through to many Osaka people.

Three days after the dropping of the warning leaflets, General LeMay gave the orders that would begin the firebombing of

Japan's four major urban areas, without regard to military targets. The purpose as announced was to start fires and burn up the cities. The greatest burning in history was about to begin.

March 13, 1945. The maintenance crews at the B-29 airfields on Saipan, Tinian, and Guam had worked day and night at top speed to make the Superfortresses ready for this third big fire raid on the Japanese homeland within a week. As General LeMay knew very well, the element of surprise was important, and it would not be long before the Japanese began adjusting their defense measures to meet the new American tactics. Just now, surprise was on his side, but time was not. To achieve full effect of his plan to blast the four important cities with fire, the XXI Bomber Command must move with celerity.

Four areas of Osaka were set as targets for this incendiary raid: Kita, or north district; Nishi district, on the west; and Minato and Naniwa districts. Kita was on the left bank of the Yodo River and ran to Toyo Cape. Here the main targets were the headquarters, buildings, and yards of the Eastern Sea District's main railroad. Also the main Osaka railroad station was here, and the Nishimaru line passed through the area, along the bank of the Yasuharu River, to circle Osaka's inner harbor.

On the south were the Tachugen and Sano districts, through which the rail line also passed, as well as Matsuya and Kaku. A big river, the Yadakawa, flowed north there. The Kema track enclosed the areas then. In short, this was the absolute heart of old Osaka in terms of population and industry.

And, as in Tokyo, in accordance with the requests of the Japanese Army, the production of war materials had been changed over, so that subcontractors and household-contractors were doing a good deal of the subassembly work, thus enhancing the ability of the major contractors to speed up their assembly lines.

These areas were carefully plotted out by the intelligence officers, and the marked maps were given to the pathfinder navigators.

By nightfall, 295 planes were in the air, again heading north-west toward the Japanese Inner Empire. One plane crashed and burned on the runway on takeoff, and one was lost to causes unknown. Fifteen turned back for mechanical reasons, but the other 279 Superfortresses moved in to the target with more than two thousand pounds of incendiary bombs.

The weather was rough again this night, with many thermal disturbances. One plane was jolted so badly that the wing rivets loosened, but the Superfortress was a sturdy aircraft; this one still made it home. Japanese fighters followed the returning aircraft back a hundred miles from Nagoya, but most did not attack. One plane—WSM 276—was hit, and the left waist blister was loosened so badly that it blew out over Kyushu. The gunner, who was also a photographer and thus was carried along on this trip, had worn two safety belts, one fastened to the seat and the other to the floor of the plane. He was taking pictures with an aerial camera and had unfastened the seat belt for greater movement. The floor belt, although rated to withstand nearly 3,000 pounds of pull, broke and the gunner was sucked out of the plane. He was wearing his parachute, and the last his comrades saw was the billowing white silk as the parachute began opening below and behind them.

Several aircraft did not make Osaka. They bombed Kushimoto, Shirama, Chichi Jima, and Uji Yamada. One plane failed to return, a victim of enemy action. Some forty Japanese fighters were seen over the target area, and several attacks were made there. One Japanese plane tried to ram a Superfortress of the 73rd Wing, but did not succeed.

On the ground, the Japanese defenders were waiting for a high-altitude attack, and every gun that could reach 21,000 feet was manned. But when the bombers came, it was a complete surprise. The air-raid alarm had sounded and then it was turned off. The planes came in, not at 7,000 meters and more, but at much lower altitudes. The Japanese antiaircraft gunners were flab-bergasted, and their weapons were of virtually no use at all.

Osaka had 157 high-altitude guns. The radar installation was primitive and not working well. The searchlights were not operating properly that night, either.

In the previous two raids, the Americans had discovered that the Japanese automatic weapons were most ineffective. There were eighty-eight such guns around Osaka, and their radar simply did not penetrate the high overcast that was hanging over the city this night. Also, the Japanese in central Honshu were suffering from the same problems that the army faced in the east: inadequate night fighter squadrons. In Central Honshu the Japanese could put up 192 single-engine fighters and only twenty-four twin-engined fighters. It was unthinkable that squadrons from other areas could be called in to help—the Japanese Army just did not work that way.

Late that night the American bombers began to approach the Japanese home islands, or Hondo, as the Japanese called them. The term had a special meaning. The Ryukyus, Korea, and Taiwan were all a part of the Japanese Inner Empire, but the central islands of Honshu, Kyushu, Shikoku, and Hokkaido had a special significance, a truly religious meaning of their own. This was the sacred territory of Japan from time immemorial. This was the land that had never been successfully invaded by any other nation. Now the Americans were invading Japan in the air every day, and for three days had been waging the most destructive bombing campaign in the history of this war. Osaka was now about to receive its immersion in fire, and its citizens were half expecting the blow.

Kinoseko Imajiyo was a twenty-three-year-old worker in the Osaka Imperial Gun Factory down by the harbor. Her father was a member of the harbor board of Osaka and a distinguished citizen. They lived in the Suiki district of Minato-ku. (*Ku* means "ward"; every Japanese city is divided into such wards.) It was a completely residential district; their neighbors on both sides were young married couples, or, rather, they were the wives of young married couples, for the husbands were off serving in the armed forces.

Kinoseko's house was within walking distance of the factory where she worked, near the Number Two Osaka pier, which meant it was right inside the prime target area selected by General LeMay for this first big Osaka firebombing raid.

Kinoseko was outside her house that night when the first air-raid-warning siren began to blow. She was wearing the heavy padded air-raid hood that the neighborhood association had given her, and *monpei* and a heavy cotton jacket. The warning came from the sirens around the city when the planes were over Kii Minamichi and Atsushi Prefecture's Cape Komata. That the bombers were heading for Osaka was confirmed a few minutes later when they passed over the south side of Awaji Island, moving toward the Seidan district.

The sirens blew for four seconds, then stopped for eight seconds, then blew again. This was the warning signal. An air raid was coming, and the people were being told to prepare. From the upper stories of the factories, a stream of humanity began to emerge onto the streets down by the harbor. Work was naturally suspended, and the workers were moving out to find some sort of protection. Ten times the warning siren blew. The tension throughout Osaka increased, as the people knew now that they were to have the same sort of treatment that Tokyo had received on March 10 and Nagoya on March 12.

As the bombers droned on toward their target, the tension and activity in Osaka's streets increased. Civil defense and ward officials came out with megaphones to direct the people to move out of the area down by the harbor. Some shouted orders that were usually ignored as the people streamed along, hurrying to get away.

The sirens began to sound again, this time more urgently. It was the air raid *alarm* this time, more than a warning, the news that the bombing was about to begin.

The B-29s were moving in over Osaka Bay. The men with the megaphones continued to shout. The lights of the buildings began flashing on and off, another signal to the workers in the factories and offices to beware and get away. The radio station at Kii Minamichi began to broadcast, announcing the movement of the B-29s, and their destination: Osaka.

"The enemy planes are on their way. . . ."

Osakans had heard that air-raid alarm many, many times before, but there was something different about it on this night of March 13. They knew that firebombing was to be their lot this night.

The people thought they were ready. They had been taught how to fight fires. They had been bombed before, although not very effectively. Neighbor would help neighbor, and they would beat out the fires with the flails given out by the neighborhood associations, and with old mats they kept at home for the purpose. Both of Kinoseko's next-door neighbors, young housewives, were at home, waiting just as she was.

Kinoseko Imajiyo went out of her house. She thought about going into the garden and climbing down into the underground shelter the family had built there. But she paused and looked up at the sky. Overhead, flying low, she saw a single B-29. (Obviously it was one of the pathfinders, although the term meant nothing to Kinoseko.)

As she watched, the bombers began to come over in groups. She could see the tips of the wings of the aircraft, the wing lights, and the exhausts of the engines glowing red with fire. One after the other they passed over, a great procession of aircraft coming into her city. Hitoshi Koyama, the historian of the Osaka bombings, wrote that Kinoseko gritted her teeth in silent rage as she watched the American planes invading Japan's sacred air space. Perhaps she did. She was a product of the Japanese educational system, taken over early in the 1930s by the militarists, and she had truly believed until recently that Japan would emerge victorious from the struggle for a Greater East Asia, and that it was impossible for Japan to be invaded, or even bombed. She had already been disabused of the latter idea, and this night's events so far were already a sad blow to her confidence in the future.

As Kinoseko watched, the B-29s' leaders approached their aiming point. She counted sixty-one planes coming in over Osaka Bay, traveling northeast, toward the mouth of the Yasuharu River.

The noise overhead grew thunderous as plane followed plane across the bay, heading for the city.

The 314th Air Wing planes came in bunches, one, two, three of them, and suddenly the sky began to rain firebombs. Kinoseko watched as the bombs fell by the hundreds and thousands around her neighborhood, and where they fell came splashes of red and yellow light and then the spreading of fire. In the darkness, the overpowering roar of the B-29s' engines echoed through the streets of Osaka. A cascade of fire rained down on the city, as the 314th Wing and then the 313th and then the 73rd dropped their bombs.

The air defenses were of very little use. The high-altitude anti-aircraft guns could not fire on the invaders. Actually, the Japanese got only twenty-five planes into the air that night and they made thirty-nine round trips, but that does not mean thirty-nine attacks.

Army officials on the ground watched in awe as the aircraft came in, not in large groups, as had been the habit of the B-29s in the past, but in twos and threes and even singly, and dropped their firebombs. The fires hit the edges of the residential area and began to spread until it was as light as day in the whole Osaka area. "They came down like rain," said one civil defense official, as he watched and pondered what might be done. The answer was really that there was nothing to be done. As with Tokyo, and to a lesser extent Nagoya, the firebombs were too many to deal with: 1,733 tons, most of them six-pound bombs. Thousands and thousands of bombs, raining on the tile roofs of Osaka.

The planes came in at 4,500 to 8,000 feet, again operating

individually. The first B-29 arrived over target at three minutes before midnight. The last left the Osaka region at 3:25 on the morning of March 14. In between, 272 other B-29s bombed. They dropped 1,700 tons of incendiaries on Naniwa, Nishi, Minami, and five other districts of Osaka.

Takako Oshima was thirteen years old in 1945, and a student at the Ichiryo Kyogawa girls' school of commerce. She lived with her family in Naniwa in the center of Osaka, where her father kept a tailor shop that adjoined their house. The family consisted of her mother, Shiyo, her father, Shinichi, and her seven-year-old brother Sanjiro. There was another brother, older, but he was off with the army somewhere "at the front." He was talking about getting married to a girl he had known all through five years of school at the National People's School—if and when he came home. There was another sister, but she had been sent off to Shiga Sakamoto in the mass evacuation of students from the Osaka area earlier because of the bombings.

On the night of March 13, Takako's father was working in the tailor shop, her mother and little brother were asleep in the family air-raid shelter, which had been constructed in the tailor shop by digging beneath the concrete floor and putting down wooden flooring and a wooden cover over the shelter. Takako had a mountain of homework to do for school, and she was in the house studying when the air-raid warnings began.

When the warning signals turned to alarms, Takako and her father stopped what they were doing, and joined her mother and little brother in the shelter.

Then Takako's father decided he had best go out and take a look at the house, since the bombs were beginning to fall. He went out. He could see the light from the fires blazing all around their neighborhood. The B-29s were directly overhead now, and dropping their firebombs by the thousands.

In a few moments the family heard Papa Oshima shouting. The

west side of the house was on fire. He rushed into the shop, grabbed a ladder, and went out again. Takako went to the other door and looked out. She saw him trying to beat out the fire with a flail. But by this time the west wall was blazing redly, and the whole neighborhood was lit up like day from the fires all around their block. Up above, the B-29s sailed on through the night. Takako could hear the enormous racket their engines made as the planes dropped their messages of death. Her father shouted at her to go back into the shelter, and she hastened down into the hole again.

In a few moments her father came running into the shelter, followed by the neighborhood association block leader. The fire was too far gone, said the block leader. They must now evacuate the house and go out into the garden, where they would be much safer.

So the four members of the family went into the garden. The house was blazing, but the B-29s were gone—or seemed to be. Takako's mother threw a steamer rug over her to protect her from sparks. They stood and watched their house burn.

Just then, another B-29 came over, and more bombs came down. Just as Takako was stepping forward to adjust the steamer rug around her shoulders, a bomb burst at her feet and fire shot out all around the family. Takako stood like stone. She thought she was dead. Fire began to break out all over the steamer rug, and she threw it off. The flames then spread to her *monpei* and long-sleeved shirt. Her air-raid turban was burning, but her mother snatched it off and put out the fire in her hair. While all this was happening, Takako was standing like a log, mesmerized, still thinking she was dead. Facing her was her brother, who was also on fire, and her mother and father were moving around desperately to help. Her father seized two buckets that stood beside the family cistern of water kept, as ordered by the neighborhood association, for the purpose of putting out fires. He dipped them in the cistern, filled them, and dashed the contents over Sanjiro, putting out the fires that were ravaging his clothes. Takako stood dumbly, numbly, unable to speak, unable to move. She just watched as her father saved her brother's life.

In the confusion, Takako's mother had disappeared, and no one knew where she had gone.

Takako's body was burned in many places. The fire had burned through her turban, and had burned her *monpei*. She was wearing another pair of trousers under the *monpei*, but the fire had burned through both pairs, Her shoulders were blistered, and so were her hands. She went over to the cistern and her father poured water over her shoulders to put out the flames there. Her left hand was burned right through the glove, and this, too, was dipped in the water to cool. As she stood there, she saw that skin was literally dripping from both arms and hands, hanging down in strips. From the shadows came a next-door neighbor, who came up to Takako and helped her get closer to the cistern. The neighbor— *oba-san*, or "auntie," she was called—splashed water over all of Takako to be sure the fires in her clothing were all extinguished. Then she bathed Takako's hot face and hands with more water. The lady herself was burned on the thighs by sparks and flames from the burning house. She had a child with her who was also burned, and they bathed this baby to cool it off. Oba-san's own house had begun to burn, and she had escaped by throwing herself out of it with the baby in her arms.

After Papa had turned up, he had begun calling for Mama Oshima, but she did not respond. He thought she must be with a neighbor. At the moment, Shinichi Oshima had too much on his mind to worry. Something had to be done about Sanjiro. His papa picked him up and immersed him in the cistern. It seemed to relieve the boy's pain.

Now Takako began to cry. Later she did not remember that at all, but she cried very hard for a long time as she watched their house burn down.

Papa Oshima started to try to put the fires out with buckets of water, but he soon saw that it was useless. Water did not affect the firebombs, they continued to burn, no matter how much water was poured on them. Seeing that it was hopeless, Papa Oshima then turned all his attention to the family. Takako had decided to help put out the fires. He pulled her away from the house, and back to the cistern again. He looked at his seven-year-old son, the boy who had only been going to the National People's School for a single year, the pride and hope of the family, for once the oldest son had gone into the army, no one expected him to return to Japan alive. Sanjiro, then, was the Oshima heir, and in him rested all their hopes.

The boy was so badly burned that not even his mother would have recognized him, had she seen him on the street. The shape of his face was completely changed, swollen so that his eyes were mere slits. Large blisters were rising all around his head and neck. His hair was burned away. He said nothing at all, but stared fixedly at Takako, and Takako stared back at him as though he were a stranger. Neither spoke.

Papa Oshima saw that Sanjiro's body was covered with burns His belt had been partly burned away from his waist. His *monpei* and shirt were burned and the flesh was charred beneath them. Actually, most of his clothing was burned off. The boy's face had turned a dark red, and so had Takako's. She could see that Sanjiro's face was darkened, and he could see that hers was also, but neither could sense the damage done to themselves. As time went on, however, the pain began. Her left hand was badly burned, her right one less so. She had burns on many parts of her body—shoulders, legs, neck, face, and even feet.

Papa Oshima was also badly burned. His face was blistered and blackened and his lips were split. Both of his hands were scorched from his efforts to put out the fire that burned his house.

But as the night wore on and daylight began to appear, the Oshimas realized that at least they were alive, and that the bombers were gone. That was the great blessing of March 14, 1945.

Or so they thought.

As the fires burned down, and for the moment at least Sanjiro seemed comforted by the water, Papa Oshima had time to worry about his wife. Leaving the children, he began searching.

No, she was not with a neighbor. No one had seen her.

With growing apprehension, Papa Oshima moved through the ruins of his house and tailor shop and down into the shelter. Perhaps she had stayed in there when the others came out, he thought. He went down through the smoldering boards into the interior, where a vault had been made in the back. Inside the vault was a wicker trunk that held his wife's precious kimonos, some of them handed down in her family for generations. He opened the trunk, hoping to find her inside. But no, she was not there.

Papa Oshima felt his heart sink, and in an instant he knew that she must have fled back into the burning house and been killed there. The house was still smoldering, and there was no way he could go inside to look for her, nor, if she was there, would there be any use in doing so. He went back outside, pulled Sanjiro out of the cistern, beckoned to Takako, and put the boy up on his back.

"Let's go," he said.

Takako hung back. She began calling for her mother.

"It's no use," he said. "Let's go."

Still, Takako delayed. At that terrible moment she realized that her mother was dead, and she felt an unbearable weight of responsibility. Why hadn't anyone helped her mother? Forty years later, Takako would be asking herself that same question, but the fact was that no one could have helped Shiyo Oshima from the moment she made the turn that took her back into the burning house instead of outside into the garden.

The Oshima house was very near the avenue that led to the center of the community. Papa Oshima led them out into the street, and they began walking. After a few minutes they came to the business section. The fish market was burned down, they saw, and the fishmonger was standing outside, his *monpei* badly burned, looking blankly at the ruins of his life.

They walked on.

Sanjiro began crying, calling for water. Papa Oshima knew that the burned boy must have water, and very soon. He knew a man who lived in this area, near the main gates of the Eikoko Public School, and he turned that way to find help for the boy. They seemed to be walking through a strange land, through a forest of trash. Everywhere around them they saw rubbish, from wheelbarrows and packs full of deserted belongings to futons and quilts and suitcases, bits and pieces of luggage, and the personal belongings discarded by fleeing people. The streets were full of people rushing this way and that, and it seemed that no one was paying the slightest attention to anyone else.

Papa Oshima then turned into the gates of the school. Inside, he saw that he had come to precisely the right place. There were two doctors inside, one of whom he recognized. He walked into the room where they were working. He stopped and brought Sanjiro, who was asleep by this time, down off his back.

As Papa Oshima lay the boy down, Sanjiro's shirt came up from his *monpei*, revealing his midriff. Takako took one look and screamed. Papa Oshima had believed that Sanjiro had been burned on his face and neck for the most part, but now the naked body showed the truth: the boy was burned from head to toe, his whole body covered with enormous blisters. The sight was too much for Takako to bear, and she turned away.

The doctor took one look at Sanjiro and separated Takako from the father and son. She was to go into another room for medical treatment, he said.

Takako did go to another room, and there the first-aid attendants treated her burns. She also had burns on her feet from the hot asphalt of the streets, because her shoes had burned away.

The family remained at the school overnight. In the morning, Papa Oshima went to his brother's house and brought the children's uncle back to the school. The men found a stretcher and carried Sanjiro to the uncle's house, and Takako went along as well. That day, Papa Oshima left the children at his brother's house while he and his brother went to the Oshima house to try to find Mama Oshima. They searched through the cooling ruins, but they saw nothing in the house. Finally they went back down into the shelter again, and into the vault. They found nothing. But beneath the stairs in the shelter, they finally discovered the body of forty-eight-year-old Shiro Oshima. She had died of smoke inhalation. It was not hard for them to piece together what had happened. In the darkness and smoke and fire of the great bombing raid, Shiro had become disoriented and begun groping her way around in the air-raid shelter, not knowing how to get out. Before she could find the stairway, she had been overcome by smoke, and then asphyxiated.

Sadly, Papa Oshima returned to his brother's house and broke the news to Takako. She collapsed, and actually fainted. When she regained consciousness she began to cry. For years she was obsessed with the thought of her dying mother fumbling in the shelter, trying to get out, with no one to help her, while the others stood by the cistern in the garden.

At the aid station, the doctors had looked at Sanjiro with solemn eyes. He was horribly burned, but there were virtually no medicines available, and nothing could be done for him except to bathe his wounds and treat them with salve and bandages.

He was now bandaged from head to foot. All that day, March 14, Sanjiro was very restless. His face was swollen and his eyes glued shut. The doctors had bandaged him, but privately they knew that the boy's chances of survival were practically nonexistent. Too much of his body had been burned, too much fluid had been lost.

Most of the time since, Sanjiro had been mercifully unconscious. Takako stayed with him, although her eyes were swollen shut so that she could not see. But she could hear him, and when he called out for water, she cried out to the household in a loud voice. Her aunt came with water, but then Sanjiro was too weak to drink it. Several times that day, Sanjiro called for water, and each time it was brought, but he could not drink.

Takako knew then that he was going to die. All night long she stayed with him, and then on the morning of March 15, Sanjiro died.

On the night of March 13 and the morning of March 14, very few people in Osaka could really see what was happening. Their perception was confined almost totally to their own immediate surroundings. But some of the authorities were watching from the tops of buildings as the American bombers came.

What they saw was a sea of fire that engulfed the central section of Osaka. Along the North Canal, men and women were fleeing in both directions. Some were going into the water. Some were hurrying to the West Bridge to cross the river and thus escape the fire area.

The police, who would be responsible for making a formal report on the events of that night, were on the rooftops, watching and keeping notes. When the raid ended, for three days they worked to discover all the details. Finally, on March 19, they made their formal report to the army.

The planes had come in over Shoryugensho Island at 11:15 P.M. They came up from the southeast, heading for the northwest. They appeared over Osaka at 11:44 and, for the next three hours and fifteen minutes, created and maintained their sea of fire.

Next morning the local newspapers all had almost the same headline: OSAKA INVADED BY OCEAN OF FLAME.

And then there were subsidiary headlines, telling of the efforts of suicide pilots to destroy the enemy bombers. Unfortunately, however, the "wild eagles" were all too few in the sky that night, and the only plane shot down over Osaka seems to have been destroyed by an antiaircraft gun.

The best panoramic view of the air raid was afforded several journalists from *Asahi Shimbun*, the big Tokyo newspaper, who climbed up to the roof of the *Asahi Shimbun* building in west Osaka. From there they could see the planes as they came in from a distance over Osaka Bay. They could hear the noise of their engines. Suddenly, as they watched, from the bellies of the airplanes came an avalanche of what looked like gravel. But as the "gravel" fell and hit the ground, it sprouted into light. At first there was a point, and then a growing reddish spot blotting the city, and then the spot spread and spread until the redness was everywhere. One *Asahi* reporter looked at his watch. The time was 12:05.

The 314th Air Group from Guam hit Minato and Minami districts. The 313th from Tinian hit Kita and Nishi. The 73rd Wing from Saipan hit the center of the city, and soon Osaka was transformed into what the newspapers called "a sea of wild fire and raging smoke." The B-29s bombed an ammunition dump, and the ammunition began exploding in all directions. The fires spread to the army stores, and destroyed most of them.

The police report of the Osaka raid spoke of machine gunning, but as in the Tokyo and Nagoya raids, the B-29s were not supposed to be equipped with machine guns or ammunition for this raid.

The fires and other damage hurt the city everywhere. Even the "water people," those who lived on boats in the Ushizu and Yasuharu rivers and Osaka Bay, had casualties. Some of their houseboats were burned up, and so were many of their sampans. About seven hundred of the water people died in the fires.

As was true with all these great air raids, the figures of victor and vanquished did not agree. The Japanese police reported that in Osaka proper the firebombs destroyed 134,744 houses and damaged another 1,363, and killed 2,987 people. Seriously injured were 763 people; 7,737 were less seriously hurt, while 687 were missing. In terms of death, the Osaka raid was as nothing compared to the great Tokyo raid three nights earlier. There were no high winds and there was no fire storm. But in terms of suffering to the living, the Osaka raid was as disastrous as the Tokyo raid: 500,000 people were left homeless this night; many of them saw their shops and businesses burn up and were then without a way to earn a living.

When morning came, the police began to move around and pick up the bodies. Many were found in the rivers and the bay.

The American air force figures never jibed completely with those of the Japanese. The Americans' interest was different in the first place. The B-29s, they said, destroyed much of twenty-one square kilometers of the big port city, burned 136,000 houses, made 501,000 people homeless, killed nearly 4,000 people, again mostly women and children, wounded 8,500, and left nearly 700 people unaccounted for—obviously blasted into oblivion.

The bombing raid lasted for three and a half hours before the last bomber moved away into the eastern sky. The results lasted much, much longer, as the fires set by the bombers burned and burned.

Imperial General Headquarters made one of its usual sententious announcements of the raid, claiming that 90 B-29s had struck Osaka and that a large number of them had been shot down. Of course the number of bombers was three times as great, and the number of planes shot down was very small: the 73rd Wing lost three planes, the 313th lost three also, and the 314th lost four. The surprise element had continued to work for the B-29s. The army had failed to learn—or at least to report on—the manner in which the bombers had behaved at Tokyo and Nagoya.

Would it have done any good if the army general staff had put out all-points bulletins about the new B-29 tactics? Probably not. It would take the Japanese some time to figure out how to meet such a menace as the B-29 firebombing, if they ever could. It was not something that could be managed overnight. And General LeMay's plan had only been put into action five days earlier.

The Oshimas had the bodies of Mama Oshima and Sanjiro cremated and their ashes preserved in boxes. Takako went to the services, although she still could not see. It was ten days before her eyes opened and many months before her burns healed.

As for Osaka, the propaganda from Imperial General Headquarters and Radio Tokyo claimed that within hours after the raid it was business as usual on the ground and that the public had been aroused to new fury against the Americans.

The truth lay in a super-secret report made by the Osaka branch of the thought control police. They told the Home Ministry in Tokyo that a survey made between March 18 and March 20 indicated an almost total war-weariness on the part of the public, a feeling of hopelessness and terror in the face of the B-29 bomber attacks and a disturbing new antimilitarist feeling among the mass of the people. The thought police had begun their investigation with the usual idea of rousting out a few troublemakers and putting them in jail, but they had soon changed their minds. They could not put half the population of Osaka into jail, could they? That was the sort of resentment and fear they were encountering.

Yet the results of the Osaka raid were not particularly effective in shortening the war by eroding the public support of the military. The Americans had made one move that did not sit well even with the most liberal Japanese enemies of the *Gunbatsu*, as the militarist government was called. In leaflets they had dropped on March 4, the Americans had claimed that they had no quarrel with the Japanese people, or with the citizens of Osaka. They had warned the people to keep out of military areas and promised in the leaflets that military areas alone would be attacked. But when the attack came that night of March 13, it was general, and the most heavily bombed areas were residential, not factory areas.

Thus, although the B-29s aroused fear and resignation in the hearts of the people, the awe was somewhat tempered by the knowledge that the Americans were showing no quarter. Women and children were as much at risk as soldiers of the line. General LeMay's bombs were aimed at Sanjiro Oshima just as much as at the Imperial Gun Factory. And Mama Oshima and Sanjiro and thousands of other Osakans died horrible deaths because General LeMay was their enemy.

Osaka

* * *

As for Kinoseko Imajiyo, the young factory worker who had stood in her garden with clenched fists and watched the American bombers invading the sacred sky of her Yamato—the spirit of Japan—she was not hurt this night of nights. But there would be more raids, and on one of them, Kinoseko would see nine people die the same horrible deaths by fire.

As the people of Osaka knew on the morning of March 14, 1945, their war with the Americans was just beginning.

14
KOBE

THE B-29S CAME BACK OVER OSAKA ON MARCH 14 FOR A LOOK at what they had done in the third of what would go down in history as the most destructive series of aerial attacks of all time.

The aerial photographers took their pictures, and back at the Marianas headquarters they were shown to General LeMay. The smoking ruins showed that 8.1 square miles in the center of Osaka, containing 119 large factories (and 200,000 houses) had been wiped out. General LeMay was immensely pleased, particularly because the orders to return to the Tokyo bombing pattern (closely placed incendiaries) had corrected the error committed at Nagoya on the second raid, where the incendiary bombs were too widely scattered to create "oceans of fire."

The Kobe raid was on. A check with the weathermen showed that good weather was predicted for the night of March 16. The every-other-night pattern could be maintained.

But why Kobe?

Kobe was the sixth largest city of Japan, and the largest port. Its shipyards made up the greatest concentration of shipbuilding and ship repair works in Japan. More marine engines were built there than at any other place. The main rail line from Shimonoseki to Tokyo ran through Kobe. The national coast highway bisected the center of the city.

All good reasons, certainly. But the deciding factors were in the XXI Bomber-Command report that Kobe was highly congested, with a population density of more than 100,000 people per square mile. Also, according to that report,

> Only about 10 percent of Kobe's buildings are of brick, sheet metal, stone, or concrete. Many of the modern buildings are surrounded by flimsy residences or themselves contain highly inflammable industrial materials. . . . With no large river or canals, Kobe is dependent for its water supply on three large reservoirs, a supply which has never been plentiful, and is considered inadequate for large-scale firefighting.

Kobe ought to go up like a Hindu funeral pyre.

That was the major reason for its choice as the fourth target in the incendiary campaign.

The intelligence and operations officers took a long, hard look at what had been learned on the first three raids, and passed along the details. Nagoya in particular, and to a lesser extent Osaka, had been marked by failure to take advantage of the concentration and merging of fires, to burn the greatest possible area. At Osaka the problem had been the attenuation of the raid itself, strung out over more than three hours. At Kobe the effort must be made to bring the maximum number of B-29s over the target at the same time.

Also, the aiming points would have to be closer together than they were at either Osaka or Nagoya, and the intervalometers must be set at fifty feet, which meant that every fifty feet a cluster of firebombs would be dropped. Further, in the cases of Nagoya and Osaka, planes had dropped their bombs in isolated areas, which meant there was no chance of achieving the intersecting fires that might create a fire storm.

Four aiming points were chosen. One was in the northwest corner of the city center. The second was south of the main railroad line. The third was northwest of the main railroad station, and the fourth was northeast of the railroad station. It was expected that the wind would be blowing from the west to sweep the fires across the city center.

Kobe presented some new problems. The area to be hit was long and narrow—ten miles by two miles. But the big advantage was that the city was strung out along the shore, which made it easier for the bombardiers. The way the mission was planned, the navigators would check at Nishina Shima to see that they were on course, make landfall at Hino Point, and cross the bay between Shikoku and Honshu. They would then fly up Osaka Bay and make a left turn along the shore to avoid the Osaka antiaircraft guns and fighter bases.

After the Tokyo raid, there had been a good deal of flak at headquarters from the individual aircrews. The gunners did not like the idea of being left behind when their planes flew, and the rest of the crewmembers felt unprotected without those guns and gunners. The argument was that every raid became more dangerous because the Japanese were soon going to become familiar with the technique and change their defenses to guard against it more effectively. LeMay had not anticipated flying his B-29s for a long period without protective armament, and even on the Nagoya raid some B-29s had carried their gunners along. On the Osaka raid, more planes had taken guns and ammunition. On the Kobe raid, guns were authorized. Intelligence indicated that Kobe's defenses were likely to prove tougher than Osaka's. General LeMay was eager to secure maximum bomb load, but there were 150 Japanese fighters located within fifty miles of Kobe and 250 within a 100-mile radius. The Japanese fighter pilots preferred to make tail attacks, as experience indicated, so the 173rd and 313th Wing planes would carry their tailgunners and two hundred rounds of .50-caliber ammunition. Guam's 314th Wing planes would not, because of the distance factor. From Guam, an extra hour of flying time was needed. That meant an extra gas tank in the bomb bay. That cut the bomb load from the 15,000 pounds of the other two wings to 10,000 pounds. To take gunners and guns and ammunition would cut the bomb load even further, and this LeMay was not willing to do.

Recently the air-sea rescue efforts of the navy and air force had been stepped up to give the aircrews a little more sense of security. Five submarines were stationed along the B-29 route for the Kobe mission, and one plane tender that managed three Dumbo aircraft, rescue planes capable of landing on the water. Picket boats and crash boats were laid on near Iwo Jima and the B-29 bases. Also for this mission three Super Dumbo planes were assigned to orbit the submarine positions. That meant, as the briefing officers pointed out, that a crew could ditch, be picked up by a submarine, then be taken off the submarine by a Dumbo, and be back at the base in time for dinner.

The effect of what had gone before was just what General LeMay would have wanted had he known precisely how the people of Kobe would react. For the fire raid on Osaka on March 12–13 had brought real fear to Kobe. After the Osaka fire raid, people had noticed a few airplanes circling over Kobe, and they had the feeling that they were going to be next on the American list. Every day the tension in Kobe grew.

Hiroko Teisaki and her family lived not far from the center of Kobe. Since the Osaka raid they had noticed that virtually everything had disappeared from the stores, even salt. People were buying up everything in sight and hoarding it. People were also so nervous about the bombing they fully expected to come at any moment that they had begun dismantling their houses. The Teisaki family tore up the tatami, the straw mats on the floors of their house, to make it more fireproof. There was nothing they could do, of course, about the wood construction and the shoji screens that served as interior walls. These could be pulled down at the time of the raid.

General LeMay had a special problem with Kobe. He was running out of incendiaries. There were only a few of the M-69 six-pound incendiary bombs left, and because of fuse problems there were no 100-pound M-47 bombs available for the pathfinder planes. So other firebombs—E-28, E-36, and E-46 clusters—were fused to open at 2,000 feet, and some E-46 clusters were fused to open at 2,500 feet. A number of four-pound magnesium bombs were to be carried on this raid, too. This would be a change for which the Japanese were not prepared. With the M-69 firebomb, an immediate attack with water could prove effective. But with the four-pound magnesium bombs, water only caused the bombs to burn faster.

There was another little trick up the American sleeve: 20 percent of the bombs contained warheads with varied delayed-explosion settings. Thus, firefighters would soon discover that when they tried to put out one fire, another would start right on top of it. And every third B-29 was to carry one 500-pound fragmentation cluster fused to open 3,000 feet below the B-29. The fragmentation bombs would harry the firefighters as well.

These would be unpleasant surprises for the people of Kobe, but they were prepared for the worst. Since that first Tokyo fire raid, even the newspapers had paid more attention to the truth than usual, a sure sign that the government was concerned.

On March 14, the day of the Osaka raid, the newspapers reported that on March 12 a lone B-29 had bombed Yokosuka, site of the big naval base, and the next day two B-29s had bombed in the Nagasaki area. The bombs, obviously, were tokens. The purpose of overflights, just as obviously, was aerial reconnaissance. Such flights, coming over various parts of Japan, kept the people on edge. Which city would be next on the American list?

Domei, the government-controlled Japanese news agency, issued a story that was run in virtually every newspaper in the land on March 13.

"If the Americans succeed in gaining control of Iwo Jima," the article said, "then even greater numbers of bombers can be expected over the mainland cities of Japan." (The Americans, of course, already controlled Iwo Jima. Mopping-up operations were in progress.)

> The enemy's intention to attain maximum results with minimum losses is revealed by his tenacious resort to raids by isolated machines and small formations. A good knowledge of his tactics, attained by studying his one-plane and small-formation raids since the beginning of November, is necessary in order to strengthen our air defense.

Raids by large formations of B-29s coming from the Marianas bases had occurred with growing frequency, Domei said, citing the following figures:

> November: 3 raids, 130 planes
> December: 4 raids, 290 planes
> January: 6 raids, 430 planes
> February: 5 raids, 480 planes

In the intervals, small formations had conducted many raids:

> November: 6 small raids
> December: 54 small raids
> January: 66 small raids
> February: 90 small raids

Most of the small raids, the Domei analyst noted, had been carried out at night. "This shows that the time people are usually in sound sleep is the exact time requiring strict precautions." And, said Domei's analyst, it was noteworthy that the Americans were not avoiding Fridays and the thirteenth day of the month, known by the Japanese to be regarded by Americans as unlucky.

So, the Domei analyst concluded, the small raids were as important as the large ones. The small raids at night brought the planes over Japan. They sent back reports of weather conditions. But the real reason for the small raids, he said, was training. He supposed that the crews were changed for each of these small raids, and that thus hundreds of aircrews were now trained to fly over Japan. Soon, he predicted gloomily, this training would make itself felt in the form of larger formations in night raiding.

> Another important factor that must never escape attention is that the enemy bases have been pushed much nearer to the Japanese mainland. Several raids during one night are no longer a rare phenomenon. This tendency has become marked since the attack by 130 planes on March 4, and mere nerve warfare has long ceased to be the enemy aim. The Americans have been gaining experience in recent months, and it is no mistake to conclude that all this portends large-scale night raids.

> The Twenty-first Bomber Command of the enemy is now commanded by Curtis LeMay, who personally directed terror raids on Hamburg and Berlin, which fact increases the probability of such raids on the mainland of Japan.

> The American air tactics are elastic, in the sense that they are modified on encountering strong resistance. Not only strong nerves but complete air defense is therefore absolutely necessary to meet the probable large-scale night raids of the enemy.

Thus spake Domei. If armchair analysis could affect the outcome of the war, Domei's expert would have been entitled to promotion. But the Japanese army, and the navy as well, were unable to do what Domei demanded, i.e., create powerful military air defenses. Four times as many guns as were then in use would give the Americans pause; four times as many night fighters would give the Americans even more pause. But there was a shortage of machine tools to build the antiaircraft guns, and a shortage of metal. There was a shortage of pilots to man the planes that were coming off the assembly lines, and the pilots were being trained these days for one-way missions. This did not make for skillful air defense.

On March 14, several newspapers, including the *Japan Times*, editorialized about the American firebombings.

> For their monstrous inhumanity, for their unpardonable crimes against civilization and decency the fiendish Americans will have to render account before the bar of history. For all time, the Americans will have to bear the stigma of world condemnation and suffer from the curses heaped upon them by outraged humanity as a result of the wanton terror they are sowing today.

In a way, the B-29 bombings were changing the Japanese government's approach to the war. Japan was experiencing minor revulsion against the government's war-reporting policies. *Yomiuri Shimbun*, one of the three largest Japanese daily newspapers, complained—and was allowed to publish—a criticism of the government reports on bombing damage.

"If such reports are made that, if only the dateline is changed, they can apply to any bombing at any time, we must say that the essence of reporting and of propaganda under wartime conditions is not being understood."

This was a very Japanese way of saying that the government

had better stop lying to the people. Most important about the *Yomiuri* article was that it was published at all. It went on to say that "stereotyped reports not only fail to give strength to the people but on the contrary rob them of their strength."

On March 15, the newspapers were allowed to publish reports of the assistance given to victims of the Tokyo fire raid of March 10–11. By this time, the news of that total disaster ("catastrophe" was the Japanese word) had seeped all over Japan despite attempts by the military to limit the discussion. The effects had been too staggering to keep secret.

The mass movement of citizens out of Tokyo had already begun. The problems were transportation and housing, because hundreds of thousands of people had no place to go.

Imperial General Headquarters was still playing down the extent of the Osaka raid. The official announcement said only that ninety (not nearly 300) planes had bombed Japan that night. And as usual, the IGHQ estimate of American casualties (eleven planes lost and sixty damaged) was an enormous overstatement. The focus of Imperial General Headquarters was on the "fearless" defenses of the civilian population. Osaka had been badly damaged, the army admitted, but people had risen up and put out the fires. "In Amagasaki city," said the IGHQ communiqué, "damage caused by the air raid was minimized by the dauntless activities of the citizens, and all the flames were put out promptly."

By March 15, the really fearsome nature of the new B-29 attack program was out in the open. After an emergency Cabinet meeting, the government spokesman announced that not just Tokyo, but all the major Japanese cities, would be evacuated of all but essential workers. Every city must manage for itself. In Kobe, the news was greeted with more than a little dismay. It would mean the breakup of families, almost the final deprivation of the war. But, *shikatta ganai*. There was nothing to be done. Everyone could see the logic of the move. The public was not used to complaining, and after nearly eight years of constant warfare, they were reduced to almost total apathy.

Late on the afternoon of March 16, the B-29s began taking off from Saipan, Tinian, and Guam. The men of the 73rd Wing had outdone themselves, loading an average of more than 16,000 pounds of bombs onto their B-29s. The 313th Wing was unfortunate in that the types of bombs available precluded maximum loading, and the 314th wing at Guam managed to take aboard only a little over 10,000 pounds of bombs per plane.

On they came through the night, through turbulence and showers, right on schedule.

Over Kobe that night, clouds had blown in from the sea, and the bombing would have to be made by radar, for the most part. More "blind bombing," the Japanese called it. More low-altitude bombing, the Americans called it, bombing between 3,000 and 6,000 feet, aiming to start fires and burn out the city of Kobe. Three hundred thirty-one B-29s were making this fourth firemission, quite a remarkable achievement for the ground crews that had had to repair and service those planes that had flown the three previous incendiary missions.

Kimiko Mikitani was walking along the street of Misaki Homachi district in Kobe that night, toward her house on the north side of Dai Wada Bridge, when the air-raid sirens began to screech. Immediately the street became a hive of panic, with people running this way and that, back and forth, searching desperately for a place to hide from the B-29 bombers. Kimiko Mikitani just kept on walking faster now, toward the bridge and her house just a few blocks on the other side. On her back she carried her one-year-old baby boy. In her belly was the embryo of a second child. Kimiko was twenty-five years old. Her husband had a responsible job with the Mitsubishi airplane factory, ten kilometers outside Kobe. They were a happy couple and were looking forward to raising their family, even though the war raged around Japan.

Kimiko walked on. The sirens wailed, and now she could hear the sounds of the B-29s as they came over Kobe. She had nearly reached the edge of the bridge. Down below and to the right, she could see hundreds of people huddling under the bridge supports and under the bridge itself, in the water. Someone had put out the word days earlier that the bridge was as good as an air-raid shelter in case of trouble, and hundreds of people had responded in this time of trouble.

The B-29s came in. They were flying low—Kimiko estimated the altitude at less than five hundred feet—as they zoomed across the river and Dai Wada Bridge. And then they began loosing their firebombs. Suddenly the air was full of falling objects. The bombs fell in the river, on the shore, on the bridge, and as they fell they exploded in blue-white light and burned fiercely. These were the four-pound magnesium bombs. Those that fell in the water burned all the faster for that, and created heavy smoke that crept around through the supports of the bridge, and hugged the ground and the water. The bridge's wooden supports and piers were now burning. Everything on that street was burning, and the smoke grew thicker and blacker. On the bridge the wind was blowing, a hot, hot wind, fanning the fires, and growing hotter by the moment. The fires made the wind whirl around until on the bridge approach the wind turned Kimiko so that she had to head into it to stay upright. Then the bombs fell all around her, and her clothing began to burn. Her air-raid turban caught fire, and her hair began to smoke and stink. Her *monpei* caught fire, her arms were burned, her legs were burned and her hands. Then she was whirled around again, and felt the loss of weight on her back as the wind whipped her baby boy out of his back pack and away, through the smoke. She never saw the child again. It was as if the god of war had swallowed him up, right on the Dai Wada Bridge in downtown Kobe.

Kimiko's shock was enormous; fortunately, nature took a hand and blinded her memory. She began to run, then stopped and rolled in the roadway on the bridge to put out the flames, and began to run again, and her clothing flamed again. Somehow she ran, and ran, and ran, and forgot where she was or what was happening. When she recovered her senses, she was wandering around near the site of her house. The block, of course, had been burned out by the fierce fires. Back on the bridge, the wooden structure was burning. Below the bridge, 500 people had either died or were dying from the fires and from smoke inhalation and asphyxiation as the magnesium bombs did their deadly work. Those fires still burned at five o'clock the next evening.

Kimiko came to her senses and realized that her face, hands, and legs were all stinging from the burns. She stopped and pushed up the sleeves of her air-raid jacket. Her arms were burned.

She began seeking medical attention. She went to a hospital, but was turned away. Not badly enough burned, said the medical staff. Others were much worse off. She wandered on and finally, early in the morning, found an aid station where they treated her burns with salves and gave her bandages for the worst of the burns. The hurt now in her body was matched by the burning of her soul, as she considered her firstborn son: dead, gone, whisked off her back by the fire storm and swept away, no one knew where. No one would ever know. Kimiko's depression became as intense as her pain.

Her husband was quite safe. He had been at work in the airplane factory outside town when the bombers came to destroy Kobe, and the factory was not hit. When he learned that the bombers had burned his section of the city, he began searching for his wife. That next day they found each other at the shelter for relief of victims in the center of the city.

Kimiko was badly enough injured that she should be hospitalized, the doctors told her, but they had no facilities. So she began searching around the city for a hospital that would take her, and finally she found one. She went into the hospital and stayed there for several weeks, until her burns healed. She became extremely depressed over the death of their child and wondered if life was really worth living. But then her new baby began to kick in her belly and those signs of new life reminded her that there was more to the world than war, death, and destruction. There was, after all, something to live for.

Shizue Nakamura lived on the beach in Nagata-ku, in a household with four people. She was thirty-three years old at the time, and seemed to spend most of her time standing in line somewhere or looking about for something that she needed to buy. The difficulties of wartime shopping had become the most important factor in her life as a householder.

On that March 17 she had spent long hours looking for goods and food, and was very tired. So she was in bed asleep when the bombers came over. The house was in total darkness, but the light from the fires that had started farther off in Kobe began to shine through the glass door. She could tell from the flashing and the flames that some area of Kobe was being devastated by bombs, but she was so tired that she decided she would go back to the futon and try to get some more sleep. Then the air-raid siren began to blow in her area, and she knew that she must get up and dress and go to the Nagaraku elementary school, which was the place of refuge designated for the people of her area. She got up then, dressed hurriedly in the standard air-raid costume, and started for the school. All around her, people were running to this place of refuge as if they could hide there from the planes up in the clouds. Offshore, off Cape Wada, she saw a ship sink that night. For days afterward, the bloated corpses washed up on the shore of her beach.

The fires burned all night long. They burned schools, hospitals, and temples. The 700-year-old Yakusenji Temple, located not far from the Dai Wada Bridge, was burned to the ground. The dead numbered 2,598 and the wounded 8,558, but this was the least of it. More than 650,000 people were made homeless, and the homes of a million were damaged. By Japanese count, the raid left 236,000 "sufferers."

Kobe

Thirty years later, the Buddhist priest Satoshi Goto would undertake a compilation of the names of the dead, the 8,000 citizens of Kobe who perished in the fire bombings of that city, and a committee would be formed to trace the history of the bombings, just as it would be in all the cities of Japan. This would become a part of the peace movement associated so closely with the Hiroshima and Nagasaki bombings.

15
KOBE
AFTERMATH

THE JAPANESE COUNTED ONLY SOME NINETY B-29S OVER KOBE that night of March 16 and early morning of March 17. Actually, 306 B-29s reached the primary target area, but since 250 of them bombed by radar, it was natural enough that the defenders on the ground and in the air did not see all the aircraft.

On this sort of mission, with aircraft operating virtually independently, there was no way of knowing exactly what had happened to the planes that did not return. What General LeMay did learn was that three of the B-29s did not return. The 313th Wing lost two planes, and the 73rd Wing lost one. One plane was seen to be under intense antiaircraft fire over the target, and observers on another B-29 saw it go into a flat spin. But what had happened to the other two missing planes was anyone's guess. They did not appear in the sea areas patrolled by the submarines or the Dumbo aircraft. The presumption had to be that they were lost over the target or somewhere over Japan. Nine other planes were damaged by antiaircraft fire, but all made it to their bases.

On the way back to the Marianas, fifteen planes landed at Iwo

Jima, proving that the Domei military analyst had been correct in his assumption that once the island was in American hands, it would become an instrument of the B-29 raiders. (Even now, the Japanese people had not been told that virtually all of Iwo Jima was in American hands.)

When the B-29 aircrews were debriefed on Saipan, Tinian, and Guam, it was determined that the Japanese had put up some 250 fighter planes, but that only ninety-six of them had attacked, and that only eight had pressed home more than one attack. The Japanese still had not learned how to deal with the new American tactic of low-level saturation bombing by incendiaries.

On the morning of March 17, two B-29s were sent over Kobe to take photographs, and they returned with indications that three square miles of Kobe's fourteen-square-mile area had been destroyed by the firebombing. The photographs showed several large fires and many small fires still burning, twelve hours after the attack. Militarily, not even the most optimistic estimate could show very successful results: the Mitsubishi Heavy Industry Plant was 8 percent destroyed, the Kawasaki Heavy Industry Plant was 13 percent destroyed, and the Arata Shipyard was 21 percent destroyed. Only the Kobe Harbor District Number Two warehouses were completely destroyed. The central railroad station was not destroyed.

But as far as houses were concerned, the mission was a roaring success. In the three square miles, virtually every house was wrecked. That meant about 20 percent of the residential area of Kobe was burned out, in twenty-three residential districts. The effect on the people's morale was all that the Americans could have hoped. The terror campaign was working very well.

On the morning of March 17, Prime Minister Koiso was ordered by the Emperor to take a more active role in the prosecution of the war. Hirohito expected the Prime Minister to find out precisely what the Imperial General Staff was doing these days, and to report back. The order was an indication of the Emperor's growing concern over the conduct of the war, and the inability of the military to protect the people of Japan from the deadly bombing.

Following the Emperor's visit to the Sumida River district after the great firebombing raid of March 10, he knew the war was lost. There was no way, given the structure of the Japanese government, that he could immediately change the course of events, but already the men who opposed continuing the war were beginning to assemble around him.

In Tokyo, the new defense ordinance of the Home Ministry went into effect. In future, any Japanese citizen who failed to turn in an enemy leaflet was subject to prosecution and a prison term.

In Tokyo also, in another emergency meeting, the Cabinet decided to evacuate the first- and second-grade children of all major Japanese cities. Originally, these youngsters had been exempted from the general evacuation of schoolchildren because the authorities felt they should remain at home with their parents. But now the danger was seen as too great to continue that policy. The youngsters would go to stay with relatives. And what of the families that had lived in Tokyo for so long that they had no relatives outside the city? The question was not addressed. In-laws, peripheral family, any connection would have to be used.

What the new ruling meant was that all of Tokyo's schools would be closed down as schools. They would now become shelters and first-aid centers.

The government assured the people that the closing of the schools did not mean the suspension of Japanese education. But, in fact, that was what was happening and had already happened in large measure. Already, the pupils of the upper grades had been sent away with their teachers, and in their new surroundings had been mobilized as student volunteers for the war effort. Hollowly as the denials rang, they were not even very important. Everyone in Japan recognized now that the war had entered a new and desperate final phase. No one expected education as usual.

The newspapers, usually so empty of the real news of the day in Japan, were now filled with articles relating to the firebombings. Immediate relief of the Tokyo fire victims had been given, said the press. Those hundreds of thousands who sought assistance in the refugee centers had all been given five-day supplies of the usual rice, miso, millet *mochi*, and pickled radishes. For the children, there was milk. Trucks had brought in rice balls and hardtack. Blankets had been brought in, and for those lucky enough still to have a roof over their heads, fuel was rationed in weekly allotments. The army was supplying towels, candles, shoes, toilet paper, and matches. Fish, vegetables, onions, potatoes, and horseradish were rationed on a daily basis.

The schools and temples had already been turned into emergency aid centers for those with no place to go. The various ward governments were taking responsibility for their own people. Victims from Nihonbashi, almost totally destroyed, had been moved into Akasaka, which was only partially wrecked. Victims from Kanda were moved to Koishikawa district.

Throughout Tokyo, the ward government had rallied. The central government had established the rules. Two sorts of certificates were to be issued to the raid victims. One certificate would entitle them to new ration books for soy sauce, rice, bedclothes—all the necessities that had vanished from their lives on the night of the terrible fire storm. The other was a new identification card, necessary so that those people with savings (and this meant most Japanese) could withdraw them from the banks. At the ward level, teams of twenty and thirty people were organized and sent to various districts to set up offices. The lines were long and continual.

That day, March 17, the Japanese government also established a special Cabinet Ministers' Council for relief of the air-raid victims. Chief of this commission was the Home Minister. Other members were the ministers of agriculture, welfare, commerce, transportation, and communication. The purpose of the commission was to bypass the usual red tape of government and to relieve the military of the responsibility for relief. Separately, a new air defense committee was established to deal with future air-raid problems. This committee was headed by the deputy chief of the army air defense headquarters, and included the Tokyo police and fire chiefs. These gentlemen would address themselves to the issue of what could be done to make the American air raids less deadly.

Still more changes came in the wake of the new emergency. On March 17 the government announced a new press policy. In future, to save paper and effort, metropolitan papers circulated in various districts would be amalgamated with the local papers of the districts. In other words, except for *Mainichi Shimbun*, *Asahi Shimbun*, and *Yomiuri Shimbun*, to name the major Tokyo newspapers, the metropolitan newspapers would no longer be national papers, but would stick to Tokyo affairs. The purpose of publication of the newspapers would be more narrowly drawn to informing the public of daily changes and government rulings, and less about general news and considerations of such cultural matters as Japan's history, linguistics, and the Greater East Asia Co-Prosperity Sphere, and the course of the war in Europe—all of which had come to dominate the press in the absence of any real information about Japan's own war as it was going in the Pacific and China.

Thus there would cease to be metropolitan papers. The equipment would be transferred to the local papers, and so would the personnel. In Tokyo, five of the new local papers would print in one plant. In Osaka, three papers would print on the same presses, and in Fukuoka, two. The Kobe raid had so interrupted communications and operations throughout Japan that it was March 18 before the general public learned of this fourth great fire raid on a major Japanese city. Imperial General Headquarters, as usual, told the story the way the army wanted it told.

"About sixty B-29 bombers indiscriminately bombed Kobe", began the communiqué. The Japanese had shot down twenty of the invaders, said IGHQ. Virtually all the rest were damaged to some degree. As for the fires, they were brought under control, for the most part, by ten o'clock on the morning of March 17, and did relatively little damage.

So Imperial General Headquarters and the Japanese central government were not precisely on the same wavelength these days. The army was determinedly ignoring the dreadful results of the American fire raids, but the government was admitting that the damage was extremely serious.

On March 18, the newspapers published Information Spokesman Sadao Iguchi's remarks to the effect that the terrible firebombings were drawing the Japanese people closer together.

> They only serve to fire the anger and contempt of our people against the enemy and intensify our will to fight on until they are utterly crushed. . . . The areas attacked were largely peopled by merchants, small shopkeepers, and artisans whose homes adjoined or were in their places of business. The incendiaries were so concentrated that the residents of three areas for the most part had no means of escape. These areas included many religious and cultural institutions, hospitals, schools, and cemeteries.

This much was certainly true. What was not was Iguchi's claim that "not even remotely were those bombed areas connected with war industries or located near military installations." Virtually all the survivors accepted the concept that they were connected with the war effort. Certainly, now that the firebombings had started, they realized there was no line any more between civilian and military; the government had been calling for total mobilization for many weeks. This was one aspect of that mobilization.

The real reason for the American "wild attacks," said the information spokesman, was the American concern about shortening the war, to cut down its terrible losses in men and equipment.

A long, grinding fight lies ahead. Try as the enemy might to cook up many tricks in efforts to shorten the war, they will find them all futile. Their propaganda leaflets are being trampled underfoot as so much trash. The destruction of our cities and our homes will not make the going any easier for them. The citadel of our national spirit, which is to be found in the hearts of each and all of our people, holds firm, generating an intense will to fight for no less a goal than total victory, with total and full composure, unwavering confidence, and inflexible determination.

Stripped of the propaganda-loaded verbiage, the Iguchi statement was another warning: Look out, more is coming.

In the Philippines, Admiral Takejiro Ohnishi, the inventor of the kamikaze concept, made an unusually frank statement about the war situation, although it was couched, as such statements always had to be, in terms of the highest hope.

He noted that Japan's early victories had come so quickly that she still controlled large portions of territory—meaning that the war was going very badly indeed. Since no one was giving up, the Japanese would undoubtedly win, he said, which meant that the Philippines battle could be expected to end very shortly in another Japanese defeat.

For people to worry about the fuel shortage, he said, was nonsense, since nothing could be worse than those days just before the war, when the Americans had cut off the petroleum supplies and not a drop of oil reached Japan for weeks. This meant that Japan could now expect to be cut off from oil again, as the war worsened.

And what about the battle against the American navy? The admiral admitted that it would probably not be possible to sink all the enemy's ships. His motive was to kill so many Americans that they would ultimately become tired of the war. That was the road to victory now, he said. "There is no way to victory other than through spiritual and ideological means."

And then he got to his real point:

> The real fighting in this war lies before us. The Japanese people have not suffered enough yet. . . . They must suffer more and become complete, full Japanese. The work of the Shinpo Special Attack Units in stirring the Japanese people was vast. Today the whole nation has become a special attack unit. The Japanese people must be turned into war power, and if the enemy should land, they should take up arms and defeat him even if they suffer losses of three and five million. This is not impossible.

Some, said the admiral, were losing heart because of the "repeated rearward movements of our forces." (Another prediction for the wary that this rearward movement would continue.) But the war would be won through the same spirit that impelled the kamikaze pilots. So many had fallen already that all Japan must hold out, so that they would not have fallen in vain. "How can they rest in peace unless we win?"

That was all the comfort Admiral Ohnishi, one of the architects of the Pearl Harbor attack against America, could now offer the Japanese people on the day after the fourth major fire raid.

The war must go on and on and on, said the admiral. But what he did not know at his headquarters in the Philippines, was that in the past ten days the people of Japan had begun to suffer intensely from this war, with hundreds of thousands dead and more than 2 million homeless from the firebombs.

16
NAGOYA
REVISITED

THE FIREBOMBING OF JAPAN WAS AN ENORMOUS SUCCESS FROM the American point of view. In Washington, the commander of the Army Air Forces, General H. H. Arnold, looked forward to the summer day when General LeMay would have a thousand B-29s for operations and could then "have the ability to destroy whole industrial cities. . . ."

But General LeMay was not satisfied. The Nagoya raid had been a failure. The fault was his own, as he admitted.

> It seemed to me that perhaps we had been concentrating our detonations at Tokyo more tightly than we actually needed to, and by scattering bombs more widely we could achieve the same results, but over a larger area. Thus the bombs had been spaced to fall a hundred feet apart, and the result was that only two square miles of the city had been destroyed.

That was not enough for General LeMay. Thus he decided to schedule a new attack on Nagoya. The orders were issued on March 18, for the raid the next day. It would once again be primarily an incendiary raid, although every third B-29 would carry two 500-pound general-purpose bombs. In this case again the purpose was to disrupt attempts by firefighters to put out the incendiary fires. General LeMay hoped that the high-explosive bombs would knock down power lines, block streets, and break water mains, thus increasing the confusion of the defenders.

The ordnance men were scraping the bottom of the firebomb barrel. A month earlier, no one had expected such a demand for incendiaries, so the pipeline had run dry. More bombs had to come from America before the firebombers could pick and choose the sort of bombs they wanted to employ. For this Nagoya raid they would have to use everything they had left, which meant nine different types of incendiaries, some much more effective than others.

Each previous raid had brought its lessons. The Kobe raid had taught the bombers that they would have to take more care to saturate the city's fire-prevention and antiaircraft positions. To do the job, they must bring the B-29s in faster and in more concentrated groups.

Each of the three wings then was assigned a time bracket. The pathfinder planes were to be over the target from 12:35 until 12:40 A.M. They would drop their big bombs, which would create large fires, lighting up the target area for the planes to follow. The main forces would come in between 12:40 and 12:51. Since 325 B-29s were scheduled to make the raid, this would mean a B-29 over the target every 13.75 seconds.

Japanese defenses were expected to be improved, since the Japanese had now experienced four major fire raids. There were about 200 heavy antiaircraft guns in the Nagoya area, plus the guns of the ships in the harbor. There were also about 170 automatic antiaircraft guns, effective at altitudes around 5,000 feet, but not above that.

What the Americans really worried about were the fifty search-lights in the Nagoya area. The Japanese were very good at using searchlights to bring the B-29s into close observation. LeMay's men hoped for cloud undercast and a lot of smoke from the fires, which would decrease the effectiveness of the searchlights.

The Kobe raid had indicated the need for some action to knock out those searchlights, and so the 73rd Wing would carry its lower forward and aft gunners as well as its tail gunners. The lower gunners would fire on ground targets to knock out the searchlights. This was a reluctant concession made by General LeMay; the 313th and 314th Wings would load only their tail turrets and they were not to fire unless fired upon. But the Japanese were now using the tail attack more and more, and for morale purposes the Americans needed some aerial protection. In this particular raid the weight factor was not quite so important, because the XXI Bomber Command had scarcely enough incendiaries left to load all the planes.

On the morning of March 19 the briefings began again on Guam, Tinian, and Saipan. All the usual points were covered: routes, bomb loads, checkpoints, times over target, weather, anticipated fuel consumption, and the hundreds of other details that go into the making of a successful bombing mission. The navy would be on hand again with four lifeguard submarines and a destroyer. Five Dumbo aircraft would be stationed along the flight path, to rescue survivors. Crash boats would be on the flight path just off the runways on Tinian, Saipan, and Guam, in case of takeoff emergency. As usual, everything possible was being done to maintain the morale of the aircrews. Soon the B-29s would begin to have fighter escort from Iwo Jima, but not quite yet.

For this mission the B-29s would have to rely on speed, surprise, and their few operating guns against the 150 enemy fighters expected to be encountered in the Nagoya area.

In Nagoya, they called this night of March 19 *yakan shodo sakusen*—"the night of scorched-earth operations." When, at around midnight, the air-raid sirens began to sound, and the officials with megaphones began moving along the streets, calling on the people to get out of the industrial area, the people responded very well. The streets were soon filled with scurrying bodies, everyone seeming to know where he was headed, moving rapidly out of the downtown district of Nagoya.

In came the planes, nearly 300 of them (although as usual the Japanese underestimated the number). The pilots had been instructed to bomb from about 5,000 feet to 7,500 feet. The Japanese maintained that they were lower, between 3,000 and 6,000 feet. They counted 1,860 tons of firebombs that night, and when the bombing was finished, the Japanese press had a phrase for it: "The heart of Nagoya has been devoured," said the newspapers two days later, when the accounts of the raid were published.

In that March 19 raid, only 826 people were killed—a tribute to the improved methods of moving people out of the target areas. Still, 2,728 people were injured, and another 40,000 houses were burned out.

The photographers of *Chunichi Shimbun*, the largest newspaper in central Japan, were on hand to watch and photograph the destruction of their city. They saw the fires blaze up, and above all, they saw the burning of three more square miles of their city. This brought the area of destruction up to about five square miles.

Several important aircraft industry targets lay within the city or north of Kagamigahara, but none of these was disturbed. That was not the purpose of this series of raids; the attempt to destroy Japan's military aircraft production had been put on a back burner.

Most of the destruction was to houses, schools, and hospitals. Several railroad sheds were burned out, and the Toyo Cotton Mill was about 20 percent burned, as shown in the photographs taken later. Downtown business areas, particularly those occupied by shopkeepers who kept their businesses in their houses, were also wiped out. A small building near Nagoya Castle was burned, and so was a barracks for soldiers in the castle area. The Yamada

Engine Works was hit. But again, the target was really the people of Nagoya, and the target was badly hurt. Burned-out streetcars and trucks, and the debris of castoff belongings and wrecked bicycles, carts, and wagons littered the streets that next morning, as the planes flew homeward.

The wind certainly helped this night. It blew from the north at thirty-five miles an hour, and fanned the blazes in the central section of Nagoya.

Antiaircraft fire over the city was fairly heavy, and the searchlights were as much of a problem as the Americans had feared they might be. A number of bombardiers reported that they were so blinded by the searchlights on the bomb runs that they did not know where their bombs went in. The flak was heavy and about twenty planes were damaged, more or less badly. One plane of the 313th Wing was hit so hard that its No. 2 and No. 3 engines were knocked out. The pilot tried to nurse the plane home, but finally north of Iwo Jima he had to ditch. The ten crewmen were all rescued.

The Japanese put up more fighters than the Americans had expected; 192 planes were sighted. But again the problems of Japanese fighter training in 1945 were indicated by the fighter planes' behavior. Only thirty-seven of the fighters attacked the B-29s, and only a few of them made more than one pass. It was not a question of will but of skill. Only one B-29 was damaged by an air attack, and one attempt at ramming failed.

The B-29s lumbered away, and some of the Japanese fighter planes followed them out over the bay for five or ten minutes, before turning back to land. The most spectacular Japanese action was an attempt by four fighters to shoot down one B-29 that was traveling alone. Thirty miles west of Tori Shima, the four planes made twelve coordinated attacks on the B-29, employing a new technique in which one used landing lights to illuminate the plane so the others could find it. But if the fighter planes were not successful in shooting down the bombers, the bomber crews were grateful enough. A few shots were fired at Japanese planes, but no Japanese aircraft were destroyed this night. On the way back to the Marianas, half a dozen B-29s landed at Iwo Jima, largely because of fuel shortages.

The results of this raid were declared by General LeMay to be eminently satisfactory. The total area of Japanese industrial cities destroyed in the five firebombing missions was more than thirty-three square miles.

The conventional history of the B-29 operations indicates that General LeMay had used up his supply of firebombs. The navy had scoffed at him when he said he could operate the B-29s in the Marianas for 170 hours a month, although in the European Theater, they were operating the B-17s only about 30 hours a month. Therefore, goes the story, the B-29s ran out of firebombs on March 19. Furthermore, Admiral Nimitz was demanding that the B-29s be used to drop mines in Japanese waters to help the navy destroy Japanese shipping. This program was undertaken only reluctantly by General LeMay, who now believed he could firebomb Japan out of the war if he were given adequate planes, bombs, and no interference from the navy.

But was this the end of the firebombings?

Sensako Sugiyama of Nagoya would challenge the conventional historians. And so would Japanese records. For on March 24, at 11:56 P.M., the B-29s came again.

March 24. The B-29s headed out again from the Marianas for Nagoya. At 10:44 P.M., Radio Tokyo opened up with its early-warning system.

"It is suspected that large formations of large type enemy planes have headed toward the Bonin Islands group. If these planes are headed for Nagoya, it is believed they will reach Nagoya between 11:30 P.M. and midnight.

"Although these instructions are frequently given," the announcer added, "have every possible container filled with water, keep the things both inside and outside your house in order, and have everything prepared so that you will be able to fight without anxiety.

"As soon as the movements of the enemy planes become clear, they will be announced promptly. Hence, rest yourselves and be calm just before dashing out to fight. . . ."

Two minutes later the radio confirmed the heading of the planes toward Nagoya and the time of their arrival over the city. At 11:08 P.M., the radio announced an air-raid warning for the Tokkaido area, extending from Tokyo to forty miles west of Nagoya, not including Osaka and Kobe.

At 11:37 P.M., Radio Tokyo identified four planes as heading toward Nagoya, but erroneously predicted their arrival before midnight.

At 11:47 P.M., the announcer asked if the public was ready for the coming battle. "Let us fight tonight again. Are you sure there are no obstacles in your path?"

He also cautioned his listeners to be careful with wooden houses, and asked the civil defense teams, "Are you sure all your men are at their stations?"

More and more planes were identified as heading for Nagoya, and the announcer continued on the air for several minutes. Then he broke off. But he was back on the air again at 12:15 to warn his listeners that the Americans were changing their tactics. This time, he said, they would be entering the Nagoya area from many directions. But Japanese planes, too, he said, were now heading for Nagoya to intercept the enemy.

At 12:55 the announcer warned that the planes would be arriving at any minute. One minute later he was back on the air.

"Number one has penetrated Nagoya. Number two will soon penetrate Nagoya. Number three is heading north over the waters north of Tsu.

1:11 A.M.: "The enemy planes are dropping incendiaries and explosives. Be sure to wait in the case of the explosives for them to go off, but dash in to put out incendiary fires."

1:21 A.M. : "Our intercepting units are fighting gallantly. One enemy plane has been shot down. Some people must have seen the plane go down, with black smoke streaming behind it. Please do your best."

1:26 A.M. : "The fight against incendiary bombs is decided in the first five minutes. Please extinguish fires before they spread."

1:30 A.M. : "Taking out your household goods is important. In order to minimize the number of fires, let us all work to put out fires promptly. Let us concentrate on the surrounding of central fires."

1:33 A.M. : "You must not hesitate to destroy houses in the vicinity of fires."

2:06 A.M. : "Our air defense units have shot down another plane. All officials and civilians: let us fight hard. It appears there are still several enemy objects over the waters."

Finally it ended.

2:31 A.M. : "The air-raid warning is hereby lifted for the Tok-kaido area."

3:03 A.M. : "By the vigorous activities of our air defense units, a considerable degree of war results has been achieved. When the sun rises, enemy planes shot down should be seen on the ground by all citizens. I pray for your best efforts."

That night, the Japanese counted 130 B-29s, which hit the eastern section of the city around the Mitsubishi engine factory with 1,545 tons of firebombs, killing 1,716 people this time and injuring 770. The bombers burned another 7,600 houses.

This time they used flares, the Japanese said, to illuminate the targets they were attacking. (The Americans charged that the Japanese used the flares to light up the aircraft.) The most tragic element of the night's bombing was the burning of an elementary school, which, under the new regulations laid down in Tokyo, was now used as a shelter for the public. The school burned fast, and broiled several hundred Japanese women and children trapped inside with no hope of escape.

* * *

This was the night that Sensako Sugiyama was caught in the open by the firebombs. After two raids that month, Nagoya was not expecting still another, and the defenses were down. Many people chose this quiet evening to go for a walk in the open areas around the industrial district. Sensako was one of them. She was badly injured. Her hands, arms, and face were badly burned. She was in enormous pain and rolled over and over on the ground to extinguish the flames. Nevertheless, Sensako continued to believe that somehow Japan would win the war.

After this raid of March 25, relatively few houses in the center of Nagoya remained standing. But, of course, the Mitsubishi plant continued to function, at about 80 percent of capacity.

Nagoya was becoming inured to the attacks. Morale was dropping all the time. Production at Mitsubishi fell, not because of damage to the plant, but because more and more workers were absenting themselves from the job in order to be with their families when the air-raid sirens sounded. And then, when the raids were over, came the tedious tasks of trying once more to pick up the threads of life, to find food, fuel, and medicines.

By the end of March, Sensako had just about decided that Japan had indeed lost the war. She told this to friends, but, of course, not within the hearing of the dreaded thought police, who had become more active than ever, now that the Home Ministry knew trouble was increasing.

The B-29s were back over Nagoya again on March 30, with their deadly rain of fire and explosives. This time they came earlier, at 10:00 P.M., not so many this time, just twenty-seven planes, from the east, and they bombed Showa district. It was not a big raid this time, only twenty-nine people were killed. Now it was not so much the size but the frequency of the raids. On April 6, five people were killed. But on April 7 the B-29s were back over Nagoya in force. This time it was a morning raid. The Japanese counted 160 planes. They dropped high explosives and 153 tons of firebombs. The central Nagoya railroad station was completely burned out and thirty-three people were killed inside. Altogether that day, 302 more people died, and 5,191 more houses were burned out.

Nagoya was now almost completely numbed to the bombing. People could scarcely remember when they were not being bombed day after day.

の時に困が来て、

軍を締めて掛る

No toki ni komari ga kite,
fundoshi o shimete kakaru.
(When trouble comes, pull up your socks.)
—Old Japanese saying

17
TROUBLE
COMES

ALL THAT GENERAL LEMAY WANTED WAS A HANDFUL OF CIGARS, the thousand B-29s that General Arnold had promised him by summer, and a license to burn up all the cities in Japan. He was convinced that he had found the perfect "strategic bombing" weapon, and that firebombing would force Japan to surrender.

Certainly the Americans were not wrong in their assessment that the fire bombing was creating serious morale problems in Japan. But they did not understand one aspect of the Japanese character: the apathy with which the Japanese people accepted the war. The firebombings convinced many Japanese that the war was lost, but that did not mean they were willing to stop fighting and surrender "unconditionally" to the enemy that was trying to kill the civilian population, and that could be expected, according to the Japanese government, to enslave or murder the whole nation.

If, to a westerner, this concept seems ridiculous, then he should read the accounts of the end of the battle for Saipan, when thousands of Japanese civilians, women and children for the most part, killed themselves rather than fall into the hands of the Americans.

Saipan was a part of Japan's Inner Empire, that is, it was settled by Japanese, who drove out most of the native Chamorro population after the island was taken over by Japan from the Germans at the Treaty of Versailles in 1919. The attitude of the Japanese on Saipan was precisely the attitude of the Japanese in Japan. The mass suicides at Marpi Point, Saipan, were a harbinger of things to come.

Thus, while General LeMay's aim was to shorten the war by prompting a rapid Japanese surrender, the effect he was achieving was quite the opposite. By April 1945, most Japanese believed they were going to die anyhow, and the government's call for them to prepare to fight on the beaches struck a positive note. The recruitment of kamikaze pilots never slackened. The eagerness of the "wild eagles" to throw themselves into their suicide missions in the Philippines and elsewhere did not diminish; rather, it grew with every new blow struck against the homeland.

The B-29 was on the mind of virtually every Japanese in the homeland. Late in March, Imperial General Headquarters suggested that the Americans had lost 278 B-29s in the recent raids, and that this was more than the monthly production of the Superfortresses. The figures were made of whole cloth, of course. On that second Nagoya raid, for example, the B-29 force had lost one plane. But the attention given the Superfortresses by IGHQ is an indication of the public concern.

At the same time, many American publicists were assessing the future of Japan, now that the war with the Germans was coming to a close. Otto Tolischus of *The New York Times*, whom the Japanese knew well as a former Tokyo correspondent for the newspaper, made a radio address in New York on the public-service program "America's Town Meeting of the Air," in which he called for "unconditional surrender" as the minimal condition for Japanese withdrawal from the war.

To the Japanese people, "unconditional surrender" posed one question that was not addressed by the Americans: What would happen to the Emperor, the symbol of the Japanese nation?

Japan's publicists, of course, pulled out all the stops and threatened the people that Hirohito would be tried as a war criminal (a likely enough prospect, and one that had been discussed endlessly in the American media throughout the war years).

Every nuance, every innuendo about the American attitudes reached Japan from Lisbon or Sweden or Geneva. Concern for the future grew rapidly.

In the cities and towns, women and children were training to fight the enemy landings. Hundreds of home factories were manufacturing simple grenades that the children would attach to their bodies and then throw themselves under army vehicles. The women were training with sharpened staves that approximated bayonets, and they were promised that they would have rifles when the time came. Some were training as sharpshooters, and they actually had the use of weapons. Fortunately for the Japanese people, General LeMay did not get his way, not because of any innate revulsion of the American military against the fire-bombing of Japan, but because the Joint Chiefs of Staff saw other uses for the B-29s that should help to win the war for the Allies.

First, for months Admiral Nimitz had been asking that the B-29s be used to lay mines in the sea around Japan. The Air Corps had resisted this overture on the claim that the laying of mines was a navy job that could be accomplished by submarines.

True, said Admiral Nimitz, but he did not have enough submarines to lay enough mines rapidly enough to ensure the sort of effect that was needed, i.e., cutoff of Japan from her overseas colonies. The only aircraft capable of doing the job were the B-29s.

In March 1945, the Joint Chiefs of Staff were convinced, which means that General George C. Marshall of the United States Army was convinced, and then he sided with Admiral Ernest J. King, the chief of the United States Navy, against General H. H. Arnold, the chief of the U.S. Army Air Forces. So, in the last week of March, the B-29s set forth to sow the entrance to the Inland Sea and all other major Japanese waterways with magnetic and acoustic mines. Altogether they laid 12,000 mines, which sank about 200 ships in the next three months and virtually paralyzed Japanese shipping.

That minelaying job having been done by the 73rd Bomb Wing, LeMay again wanted to go back to firebombing. But the Joint Chiefs of Staff had a new use for the Superfortresses. The invasion of Okinawa was imminent, and Admiral Nimitz wanted bombing support, which meant the plastering of every Japanese airfield within the empire with bombs to inhibit Japanese use of fighter planes and bombers against Okinawa.

In the beginning, General LeMay was cooperative. But after he had bombed all the Kyushu, Taiwan, and Honshu airfields a time or two, he thought that was enough. Virtually no planes could take off from these potholed fields, he said. The fact was, and the U.S. Navy seemed to recognize it very well, that throughout the Okinawa campaign, and up to the last day of the war, hundreds of kamikazes were taking off from these "destroyed" airfields. The Japanese were masters at the art of camouflage and dissimulation. They moved the fighters as far as a mile from the airfield, and then brought them back in the hours of darkness to take off at dawn. So Admiral Nimitz insisted that the B-29s be kept available for tactical support of the Okinawa campaign.

Even so, General LeMay managed more firebombing raids, of which some, like the Nagoya raids of late March and early April, were small.

The Japanese quite accurately characterized these as "nuisance raids." They did not understand why the B-29s were not hitting their cities; they were not privy to the American logistical arguments between navy and army, and thus did not know that the XXI Bomber Command was suddenly embarrassed by a shortage of firebombs.

But in a few day, LeMay decided, the B-29s would return to Tokyo to try to burn up the remainder of the Japanese national capital.

This time the target was to be the northwest section of the city, which housed the largest arsenal complex in the Japanese Empire and many other military targets, the Diet and other government buildings, and the Imperial Palace, easily distinguishable behind its enormous moat, which had been declared off limits to the bombers by President Franklin D. Roosevelt.

The raid was planned for the night of April 13 and the early hours of April 14. Once again, it was to be a firebombing raid. Once again, more than 300 B-29s would take part in the attack.

Following the disastrous fire raid of March 9–10, the Tokyo civil defense officials undertook a far more stringent program to reduce the damage of firebombing, and to prevent another fire storm of the sort that had wiped out those hundreds of thousands of lives.

Agents moved through the streets of Tokyo, marking houses with the word *Execute*, or fastening chains on the doors. The residents were told they had about a week to evacuate. Then the house would be torn down.

Whole city blocks and streets were thus selected to become new firebreaks. On the appointed day, a work gang of ten to twenty men, women, and children showed up, fastened a heavy cable to the house, and began to heave. Usually the effort was enough to bring down the wooden house, but if not, then a bull-dozer or an army tank was brought in to finish the job.

Two million yen had been allocated for this work. When it was complete, twenty new firebreaks, from 100 to 200 meters wide, and eighty more firebreaks fifty meters wide, slashed through the center of the city. The main Tokyo railroad station was completely bared, every house in the vicinity pulled down. Whole new plazas now graced the center of the city in the heavy traffic areas such as Chiyoda, where the Diet and government buildings were located. Furthermore, every factory was protected by destroying the houses immediately around it.

"The face of Tokyo is changing every day," announced Radio Tokyo on April 5, 1945. "Anyone who has been away from the city for even a few months will return to find that he does not recognize it."

The registration and handling of homeless refugees was proceeding, but it took time to get them out of Tokyo. There were shortages serious enough that the officials addressed them publicly in the newspapers. The worst problem was transportation throughout the city. Still, the promise was made that rice would be distributed every five days and miso every three days, and that fresh or salted fish would be available to householders and refugees every six days.

The government announced a year's remission of income taxes for sufferers from the great fire raid. If a house was heavily damaged, taxes would be remitted for five years.

New attention was given to air-raid shelter construction, and renovation of basements to become air-raid shelters. The usual concrete building's basement was not an adequate shelter, the press warned (a fact that Saki Hiratsuka knew very well after his terrible struggle against suffocation and drowning in the basement of the Yasuda Bank building on the night of the fire raid).

The changes in Japanese life came thick and fast. On March 20 the government announced the official mobilization of all students, and the closing for the next year of educational institutions at every level except the junior grades. This meant that Japanese youth would learn to read and write and virtually nothing else. The children were to be put to work increasing the production of food and munitions. "Total mobilization of students" was the government term.

"This is the time that all the 100 million people must rise as one to defend the Divine Land," said Education Minister Count Hideo Kodama.

> Some of the weighty responsibilities of the defense of the country must be shouldered by students who are imbued with peerless patriotism and a spirit of service to the nation. The daily training of the people has been conducted in accordance with the Imperial Way* so that they may be able to serve the state in critical times.
>
> The day has come when this training will bear fruit in action, and the students will perform their duties of defending the Divine Land.

Such ominous warnings were almost constant in these days. The Great Tokyo Air Raid, as it is always called by the Japanese, marked a basic change in the national policy of the people of Japan. After that terrible night, the progression of battlefield losses had been adumbrated, more with each successive fire raid, until by the end of March a picture had emerged of a Japan with its back to the wall, a Japan that might well disappear from the face of the earth as a nation. The Japanese people really believed in that possibility, and so, with growing conviction that the danger was real, did their Emperor.

*"The Imperial Way" referred to the policy laid down by the military dictatorship that the lives of all Japanese must be sacrificed to the will of the Emperor at any time. The catch, of course, was *who* was to interpret the will of the Emperor.

The fall of Iwo Jima was announced to Japan on March 23. What was the government to say?

Prime Minister Koiso assured the people that like the fall of the islands of Oki and Tsushima during the Mongol Invasion of the fourteenth century, the fall of Iwo Jima to the enemy "must be the premise for the gaining of final victory in the war of Greater East Asia."

He warned the Japanese that they must expect still more damage from air raids, and that ultimately they would have to fight on the beaches of Japan. And there they would win the war. "The fighting must not cease as long as a single Japanese remains," he said.

On March 22, Lieutenant General Kenshiro Shibayama, the Vice-Minister of War, warned the people to get ready for the invasion on the beaches. Indeed, the attitude of Japan had suffered an enormous change in less than two weeks.

On March 22, the Tokyo Metropolitan Assembly voted 2 billion yen for the dispersal of industry in Tokyo. Within the month, another 100 firebreaks would be built in the city. That same day the Tokyo city government announced the discontinuation of all activities not directly concerned with defense. There would be no more training of officials for welfare work; there would in fact be no more welfare work, such as counseling for juveniles, midwifery, or assistance to prospective mothers. Libraries would be all but closed down. There would be no more agricultural exhibitions. Museums would be closed down or made into places of sanctuary. All of Japan was going on an emergency footing.

In Parliament, the Prime Minister remarked that work was afoot to make the various regions of Japan self-sustaining for the coming battle of the beaches, plains, and mountains. By March 24 the population of Tokyo had dropped to fewer than 4 million, a decrease of more than 3 million people. Home Minister Shigeo Odachi predicted that the population would continue to decline as the government encouraged all nonessential workers and their families to leave the city.

The Japanese government was in ferment, and so was the army. The Military Affairs Bureau, the controlling internal faction of the army, went into the hands of Lieutenant General Masao Yoshizumi, and eleven other young lieutenant generals were promoted into important army jobs, signifying a wiping out of the last of the Tojo faction. The army was determined to fight on to the end, all these generals being the products of the Japanese educational system of the late 1920s and early 1930s, when the army was seizing power in Japan. More than any previous generation, these generals believed in the Imperial Way and the superior power of moral strength over even B-29 firebombing.

On March 27 the Americans invaded Okinawa. The B-29s now began hitting the Kyushu air bases from which the hundreds of kamikaze suicide planes were emanating. General LeMay did not like it, but Admiral Nimitz had been proved correct. There were hundreds of aircraft on those Kyushu fields. The B-29s would be kept busy for a long time yet.

Or so the people of Tokyo thought.

18
TOKYO
AGAIN

AMONG THE SURVIVORS OF THE GREAT FIRE RAID OF MARCH 10, 1945, was the schoolboy Katsumoto Saotome, who had been lucky enough to be unhurt. But after the smoke of the air raid had died away and the fires had become cold ash, he looked around and found that his school had burned down and that all his teachers and friends at school had disappeared.

What was he to do with himself? Theoretically, he, like all the other students, was recruited into the Volunteer Students' Brigade. His place of employment was the Kubota manufacturing plant on the west side of Tokyo. But the plant was now closed down. He had spent many a sweaty hour in the great long machine shop with its steel beams and corrugated iron roof, emerging from the morning stint for luncheon covered with grease and sweat. But the plant was not operating at the moment. Its roof had partially collapsed in the firebombing of March 10. When would it reopen? When the bombing stopped, said the company authorities. So Katsumoto Saotome found himself with plenty of time on his hands and nothing to do. He was, he observed ruefully as he gazed at the rubble around his house, like the captain of a ship, relegated to loneliness.

Shortly after the fires of March 11 were extinguished, Katsumoto Saotome went down to the Sumida River area to see his old school. There was nothing left of the building but rubble and ash. It had burned down completely, and all that was left was the playing field. He could still see the white stripes of the tapes that had marked the field's north and south boundaries—the south side of the playing field for the boys, and the north for the girls. But that was all. The buildings were gone. The situation map in his old home room, which had caused so much snickering among Katsumoto and his friends over the absurd claims of the military, buttressed by the teachers, where was that now? A bit of ash, perhaps, flying out somewhere over the Pacific, that was all it could be.

The school was gone. There was no more school. The playing field had already been turned by civil defense authorities into a sweet potato field. A solitary tree stood on the boundary of the old grounds, above the mountain of rubble that had been the buildings. Rubble and pebbles and gray earth. Once the area had been splashed by color, the pink of cherry blossoms, the white of plum, the pink and white of begonias, and the yellow of spring anemones. Now all was a drab gray brown, dotted by black charcoal and gray ash.

Where indeed were the teachers? In his home room a class of sixty had studied day after day. And where were they now, those sixty friends? Gone, probably dead, or hiding somewhere in the countryside, away from the deadly embrace of the B-29s.

Katsumoto walked to the bank of the Sumida River, which only a few nights earlier had been a river of fire. Its current was gray and muddy. He had forgotten the crosscurrents that flowed through that river, but he saw them now, and he saw the bodies of the dead still stacked up like cordwood on the banks. He wandered down there among the bodies, half wondering if he might see the dead likeness of someone he had known. But who could tell one body from the other? They were like ironwood, those corpses, blackened trunks that had once been alive. Only an occasional outthrust limb, or a fire-etched profile, indicated that these had been human beings.

Katsumoto walked through Sumida Park. The beautiful cherry trees were all burned up, the buds long dead. Those trees would never again bear the pink blossoms that Tokyo had loved so well. The kamikaze pilots in the Philippines had chosen the cherry blossom as their emblem; they would fall as gracefully as the cherry blossoms, they said in the poems they wrote home to Japan, they would assume that same beauty and grace as they died to save the motherland from the enemy. But there was no beauty or grace in those gnarled, twisted remnants of living trees.

Katsumoto trudged past street after street of gray, drab ash. Block upon block was reduced to rubble: a bit of piping here, a pile of roof tiles there, where someone had decided to try to make something from this residue of destruction. A bicycle frame, a seat cushion, a broken teapot. If one wanted to sift through rubble, it could be a full-time occupation. But how useless. For the glass would be fused, the wooden implements burned up, the pottery cracked; the oven heat of that fire storm had rendered virtually everything it touched quite useless for any purpose.

Tokyo had a month's respite from the firebombing, but not from the B-29s. At 2:00 A.M. on April 2, the Japanese counted fifty B-29s over the western sector of Tokyo. The planes were dropping a mixture of high-explosive, incendiary, and delayed-detonation bombs.

Next day the Tokyo newspapers reported on this raid, claiming seventeen planes destroyed, and also on the big raids on Kyushu to try to stop the Kamikaze flights to Okinawa, and on the mining of the Japanese shoreline. All of this was reported in the Japanese press; the people were getting more real news since the advent of the B-29s than they had during all the rest of the war.

But of course, even that was not saying very much. A typical report on defenses against the B-29s would begin DOMEI . . . (FROM A CERTAIN BASE). . . . and then go on to spin a tale of some "wild eagle" rising into the sky to challenge the B-29s. The "heroes" were never mentioned by name, unless the report came directly from Imperial General Headquarters or, more likely, in a list of honors from the Imperial Palace. Those honored by the Emperor were nearly always dead; usually they were promoted two ranks in their service, a fact that gave their families some solace.

But usually the tales were anonymous. The military habit of secrecy was retained even now, when it did not make much difference what the enemy learned about the Japanese home defenses.

Into the very thick of the fray the two young Japanese airmen piloted their machine, a Toyu fighter plane. All about them soared the B-29s that had come to attack North Kyushu. It was the night of March 27 when in all more than ten of the raiders were shot down. One among this number was accounted for by these two youths, and the story of their exploits was given in a telephone message from Fukuoka to the *Yomiuri Hochi Shimbun*. The two, a sergeant major and a petty officer, members of an air defense unit stationed in that area, had been eagerly awaiting a chance to strike at the enemy since the first day of their training. And now the opportunity had come. They plunged into the attack and fought fiercely at every turn, but at crucial moments the enemy planes managed to slip away. Soon their supply of bullets was exhausted and they were forced to descend to the ground for a fresh supply. A second time they were forced to descend, and when they arose into the air for the third time they were determined to make a kill.

By a more cautious maneuver they were able to segregate one of the raiders beyond the city of Yawata. The time was about 11:30 P.M. Now had come the opportunity the two boys had waited for. Following the enemy closely until the right moment was at hand, they crashed their plane into the enormous form of the B-29, which immediately crashed into a hill to the west of Yawata.

Of course, the plane of the "wild eagles" crashed too. In a few weeks their names would be known when they were granted posthumous honors by the Emperor.

Such tales grew more frequent in the press these days, as the authorities tried very hard to assure the Japanese people that the air defenders were doing a good job. It was hard for the Japanese to believe, when they saw the evidence in their cities. The Home Ministry was growing very much concerned by the open criticism of military and especially air defense policy encountered in the streets.

On April 4 the B-29s were back in the Tokyo area again. The Japanese saw a new technique emerging: the Americans were dropping time-fused bombs, high-explosive bombs, and fire-bombs. It was true that the mixture did represent a change in policy, but the reason was that there was still a shortage of incendiaries. Out of this change, however, came a realization that the mixture was a good one. The Japanese could have attested to it. Firefighters were becoming very shy of sustained efforts in any area, after a few of them had been blown up by the delayed-action high-explosive bombs. The official report of the Tokyo fire department mentioned this specific problem as one of the most serious they now faced.

The B-29s were trying to destroy the munitions factories on the Kanto Plain, said the Japanese government. The raid began at 1:00 A.M. and lasted about three hours, and some ninety B-29s were counted by the Japanese over the target areas. "Practically no damage was caused by the enemy," said Imperial General Headquarters.

It was generally true that damage was slight, but there was a deeper damage: the psychological effect of the constant raiding that prevented people from sleeping at night.

It was the B-29s, as much as the deteriorating situation on Okinawa, that forced the resignation of the Koiso government of Japan on April 6, 1945. Admiral Kantaro Suzuki undertook the task of steering the Japanese course. It was significant that a navy man was chosen; public and Imperial confidence in the army had hit a new low.

The B-29s were back again over Tokyo on April 7, this time in a daylight raid. Something new had been added: fighter protection from Iwo Jima. From this point on, the Japanese would get used to seeing fighters as well as the big bombers over their cities.

The claims grew ridiculous. Imperial General Headquarters claimed 100 B-29s shot down in that April 7 raid on Tokyo. In fact, no one believed that claim.

Nor could the public now believe the tales of the "wild eagles," for they had become so completely exaggerated as to challenge faith. The Emperor was again brought forth to lend verisimilitude to the tales of four army air force pilots who had gone to glory by ramming B-29s: Sublieutenant Toshizo Kurai, Sublieutenant Osamu Hirose, Sergeant Major Kenji Fujimoto, Captain Junichi Ogata.

On April 12, about 120 B-29s staged another daylight raid on Tokyo. Once more, Tokyo was knocked a little off balance by the change in tactics.

Tokyo Again

What were the Americans up to?

In these recent raids, the firefighting had been easier because fewer incendiaries were used. But the bombs still rained down. And every day B-29s appeared.

They snooped and snooped, and no one knew when they were coming again. The people who had to remain in Tokyo were doing double duty. Sleep at night was very difficult; the bombers came too often. Day and night the army and the civil defense workers cut their fire lanes through the city, and pulled down houses by the hundreds. By the second week of April, people's nerves were on edge. The psychological warfare campaign waged by the bombers was working very well, even if it was inadvertent, the result of demands by the Joint Chiefs of Staff for the B-29s to be used for three different purposes.

The firefighters were now practicing some lessons they had learned in the raid of March 10. If intense fires got going in an area, there was no use in trying to save it. It was preferable to retain the effort and the equipment for intensive work on some area that was less threatened. But the first thing to do was to get as much industry out of the center of Tokyo as possible. Mitsubishi and other big company factories were moved, lock, stock, and barrel, out of Tokyo to the suburbs and to little towns twenty and thirty miles away. Of course, this could only be done where there was a facility that could be converted. And so, even with the changes, when the middle of April neared, a large segment of industry remained in Japan's capital, including a very intensive concentration of munitions factories in the northwest sector of the city.

The government was really preoccupied with the defense of industry, to the point that very little attention was given even now to the people's defense. Warnings were put out about the unsuitability of basements as air-raid shelters. But what were the alternatives? The fact was that movement out of the city was the very best course. And this was already causing serious difficulties in Tokyo industry. Every day the foremen reported more absenteeism in the factories, as the workers took their families to safety or went into the countryside to search for food.

After many discussions, the Home Ministry authorities decided that the neighborhood air-raid defense units would be disbanded. The system was just not suitable for fighting the intensive fires created by massed incendiary bombs. The People's Defense Corps was all but abandoned. The concentration of air defense was to be on the professional firefighting by the Tokyo fire department and the army.

At the end of the first week of April 1945, General LeMay foresaw a little respite from the demands made on his XXI Bomber Command by Admiral Nimitz in behalf of the Okinawa invasion effort. He seized the opportunity to lay plans for another raid on Tokyo. It would be staged on the night of April 13.

This time the target area was to be in the northwest part of the city, and the justification was that Japan's largest arsenal was located in this district, which housed a dozen arms factories. Much was made of that in the plans, but it smacks of self-justification, probably not by General LeMay, who believed thoroughly in what he was doing, but by staff officers who had some doubts about the morality of the firebombing program. The fact was that General LeMay had set out to firebomb Japan into submission, and that was all the justification he needed.

Three aiming points were selected for the three wings of B-29s. All were located in an area of about ten square miles in the northwest section of the city.

Once more, some of the planes would carry 500-pound high-explosive bombs to discourage the firefighters. This time the first twenty planes going in from each wing would carry such bombs, and they would be fused with the T-50 proximity fuse, which would be set to explode in the air, raining shrapnel down on the firefighters.

But not all the bombers would carry bombs for air-burst. Some would have delayed-action bombs, set to explode anywhere from ten minutes to five hours after impact.

On the afternoon of April 13, everything was ready, and General LeMay could be satisfied that no emergency had arisen to prevent him from going back to the destruction of Japan by fire. Once again, 327 B-29s from the three wings of the XXI Bomber command left their Marianas bases loaded with firebombs, plus those nice little extras, the time bombs and the airburst high-explosive bombs.

General LeMay had now told Washington that he could win the war for them with his B-29s alone: "I feel that the destruction of Japan's ability to wage war lies within the capability of this command, provided its maximum capacity is exerted unstintingly during the next six months."

That would mean firebombing every Japanese city, and destroying every possible house in Japan.

On April 13, 1945, the B-29s took off once more from the three Mariana Island bases, bound for Japan. That night the B-29s were carrying more than 2,100 tons of firebombs, or somewhere around 500,000 individual bombs, each capable of destroying a building, and the magnesium bombs capable of burning through steel.

The planes came in through cloud cover, low over Toshima, Oko, Adachi, Itabashi, Arakawa, Tokinogawa, and other areas. Soon, people were watching the rise of dreadful fires and the whirling eddies of wind that suggested another fire storm, a storm that would suck the oxygen from the air over Tokyo and bring about the same sort of destruction as that of the night of March 10.

But it did not happen this night, largely because of the precautions taken by the Tokyo Fire Department. The fire lancs held the fires, and although the destruction of buildings was enormous— 11.5 square miles of Tokyo were burned up in this night's raid— still, the effort of the firefighters was much more successful, and the numbers of casualties for the amount of damage (105,000 houses burned down) were remarkably slight. The number of dead was 2,459. The number of persons directly affected, of course, was enormously greater: 257,000 people injured or made sick or homeless, or in some other way affected by the bombing.

The firefighters had done the best they could. In the Toshima area, rescue units saved many lives. In Kanagawa and Chiba, sixty different rescue calls were answered. The factory workers had been trained now to fight fires in their own plants, and this helped. Within the buildings, new compartments had been segregated and all combustibles moved to the places of greatest safety. The firemen were very proud that they had been able to save one major wool-weaving factory that made uniforms for the army. But measured against the destruction, it was really almost pitiful. Against 330 bombers carrying thousands and thousands of firebombs, there was really no defense possible. The firefighters used 996 pumpers in this raid, and their casualties were five pumpers and three men killed. What the pumpers could really do was to save areas along the outskirts of the fires. But it was apparent that as far as the people of Tokyo were concerned, the policies of evacuation and fire control were an enormous improvement.

As *Asahi Shimbun* trumpeted the next morning, the Americans had dropped to new depths of depravity. Something new had been added to the fire raid on April 13. A single bomber dropped part of its incendiaries within the moat of the Imperial Palace in Chiyoda, burning down one wing of the palace. The Imperial Family was safe enough in its bomb shelter underground, but the raid on the palace was a shock, because the Americans had carefully avoided this prominent landmark in times past. In the same raid, the bombers damaged a part of the Meiji Shrine's inner sanctuary, as well as the outer worship area. One other Imperial Palace in Tokyo was also damaged. The bombers had moved out of the slums and the industrial district into the heart of the capital.

On April 14, Tokyo licked its wounds. The air defense crews were out, tearing down damaged buildings, removing burned-out vehicles, and improving the fire lanes. The ruins still smoked where eleven more square miles of the capital city had been burned out.

General LeMay was remorseless. He wanted to prove his point that the B-29s could end the war in victory for the Americans. The bombers were back over Tokyo on the night of April 15, this time concentrating on the eastern area, another area of small factories, home industries and thousands of wooden houses. They came in just after 10 P.M., another 300 aircraft, carrying the now-usual load of incendiaries and timed explosive bombs.

The firefighters had early warning this time, and were as well prepared as they could be. But the raid proved once more that the defenses against a sustained fire-bombing attack were minimal at best. The Kabata district was badly hit, and so was Omori. Another 52,400 houses burned down on the night of April 15, and another 213,000 people were listed by the government as "sufferers." But, almost miraculously, only 841 people were killed in this raid. It was a result partly of further evacuation of the city and partly of much better dispersal of the civil population and better management of rescues.

The B-29s very nearly started another fire storm this night. Had the winds been a bit higher, the destruction could have been much worse. As it was, Kabata began to blaze, and before the firemen could get going, it was a fire out of control. They headed for Omori, only to find that the raging fires had beaten them again. The national rail line from Yokohama to Kyoto was badly damaged along forty miles this night, too, for the bombers had two targets, really: Tokyo and Kawasaki, to the south. And when the bombers left, about eighty fires were still burning fiercely, and they burned all night long.

Next morning, the defenders checked the damage. More than four square miles of Kawasaki had been burned out, as well as more than five square miles of Tokyo. The notable fact was that Tokyo had been visited by only one wing of the XXI Bomber Command that night, and Kawasaki by two wings.

The bombers were improving their techniques. In the Tokyo zone attacked, the problem had been to set fires in large multistory buildings of modern construction. The mixture of bombs was refined: in the Tokyo area, the bombers carried mostly the M-47 100-pound napalm-filled bomb; it was used more than any other. For the Kawasaki area the bombers carried the smaller four- and seven-pound firebombs that were so very effective against the wooden houses that would be found there.

The results were all an arsonist could have asked for. It had been proved to General LeMay's complete satisfaction that he could do exactly what he had promised the Air Corps and the Joint Chiefs of Staff that he could do. Let them give him the bombs, and he would destroy Japan.

19
KOBE
RERUN

GENERAL LEMAY WANTED DESPERATELY TO CONTINUE THE tempo of the firebomb raids at the level of these last Tokyo assaults, but it was impossible. The United States Navy was suffering heavily from the success of the kamikaze attacks against ships off Okinawa, and Admiral Nimitz insisted that the B-29s continue to strike at the Kyushu airfields and the Japanese aircraft industry. Even so, LeMay managed to continue the firebombing of Japan on a limited scale.

On April 24 his B-29s hit Tatsukawa and Shizuoka. On May 5 they bombed Kure. On May 11 they bombed Kobe again. There were only sixty planes involved in this raid—the others were off on Admiral Nimitz's business that day—but they were very effective. They destroyed the Shinmeiwa munitions factory in Kobe that day, killing another 1,100 people.

On May 14, General LeMay's planes bombed Nagoya again. By this time the bombing operations out of western China had been suspended and the 58th Wing had been moved to Tinian. This change gave General LeMay a big increase in strength. On

May 14, 529 B-29s took off from the Marianas airfields, some bound for Okuzaki and Oita, but most for Nagoya. Their target was, as usual, the area around the Mitsubishi factory complex.

Or was it? The Japanese did not believe this to be true. This attack began before dawn and continued until 8:00 A.M. The rain of bombs in the residential area was the worst Nagoya had seen, and soon fires were raging so fiercely that the rising sun was blacked out, the city filled with smoke and devastating fires. The north district was the main target this time; 470 B-29s dropped 2,700 tons of bombs on the city. If the ancient and historic Nagoya Castle had been the target, the bombers did a great job. They burned it to the ground, so that only the stone foundations and the great golden dolphin that had adorned the castle tower remained. The dolphin was saved because although the supports burned away for the most part, one held, and so the golden dolphin dangled above the flames.

Some houses actually were hit by twenty or more bombs, and of course that sort of incendiarism was impossible to combat. In all, 22,000 more houses were burned down in this raid, but, remarkably, only 237 people were killed. The Japanese had learned a great deal about air-raid discipline in the past few months, and Nagoyans had learned more than anyone else, because this was the forty-fifth air raid on their city. One thing it proved was that while General LeMay could indeed burn down the cities of Japan, he was not doing much of a job of destroying the aircraft industry. A small part of one Mitsubishi engine factory was knocked out by this particular raid, hardly enough by itself to justify the effort. Again, it was proof that General LeMay's major interest was not Admiral Nimitz's. The general did not waver from his self-appointed task of burning up Japan. The important statistic was that 3.6 more square miles of Nagoya were burned in this attack.

Two nights after the Nagoya raid, the B-29s were back, this time 457 of them with 3,600 tons of firebombs, and they destroyed another 3.8 square miles of Nagoya.

Kobe Rerun

General LeMay had all those extra planes now, so on that same night the bombers attacked Kobe, Numazu, Oita, Kushimoto, and Yokohama. Small numbers of planes had been hitting these and other cities almost every day.

LeMay had his head now. By the middle of May the struggle on Okinawa had settled down to a slugging match on land, between powerful Japanese army forces and the American army and marines. The American navy was still having serious difficulties with the kamikazes attacking the fleet forces off Okinawa, and General LeMay's B-29s had not really been very effective in stopping those attacks.

In the first week of May, the Japanese had launched their fifth Kikusui attack—which meant that they sent hundreds of kamikazes against the American fleet off Okinawa. The U.S. fleet lost two destroyers, two landing ships, and 370 officers and men. Casualties for the Okinawa campaign were already higher than those for any other naval operation in the entire war. On May 11, 150 more Kikusui suicide planes had come over the American fleet. The destroyer *Evans* was hit by eight suicide planes that day.

In the third week of May, Nimitz consulted his intelligence officers and learned that he could expect no change, except for the worse. Nearly every day the suicide planes were out hunting for game. Every day the Japanese were gearing up for the invasion of the home islands, and most of their efforts were now being turned toward production of suicide weapons.

Thus, Admiral Nimitz decided on a new strategy. He would send Admiral William F. Halsey with the Third Fleet to make a series of attacks around the main islands of Japan, to hit at airfields and aircraft production facilities, and try to do what LeMay had failed to do—put the kamikazes out of business.

Big plans were afoot at Admiral Nimitz's advance headquarters on Guam and back at Pearl Harbor. Preparations were being made for the major assault on Japan in the autumn. The Germans had surrendered on May 7, and all the might of the Allies could now be turned against Japan.

So Halsey left Guam with orders to "go out and get 'em" where they were, to attack Japan itself. His task force headed for the Japanese islands. He was going to undertake the harassment of Japan. General LeMay was freed to go back to his attempt to destroy Japan's cities and people.

On May 24, LeMay's bombers burned another 5.3 square miles of Tokyo. About 250 bombers made the raid, at one o'clock in the morning. This time they hit a teahouse on the grounds of the Imperial Palace and burned it to the ground. They also burned a building in the Akasaka Palace compound. Ironically, it was the building in which the firefighting equipment for the palace was stored.

The Japanese claimed that they shot down twenty-seven bombers and damaged thirty, but no one saw them fall. Imperial Headquarters found it noteworthy that this was the first raid on Tokyo in more than a month. And on May 25 the B-29s burned another 16.8 square miles of the Japanese capital. On May 29 they burned 6.9 square miles of Yokohama. Then came June 1, and another big raid, this time once again on Osaka.

The Americans had found the M-50 thermite magnesium bomb to be so very effective when they were more or less forced into employing it during the days of the firebomb shortage that they now regarded it as a superior weapon because of the nature of the fire it produced, which was not extinguishable by water. Therefore, many of the 509 planes that assembled from the four B-29 wings were loaded with M-50 bombs.

But the XXI Bomber Command had gone a long way further in the creation of sophisticated weaponry. The M-50 bomb could be set for delayed explosion of from forty seconds to a minute. That created a new effect: it would explode with the power of a grenade, spreading fiery bits for as far as fifteen feet in all directions. Certainly that would be a deterrent to firefighters.

And the sheer range of sizes of the firebombs was another deterrent. The TE-4 was a twenty-pound bomb. The M-17 weighed 500 pounds, and the M-47 weighed 100 pounds, while the six-pound M-69 that had done most of the destruction in the first Tokyo raid was the old standby.

Besides the firebombs, every third or fourth plane would carry a 500-pound high-explosive bomb, and most of these were set for timed destruction, another factor the firefighters had to consider. The reality was that once the bombers came over with their thousands of pounds of bombs, there was not a great deal that the defenders could do except clear people out and rescue those who were injured or trapped. A peripheral area might be saved, but not when twenty or thirty bombs per house came down in block after block. Then it was simply a question of trying to establish a perimeter for the fire and letting the inner sector burn itself out.

On the night of May 31, the bombers moved out of their bases in the three Mariana Islands. They carried 2,788 tons of firebombs toward Osaka that morning as they came in to make their high-altitude bombing raid. No longer was there much talk about aiming points. The pathfinder planes would come in and start some fires, and the rest of the planes would drop their bombs around the fires, and the general conflagration would begin. It had become a very simple system of destruction. For this raid the planes would be bombing at between 18,000 and 28,500 feet, much safer in terms of antiaircraft and fighter resistance.

They came in over Kii Island and Cape Kisa. The army defense stations there spotted the planes and put out the first air-raid warning. But the warning system was not working very well on June 1. Osaka was very slow to get the word.

The Central Army Command then sent messages to its various fighter squadrons in the area. The word had been passed by Imperial General Headquarters that the fighters were to concentrate on *tokubetsu* or "special attack" techniques. This, of course, meant suicide attacks, ramming for the most part.

Before the day was out, Tokyo would claim that the "wild eagles" had shot down twenty-four B-29s and damaged thirty more. But the claim was almost complete exaggeration. For one thing, now that the Americans had captured Iwo Jima, they had rebuilt the Japanese airfields there, and fighter squadrons of U.S. Army Air Corps planes were stationed on the island. The B-29s on this Osaka raid were accompanied by P-51s from the Seventh Fighter Group.

In Osaka that morning, Takisei Chujo reported to his job in the office of the Osaka Electric Light Board vehicles factory where he had been employed for the past six months. Chujo was very proud of his job and his company, and felt very lucky these days. He had recently completed a course in civil defense at the Tenno Temple Middle School, where he had been sent by the prefectural authorities, and he had studied firefighting and first aid.

This morning he was just getting down to work when he heard the air-raid sirens begin to wail. But almost immediately the sirens were drowned out by the racket of hundreds of B-29 bombers and P-51 fighters over the city, and bombs began to rain down in the district where the Electric Light Board's factory lay.

Chujo rushed outside to look. The air was darkened by falling objects, firebombs by the thousands, and they were coming right down into the yard of the factory. By the time he got back into the office, it was aflame, and outside an ocean of fire splashed about the yard.

Through the smoke of the office, Chujo saw several buckets of water standing against the wall. He rushed in and grabbed them and put out the flames of the incendiaries that had fallen through the ceiling. But the office was so full of smoke that he inhaled a lot of it, and for the next two nights he gasped and coughed up smoke like an asthma victim.

He went outside for relief, but in a few moments forced himself back into the office to see if there was anyone left inside. He found four people sitting there dazed, and he got them up and out of the building and to the air-raid shelter deep underground by the factory's main gate. Then he went back to the office for another look. The smoke still hung in there, although there was no fire. He saw three office girls who had made their way into the room, and they were immobilized by shock and were all crying. He rounded them up and took them to the shelter too. Actually, the three girls were young students of the Volunteer Corps, and they knew absolutely nothing about what they should do in emergency.

Then he went into the foundry garage to see if anyone was in there. There was no one. He went out into the blazing factory yard and headed for the shelter, running, for more enemy planes were now overhead.

But as he ran he heard a blast, and saw that it had come from the area of the shelter. The air was full of smoke. The explosion had created a little wind storm, and the fiery wind blew him along. He heard voices raised in fear. Smoke was rising from the shelter. It had obviously taken a direct hit from one of General LeMay's high-explosive bombs, and that must have been followed by firebombs, because the shelter was burning. Chujo remembered the seven people he had escorted into the shelter. All must now be dead, for the top of the shelter had caved in, and the smoke was coming up through the cracks. Chujo tried to break in to see if anyone inside was still alive. He scrabbled at the debris with his hands, but it was no use. He could not penetrate the broken shelter.

The wind blew away his glasses and then he could scarcely see. He ran around to the side, and found himself in the old flower garden of the factory. There was no way he could help those people in the shelter.

He began, half blinded, to walk. He headed out toward the Tsuruhama Dori. That broad boulevard's houses were all burning, on both sides of the road. Everything in the area was going up in flames. He passed dozens of burning houses. On the road he saw all sorts of debris, futons and seat cushions, pots and pans. He came to one pile of futons, and saw a woman's face protruding. He leaned down. Blood was all over the futon and the roadway. She was dead. But on her breast was lying a little baby, and the baby was crying. Obviously the poor woman had given birth just before she died. Chujo picked up the child, and blindly continued to walk up the Tsuruhama Dori. Finally he got out of the area of destruction and came to a place of refuge. Only then did he realize that his face and hands were both badly burned. The first-aid crews treated his burns, but the child needed nothing more than what it had now, a protector.

Chujo took the baby home. He never did learn anything about the child's family or about the woman he had seen lying dead and bloody in the road.

By the spring of 1945, Japan was reaching deep into the manpower barrel for factory workers, and Osaka's situation indicated just what was happening.

Fukita Chiriyama Middle School had been established in 1940 with a brand-new building, and the teachers and students were very proud of it. It was located in Oyoda district in the Urakohoku. One of the students was a boy named Koji Yamaoka, a third-year middle-school scholar, which would mean in America a ninth-grader, or a boy about thirteen years old. Koji lived near the Fukashima railroad station on the national railroad line, which was always one of the target areas for General LeMay's bombers.

These days, Koji was not going to school much of the time. Theoretically he worked a half-day in the Osaka Steam Train Locomotive Manufacturing Plant, in the Osaka industrial district. It was part of an enormous complex of manufacturing, which included metalworks, chemical works, and shipbuilding yards, lined up on the Osaka waterfront. Along with about 180 other middle-school students from the school, Koji went to work every day at the factory. One of the other workers was his good friend Yoshi Sensue.

When Koji first went to work at the factory, they put him in school again. For a week he studied the theory of electric welding. Then for another week he was instructed in practical welding by an expert. Then he was put to work welding the superheater boxes of steam locomotives. It was quite a responsibility for a thirteen-year-old boy. Here he was, one of the enemies that General LeMay wanted to wipe out. And although he was just a boy, he was a formidable enemy, an expert artisan with a year's experience now under his belt.

On the morning of June 1, 1945, Koji went to work at the factory as usual. His friend Yoshi went to school this morning, but would be along at the factory a little later.

First there was a morning meeting at the factory with the army officers who laid down the schedules and made the decisions as to what was to be done. This had been the case in all Japanese industry since the day, about a year ago, when General Tojo had nationalized the munitions industries for the duration of the war.

When the meeting ended, the workers all filed out of the meeting place and hurried to their individual job stations in the various factories of the enormous complex. In a few minutes the cacophony began, and Koji could not hear anything that anyone might say. He had his welding mask on, and his gas welding gun made enough noise by itself to half deafen him.

Thus Koji did not hear the air-raid warning siren when it went off at 8:40 to announce the impending arrival of the B-29s. Nor did he hear the air-raid alarm signal, which meant the planes were just minutes away from Osaka, when it went off at 9:03. There was just too much noise.

There was another reason, also, why Koji and his fellow workers were not warned. Osaka had been raided so often by this time that the army officers in charge of production at the steam locomotive and shipbuilding complex complained about the loss of efficiency. The complaints started at the top in Tokyo and came right down the line to the factory. What could the officers at the factory do? They could not tell Tokyo that if the army would protect Osaka better, the factory would not be suffering from worker desertion and lost time—not when the army had just announced in Tokyo that the nationalization of the aircraft industry had brought about an enormous increase in production. But they had to do something. So they disconnected the air-raid-siren loudspeakers inside the plants. A great deal of time was saved then, as the results of the past few weeks had shown, but, of course, the workers would never know when the planes were actually overhead until they began to feel the results. Fortunately for the workers' peace of mind, they did not know this.

The first Koji knew of the June 1 air raid was shortly after nine o'clock, when the earth began to shake. That was the result of General LeMay's demolition bombs going off in the factory district.

The vibrations and the jumping and rattling of equipment grew more pronounced as the bombers came nearer to the factory complex. Suddenly, men stopped their work, dropped their tools, and began to run to get out of the factory. There was no question about the air raid now. They could see the aircraft and hear the thundering of their engines.

Koji had an eerie feeling that bombs were dropping all around him.

He put down his welding gun and started to walk toward the great avenue inside the factory that led off to the west. And then he began to run. Everywhere men were running, colliding with one another, dodging speeding trucks and other vehicles, as they tried to escape from the now burning factory. But the firebombs were coming down everywhere. Koji decided his best bet was to run straight north and get out of the factory area that way by going along the city railroad tracks to the Shinashitsu station. He was running toward the Yodo River. As he ran, he passed the segment of the factory where his friend Yoshi worked, and suddenly he saw a whole string of the student volunteers come running out of the factory, Yoshi among them.

Koji heard the *bump, bump, bump* of falling bombs, and he saw the sky black with firebombs. Then he watched his friend Yoshi running across the open road. Yoshi stumbled, and Koji saw that a firebomb had exploded at his friend's feet, and had slashed his head. The blood began to flow from the wound even as the boy ran. He ran perhaps fifteen steps and then he fell, and he lifted his head, but no sound came out of his mouth. Koji ran to him and looked down. Yoshi's head was split wide open and he was already dead. The blood was staining the white cotton uniform and flooding in a pool around the body.

There was nothing to be done for Yoshi, but Koji was still alive. How long he would remain alive seemed debatable, with all the bombs flying through the air. He began to run again, and he ran and ran. Later he could not remember how far he ran, but he could remember running through fire, and burning his hands. He also remembered how hot it was. When he had escaped the factory area and gotten out of the part of Osaka where the firebombs were falling, Koji looked down at his white work clothing. It had all turned gray. He felt pain in his legs. When he removed his shoes, he saw that they were burned through and that his feet were also burned. But at least Koji Yamaoka was alive. In Osaka that day, being alive was not that certain a proposition.

The next morning, all this drama was encapsulated by the Tokyo newspapers into two- or three-paragraph stories that told virtually nothing about what had happened in Osaka on June 1.

> About 400 B-29s from southern bases raided Osaka, in formations consisting of about ten to thirty, coming by way of the southern part of the Kii Peninsula and Tosa Bay from about 8:35 A.M., and carried out indiscriminate bombing, mainly by means of incendiary bombs, for about two hours. They later fled southward via the central part of Nara Prefecture, it was announced by the Central Army headquarters at noon. The announcement added that fires had broken out in the northern part of the city as well as in Amagasaki, but thanks to strenuous fire prevention measures the fires were gradually brought

under control. The results scored by the Japanese forces until noon were known to be twenty-four enemy planes shot down and thirty damaged. These figures are supposed to increase, the announcement added.

A day later, Central Army Headquarters amplified its previous claims to forty-seven B-29s shot down and eighty-three more damaged, with one Japanese plane lost when its pilot rammed a B-29 and destroyed that enemy, and one more plane that had not returned to base.

And who believed that story, either? By this time, nobody in Japan really believed the army's claims about the planes shot down. It was apparent that defenses against the B-29s were almost nonexistent.

20
REFINEMENTS

AS THE JAPANESE NOTICED AFTER THE SECOND WEEK OF MAY 1945, the American bombers were refining their techniques of destroying Japan's cities and people in every raid.

The Nagoya raid of May 17 was the most destructive of the war. The principal agent was the M-50 magnesium bomb. Twenty percent of these were fitted with the sort of explosive warhead that blew off half of the head of Kiji Yamaoka's young school friend in Osaka. Those explosive warheads on some bombs kept the firefighters away from all of that sort of bomb. The rain of fire was so effective in this raid that the Mitsubishi aircraft assembly plant was totally shut down after it. Several nearly completed "Betty" bombers were abandoned on the assembly line after literally thousands of bombs fell on this plant and gutted part of it.

In the raids of May 24 and May 25, several new systems were added. On the night of May 23 the planes had flown over South Central Tokyo, a largely residential area with some industry. So the first forty bombers carried M-47 bombs, but the rest carried the six-pound M-69 bombs in clusters to burn down houses. In the next night's raid, LeMay wanted to try something entirely different. This raid was flown against the heart of Tokyo, and was in fact called the Heart of Tokyo Raid by the Americans. Since the buildings in this area (around the Imperial Palace and the Diet) were large and modern for the most part, a different technique had to be used. The primary bombs were the M-47 napalm bomb, the M-69 incendiary bomb, and the M-76 500-pound incendiary bomb. One of the buildings hit was the modern Japan Electric Corporation Building, a six-story, reinforced-concrete structure about a half-mile from the Imperial Palace. One M-76 bomb passed through its roof. At the same time, several M-76 bombs hit two other buildings nearby, totally destroying them both.

This raid was also very destructive to the Ginza, Tokyo's central shopping district. M-69 and M-50 bombs did a fine job of destroying small buildings in that area. Two city blocks were completely wiped out. The Hitachi Airplane Engine Company plant was destroyed by small firebombs. A thousand empty firebomb cases were found in the factory's ruins. A brewery was demolished. There were just too many bombs for the firemen and the employees of the company to combat. And when the firemen came to sift through the ruins, they found the floor virtually paved with firebomb cases.

The May 25 raid was the worst so far; 464 bombers dropped 3,252 tons of bombs and burned out twenty-two square miles of the city. Tokyo, the capital of Japan, 110 square miles of sprawling metropolis, was now more than half destroyed: fifty-six square miles had been burned.

So the destruction increased, raid after raid. Tokyo, which had gained a respite of nearly a month between the April and May raids, was to have no more rest.

By the first of June, rumors were flying through the city. The supply of food was about to give out, they said. So upsetting was

this report to so many people that the government took the un-
usual step of reassuring the public through the press that the food
supplies of Japan were not giving out. It said there were large
stockpiles of rice, noodles, dried bread, canned goods, *takuan*
(pickled radish), *umeboshi* (pickled apricot), miso, soy sauce, dried
bonito (fish stock), and canned milk for babies.

The fire raids continued, but they were no longer the primary
concern of the government and people of Japan. The people were
numbed to the bombing. The government was preparing them
for much worse things to come: the invasion of Japan.

An *Asahi Shimbun* correspondent was taken on a tour of the
"underground facilities" the government had built to withstand
the invasion, and he wrote that Japan had become an impregnable
fortress. Ammunition dumps, infantry positions, kitchens, all
were moved into interconnecting places underground. No bombs
could fall on these places, said the *Asahi* reporter with great confidence. The impression he intended to communicate was that the
military had created an underground beehive, which would serve
all the people when the time came.

> Should the enemy forces invade Japan proper,
> all the officers and men will entrench themselves
> underground and, using all sorts of flame-
> throwers and explosives, will completely frus-
> trate the enemy attempt. A new kind of
> underground warfare now being prepared by the
> Japanese is so different from anything witnessed
> in the European continent that it will mark a new
> epoch in the history of military strategy. The sol-
> idarity of the fortress has no comparison in the
> history of world warfare. . . . The new method
> of fighting can be well compared to the tactics of
> Misashige Kusunoki, the well-known patriot
> warrior during the feudal era, who used original

devices in the construction of the Chihaya castle and beat the numerically much superior enemy force. . . .

All that had happened in the last three years had simply been preparation for what was to come. Japan, said the *Asahi* reporter, had planned it all:

> All operations waged since the Guadalcanal campaign ensured the time Japan needs by exacting heavy sacrifices in blood from the enemy. However, counter-operations to be staged in mainland will be completely different in tactics from anything preceding. They will be conducted to annihilate enemy invaders. . . . Are the Americans ready to combat Japan's enormous combat forces? With the fortification of Japan proper completed, the fighting men and civilians in unison are now burning with sublime fighting spirit.

Meanwhile, the people of Japan, living aboveground, were subjected to ever more air raids, ever more firebombing. Hammatsu, Tatsukawa, Takushima, Kagoshima, and many other small cities were attacked. General LeMay seemed bent on burning every city in Japan if he could. On June 5 the bombers hit the Hanshin area. Two hundred were shot down or badly damaged, said Imperial General Headquarters. Hanshin meant the Kobe-Osaka area. Imperial Headquarters did not admit it; the report was only two paragraphs, and said nothing about the wind that blew so hard it turned the Kobe area into a furnace.

Takeo Ikuma knew all about that. He lived with his old father and his young sisters in Fukiai district on the west side of the city.

From their house on a hill, and particularly from the second-story veranda, Takeo had an excellent view of this raid as it progressed. The bombers came in broad daylight. It was a hot summer day, and at first the smoke from the bombings hung in the air, rising lazily. But then the wind came up and the fires began to spread.

From his "catbird seat," Takeo could see the raid very well. He saw one Japanese fighter plane crash into a B-29 and then he saw the parachutes stringing out across the sky behind the collapsing bomber. The planes were flying high, as they had been doing in recent days. The sky was clear above the smoke, and the bombers looked like great, lazy, silver birds up there, as they moved along, dropping their pellets of death.

After half an hour, Takeo's aging father and the girls moved out of the house and walked to the refuge behind the hill. Takeo remained in the house and watched. It was his duty, as well, to remain at the house and be prepared to fight the fire if it came his way.

Somehow Takeo knew that this day his house, which had escaped all the other raids, was not going to escape again. Perhaps it was the precision with which the B-29s bombed, spreading the fires ever closer to his family's area of Kobe.

After an hour of the raid, the black smoke was moving swiftly toward Fukiai. Yes, the bombers were coming his way. He watched, fascinated, as the drama unfolded around him.

Most of the people in his area had already fled the neighborhood with the approach of the planes. This was illegal, since the Home Ministry most certainly had placed the responsibility for firefighting on the individual householders, but in the past two months the regulations had been honored as much in the breach as in the observance. As everyone in Japan now knew, once the firebombs came, it was a question of limiting the damage to areas, not of saving individual houses.

But this day Takeo remained at home, true to his trust to try to save the house. The bombers came on inexorably, and then he could see the tiny bombs dropping from the silvery planes. He recognized them as the small ones. They were, in fact, the M-50 magnesium bombs that water would not douse. All those buckets of water that had been stored around the outside of Takeo's house were going to be of absolutely no use.

And so it proved a few minutes later, when the bombs began to fall on the house. Dozens of the four-pound bombs struck it, and each burst and began its deadly work. Takeo tried a bucket of water on one place, but saw that it had no effect at all, and there were scores of places on the house now beginning to burn.

There was nothing one or two people could do at this point to save the house, Takeo saw that. His next thought was for himself. He had waited a long time to escape, and the fire was all around his area. He looked out at the smoke and fire all around, and decided that the best escape route lay along the electric railway line, whose embankment was relatively free of houses, and thus should not have fire all along the route. But to get to the train line, he had to get down through the streets, past houses that were blazing. As he ran along the street, he encountered many people fleeing toward the mountains, carrying their belongings or babies on their backs, carrying suitcases, bags, boxes, and futons. Some of the loads seemed very heavy, and Takeo wondered if these people were going to make it. He saw several policemen on the embankment, trying to control the human traffic that was streaming away from the burning section of the city. He saw firefighters valiantly, but desperately and without much success, working to stop the fires from spreading.

Down here in the valley, the sky was no longer visible; the air was absolutely filled with black smoke that ate into his lungs. Through the smoke, he could hear cries of anguish and fear as people tried to get help for themselves or for a loved one. The people moved along like a desperate wave of human bodies, trying to get away from the yellow flames.

Takeo looked down and saw that one of his hands had turned a strange white color. It was beginning to hurt, with a dull, throbbing pain. The smoke and the heat made his throat very dry. He came to a large barrel of water put out by the firefighters, and went to plunge his head into it. But the surface was covered with a scum of oil and grease, and it was obviously so filthy he could not drink it. So he gave the barrel a kick and went on.

Everywhere along the route he saw people. Some were searching for friends or relatives, walking along vacantly, calling out names. Now he began to see the debris of war, baggage abandoned along the route, clothing and pots and all the accoutrements of civilization, suddenly of no more importance in that mad rush to get away from the flames.

He reached the edge of the hills at Noda Machinaga. The whole area was abandoned. Behind the houses he found a trickle of water that refreshed him and helped ease the burning of his hand. The trickle moved on down the hill, into the plain, and to the Ikuta River. But the river area was being bombed now, and that was not the direction in which he should go. All around him on the plain he saw abandoned luggage, the flotsam of the war. He met people with bloody feet and bloody hands and bloody bodies. The place to go, he could see, was the upland ahead. There he would be safe, for the bombers were avoiding that area. The houses were too few and far between.

Takeo thought about his family, back at the shelter on the other side of the hill. But there was no way he could make his way there now. It was too far, and he would have to cross the ocean of flame. No, the place to go was the mountain. Wearily he forced himself to go on.

This time, Takeo's area of Kobe really took a dreadful beating from the bombers, and the bombing lasted all the while that he trudged up the hill, his hand hurting very badly. Finally he reached the highland, and there looked down. The green trees had turned dark brown and red from the heat and the fire. Most of them had collapsed in flames. Down below, the fires were still burning brightly, and yellow flames were licking upward from the tortured buildings. He saw Katano Kijo landing, almost totally burned out. What had once been green grass down there was now all scorched and ruined. The firebombs had fallen here too, and had done their work.

It had been a shelter area, and it had turned into an inferno, ensnaring many of the people who came to this boxlike place to seek shelter. They had been trapped and had died by the scores.

From his vantage point, Takeo could see that the town had burned from Fukiai to Ikuta. Everything was burned up. In the north the sea of fire still blazed, and the streets had the collapsed look that had become so common in the Japanese metropolitan areas.

Takeo had now fled as far as he need go. The fires were dying and the planes were leaving. With a certain peace of mind, he sat down and leaned against the stone wall of a building. He felt indignant at the ignominy of the beating his city had taken from the enemy, indignant and resentful and defeated all at once. Crushed. Routed. Utterly wiped out. That was how he felt, and how Kobe looked, that day.

But now the noise of the detonation of the enemy bombs and the noise of the B-29 engines over Kobe were dying down. The fires were gradually burning themselves out, and the firefighters were working hard. He could see their forms as they moved about below.

It was, Takeo told himself, the end of his world. Kobe had been turned into a pitiful remnant of itself.

With a start, Takeo suddenly remembered his father and sisters, and wondered what had happened to them. There was only one way to find out, and that was to go around the shelter areas until he found them. He began again to walk, this time down the hills, to search in all the open fields and plazas where the refugees from the fire were gathering.

Soon Takeo began to feel very tired. He sat down and leaned

his back against a concrete wall. For some reason he turned, and saw that his back was staining the wall with blood. Also, he was beginning to feel a pain in his back for the first time. Somehow, he did not know how, he had been wounded.

He saw a party of people in the road and stopped them. They were very agitated, hurrying to try to find surviving members of their families. But one man stopped and, when asked, looked at Takeo's back.

"Go to a first-aid station," the man said. "You had better get a doctor to look at that wound right away, it looks very deep and serious to me." And then the people went on, chattering among themselves, searching and calling to their friends and relatives, wherever they might be.

As Takeo walked down the road, looking for an aid station, he continued to pass distraught people, disheveled, faces red from exertion and smoke inhalation, some of them bleeding, all of them excited and upset. Kobe, he could tell, would be a long time feeling the effects of this latest fire raid.

Down on the plain it seemed that everyone in Kobe had congregated, looking for families, calling out names, searching, searching, searching. The people were covered with gray dust and grime, and sooty smoke still hung over the low spots. The looks on the people's faces ranged from grim despair to a sort of numb acceptance of the fact that everything they had was lost. Fukiai district had gone up in smoke: houses, shops, small businesses, all were gone.

Takeo sat down again. He was feeling very weak, and he now knew it had to be from loss of blood. But he had to find an aid station. He moved on, and finally he came to a school that had been set up for first aid. The doctor took one look at Takeo's pale face and immediately gave him some sugar. It seemed to revive him. Then the doctor looked at Takeo's back, and immediately gestured to him to lie down. The doctor and his assistants began to put lotion on the wound, and then to bandage it. That was all they could offer him as treatment. They had virtually no medical supplies with which to work.

The doctor knew what had caused the wound. One of the little firebombs had exploded near him, and the shrapnel had torn the hole in Takeo's back. The doctor had seen scores of such wounds this day.

Takeo rested for a few hours, and then began the search for his family again. Finally, after a long walk, he found them at the shelter on the other side of the hill from his house. They had remained there throughout the raid and had been perfectly safe.

Takeo and his father and sisters went to their house. Nothing was left but ashes and junk, twisted metal, bits of tatami, plus a few pieces of pipe and steel and wood that had been furniture.

The authorities supplied them with food for five days, as well as bedding and a canvas tarpaulin. They found a pleasant little grove of trees on a hillside, next to a stone wall, and set up their camp there. For two days they remained, numbly, not knowing quite what they were going to do, but only that everything they had in Kobe was gone.

Down below them, under the bridge and in the refugee camp on the plain, people crowded together by the hundreds. Also down on the plain were the people who had been too late in fleeing from their houses and the burning streets, the dead. The firemen and the rescue squads began collecting and moving the bodies. One school and three public buildings were set aside for the bodies to be laid out, and day after day people came to these buildings, looking at the seared remains, trying to find their loved ones.

Every day, Takeo and his family looked down upon the ruins of their city, where the wide-ranging, pitiless fire had wiped out so many houses. The heat remained for three days in the embers and smoking rubble. Finally, Takeo and his family awoke to realize that they must do something for themselves, for the authorities were incapable of doing more for them than they had. They decided they would go away from Kobe. There was nothing to hold them there now. They would go to Takeo's father's family.

And so, on the fifth day after the great raid, Takeo and his family went down to the Central Kobe railroad station and bought the tickets that would take them to a new life.

They got on the train and headed for Hiroshima.

21
CRESCENDO

ON JUNE 7 THE B-29S AGAIN BOMBED OSAKA, KOBE, AND FIVE other cities. On June 9 they bombed Nagoya and two other cities. On June 10 they hit Kobe and Tokyo and Tatsukawa, and four small cities. They were out to prove that they could burn up all Japan.

June 15, Osaka.

June 17, Kobe.

June 18, four more small cities.

June 19 and 20, Fukuoka, Toyobashi, and another small city.

It was a week before the next raid came, but it was against sixteen cities.

So frequent were the B-29 raids (and in July they were accompanied by raids from Admiral Halsey's carrier task force, close against the islands of Japan) that Imperial General Headquarters stopped treating the raids as major events. When the air raids were mentioned at all, after June 10, they were played down and the articles were very short, almost always placed at the bottom of the first or news page of the newspapers.

Instead, the government tried to deal with the air raids lightly, as in an article by Mitsuaki Kakehi in the magazine *Contemporary Japan*.

Tokyo had been raided so many times, said the author, that people now found the raids something of a joke.

> The other day, when I was about to get aboard a homebound electric car, I met a jovial friend of mine whom I had not seen for a long time. After the exchange of usual greetings the conversation naturally veered to air raids. At the end my jovial friend, to the accompaniment of a hearty guffaw said "Well, we sure are going to *endenizen* [make citizens of] these American fliers, don't you think?
>
> I said, nothing, but I too laughed heartily.
>
> Believe it or not, the air raid has aroused in us a feeling of cheerfulness, a kind of lighthearted buoyance such as we experience when something long expected happens.

Perhaps, but in the body of the article appeared grimmer indications:

> The women of Tokyo are exhibiting their bravery, particularly in the form of firefighting that is the most important function of the civil air-raid defense. Clad in *monpei*, with buckets in their hands, young women, together with men with their trousers wrapped in puttees and armed with firefighting implements, put out fires at the risk of their lives. When in one district a Buddhist temple was hit by an incendiary bomb, it was found extremely difficult to climb onto the roof, which was in flames. Yet the men and

women firefighters, clasping their buckets and other implements with their teeth, ascended the roof and stamped out the blaze in no time. I was much struck with the smiling face of a little girl whose house was damaged by the concussion of a bomb falling nearby and who related to me quite calmly and composedly her experience right after the dropping of the bomb. It is impossible to forget her beaming face.

Oh yes, said Mr. Kakehi, heroism and sangfroid were the orders of the day.

When in one ward a man's house was destroyed by a bomb, the neighbors went to him to offer their sympathies.

He smiled. "I am just one of the eight million Tokyoites to get a bomb hit. So I think I will draw a prize-winning *fukuken* [lottery ticket] next time."

By saying this, he not only relieved his neighbors' anxiety, but also treated his own calamity as a huge joke. . . .

So did millions of others, according to Mr. Kakehi. One of his colleagues would not stop going out to lunch, even when the air-raid sirens began to moan. "The first thing to do in an air raid," said this stalwart, "is to get something to eat. Keep your stomach full, you will then be ready for anything."

Among the other advantages of air raids cited by this writer was the fresh air that Tokyoites enjoyed, particularly in the winter, when forced out of their houses to seek shelter. This kept them from getting the flu. Also, an air raid was a wonderful time to go out into the garden and contemplate nature, as Mr. Kakehi did, looking out at the burning city through his bamboo grove.

But, of course, he was unlucky in a way, he said. His district of the city had gotten virtually no bombing. He did not really have adequate experience to enjoy the raids.

And he recalled for his readers the old Japanese saying, *Kaji wa Yedo no hana.* "Fires are the flowers of Tokyo."

What else could one expect from the barbarous Americans than that they would demolish the homes of millions of noncombatants? asked Mr. Kaheki. And he quoted Dr. Toyohiko Kagawa, a famous Christian minister: "America, which speaks of Christian morality, is today sending warplanes to those areas where she sent her missionaries to preach the gospel, and is slaughtering those 'sons of God' whom her missionaries baptized."

Every day in the press there appeared some sort of inspirational article about the tribulations and victories of those who were fighting for Japan on the home front and abroad. The perceived need for such articles was an indication of the depth of the American bite into Japanese morale. The raids came to Omura, to Kagoshima, to Yokkaichi and other smaller cities.

There was an almost frantic quality to the air raids now, and a reason for it. With the collapse of Germany, many more aircraft and many more American air forces were available to come to Japan. General Arnold was making plans to send General Carl Spaatz, General Nathan Twining, and General James Doolittle to the Pacific in preparation for the invasion of Japan. They all outranked General LeMay, who then would become a relatively small cog in a machine headed by General Spaatz. So General LeMay was trying desperately to make his mark. His announced reason was that he wanted to promote the creation of a separate air force. LeMay said that he still had some thirty to sixty industrial towns in Japan to attack, and that he expected singlehandedly to destroy Japan's capacity to make war by October 1.

The claim was, of course, fallacious to say the least, as the Strategic Bombing Survey records would later show. But LeMay indicated that he was confident he could do it. He was the only person in the Army Air Corps or elsewhere who believed in the theory. The other high officials were making plans for a desperate invasion of Japan in November, to involve over a million men and to cost hundreds of thousands of casualties.

LeMay went to Washington in June, and there was introduced to the atomic bomb. He did not quite understand what the scientists and military technicians were talking about, but he learned fast, and by the time he returned to the Marianas, he was prepared to deliver some atomic bombs.

Meanwhile, the firebombing of Japan went on. At least twice each week, the B-29s set out from the Marianas bases and hit more, and ever smaller, targets.

On July 20, General Spaatz arrived in Guam, and General LeMay was demoted to chief of staff of the Strategic Air Forces of the Pacific.

Still, Spaatz did not know the ropes yet, and so LeMay was able to continue his firebombing without complaint or interference. It was a time for experimentation, he decided, and one of his experiments was the bombing of the city of Tsu, on Honshu Island's Ise Bay, almost directly across the peninsula from Kyoto.

The attack on Tsu, planned for the night of July 29, was decided upon because LeMay wanted to test the effectiveness of the M-74 incendiary bomb. That bomb would be the only one employed in the Tsu attack. Of course, Tsu had been bombed before, but this was something different.

For several weeks the chemical section of the 20th Air Force had been trying to find a target for the M-74 bomb. Tsu was unlucky enough to fit the specifications. So was Aomori, another small city chosen for the same night's attack.

Another new technique was to be tried—it was not really new, but relatively so. The psychological warfare division and the 20th Air Force agreed that it could be useful for the B-29s to announce their attacks in advance. That decision was an indication of how effectively Halsey's strikes on the airfields and aircraft plants had been as his Third Fleet rampaged around Japan. Very few Japanese fighter planes now rose to challenge any American planes flying over the islands. So there was little danger in telegraphing the punches.

Leaflets were prepared and dropped several days before the attack date, and radio broadcasts were beamed to Japan by the Office of War Information, announcing that Tsu and Aomori would be attacked, and when and how.

The intelligence officers looked over the pictures and reports on the city. Tsu was an urban area built up of brick and concrete and wooden houses and buildings, a real mixture. Several industrial plants were located within the one square mile chosen for the attack. About eighty B-29s would be employed on this night, the planners said. Two groups from the 58th Wing should be able to do the job.

The people of Tsu had been making preparations for bombing ever since June, when it became apparent that the Americans were going to start firebombing smaller cities as well as the great ones of Japan. Thousands of families had moved their belongings into the hills above the city, and the children and old people remained there, while the able-bodied returned to the town houses with the aim of fighting the fires when they came.

On June 18 the B-29s had attacked Yokkaichi, which was not far from Tsu, and the Tsu chief of police had journeyed there following the attack to learn what he could about the experience. In the Yokkaichi attack, the Americans had used M-47 and M-69 bombs. The M-69 bombs could be extinguished with water, but the M-47s could not. So the chief went back to Tsu and informed the people about the types of bombs and instructed them that if their houses and factories were attacked by M-69 bombs, it was quite sensible to fight the fires. But if the bombs were the M-47s, then they would explode inside the roof of a house and start a fire that was almost immediately uncontrollable.

The people of Tsu were ready for anything. The Americans had already destroyed their hospital and police station in previous attacks. Most people believed the attack on the hospital was deliberate, and they gave the Americans more credit than they deserved for accurate aiming of the bombs. What they thought of American morality was another matter.

Since the firebombing began, the Home Ministry and the Munitions Ministry had been cooperating in the movement of factories to underground locations. An underground aircraft factory had been built at Tsu. The Americans did not have a clue about this, but the Japanese believed they knew, and that Tsu would be bombed because of it. The town also had a naval aircraft factory and an arsenal, another factory converted to airplane parts manufacture, and several other defense industries. Yes, Tsu was expecting trouble in July, even before the leaflets were dropped announcing the bombing to come.

Many of the leaflets fell on the hills around Tsu, which was a stroke of luck for the Americans seeking to communicate, since so many of the people of Tsu had gone into the hills.

So, on the appointed date, the bombers headed for Tsu. They came in at night as planned. The first bomber dropped its bombs at the northern edge of the city, and the second dropped at the southern edge. The other bombers used these fires to target the areas in between, and soon the city seemed to be ringed with fire. At this point, the firefighters gave up and fled to safety. In forty-five minutes the bombers dropped thousands of firebombs, and the fire spread over a square mile of the city center. The M-47 bomb was a great success. Nearly every building in the city center was either totally destroyed or gutted. The steel frames of the modern concrete buildings were twisted and torn to pieces. The machinery in the factories was destroyed—lathes, spinning machines, and other equipment. The Mie Textile Factory, which made army uniforms, went up in smoke. Here was an example of a fine modern building and what could be done to it by fire. Seven hundred thirty tons of incendiaries had been dropped on Tsu. Earlier the bombers had dropped about 600 tons of high-explosive bombs on the city, but the firebombs had done five times as much damage. Fire was the wave of the future.

There was no doubt in the mind of anyone in Japan that summer:
the "decisive battle" of the war would be fought in the homeland.
Yomiuri Shimbun discussed the idea openly in an article. It would be
the "god-sent opportunity for the 100 million inhabitants of the
Land of the Gods to finish off the enemy."

Virtually every day, one of the newspapers would publish a
pugnacious article promising that the Americans would be "totally
annihilated" once they hit the shores of Japan. The purpose was
to instill in the people the morale they needed to fight on the
beaches.

The problem of Tokyo defense grew worse as the people deserted the city. At the end of June the authorities organized a
Tokyo Volunteer Corps in all the wards of the city. The new
recruits were the old women and young children of the city. By
July 1, 1,200 such corps units were formed, with each consisting
of from 100 to 500 people.

The seriousness of the situation was made quite apparent when
the Emperor issued a special "Imperial Rescript" on June 22, authorizing and approving of the new military service regulations
that brought every Japanese under government control.

> Having appreciated the enthusiasm and ardor
> of Our loyal subjects to offer their services cou-
> rageously for the defense of the empire, thereby
> enhancing national prestige and glory at this
> juncture of unprecedented difficulties, We
> hereby sanction the Volunteer Military Service
> Law, which was adopted with the consent of the
> Imperial Diet, and order the promulgation.

All this fluffy language was to emphasize the Emperor's backing
of the military government of Japan, whose leaders now feared

that the Japanese people would not respond to their demands for them to be prepared to commit what amounted to mass suicide.

Late in June the government released some figures to show the extent of the barbarity of the enemy that the Japanese would now face. From April through June the Americans had burned 257,000 houses in Japan, thus making homeless over a million people. This was added to the more than one million people burned out by the first Tokyo fire raid. In Yokohama, not one of the worst-bombed cities by far, 600,000 people were homeless.

The Americans were bombing shrines, hospitals, schools, libraries, museums, and other public buildings in their eagerness to destroy Japan. Tokyo's Omiya Palace was burned, and all the trees in its lovely gardens were turned into blackened scarecrows. The Atsiya Shrine, the Hiei Shrine, the Shoin Shrine, the Togo Shrine, Zojoji Temple, Sengakuji Temple, Saiseikai Hospital, Matsukawa Hospital, and Johoku Hospital were all gone. Among the schools burned down were the Keio, Waseda, Bunrika, and Tokyo Agricultural universities, and dozens of high schools and primary schools.

The Chinese, Soviet, and Manchukuo embassies were partly burned, as were the old American embassy and the Italian embassy and a half-dozen others, either totally destroyed or damaged. In Chiyoda district, where the diplomats lived, much damage was done on those raids in the last week of May.

Once again the government was talking about spacing out the buildings with more fire lanes. The fact that the extent of the damage was now being revealed was an indication that the destruction was so great and so obvious that there was no point in trying to conceal it anymore.

Japan was now turned into a collection of war areas for army and navy. Even now, in the waning days, the army and navy could not bring themselves to operate under joint commands. This failure had been one of the principal weaknesses of Japan's war effort. It would continue. In Shikoku, for example, Rear Admiral Shunsaku Naboshima was appointed director of the naval division, while General Kumakichi Harada was named commander of the military division. And never the twain would meet, in all probability.

Three times in recent months, the Transportation Ministry had cut the train schedules, and on June 24 they did it again. In Tokyo, the electric trains that were the city's major transport were cut back another hour. This time it was admitted that the reason was the intensification of air raids, those glorious air raids that, according to Mr. Kakehi, brought the Tokyoites such joy that they wanted to laugh out loud.

On June 26, Imperial General Headquarters announced that on Okinawa, Lieutenant General Mitsuru Ushijima's Japanese forces had launched "their final attack" against the enemy. The people of Japan knew what that meant. It was all over on Okinawa. From this point on, the Americans would have an air base on the doorstep of Japan, and the air raids could not but get worse.

The answer?

The people must have the moral spirit to win, said Dr. Shinzo Koizumi, President of Keio University, in one of those intense propaganda articles written for the government in these desperate days.

The secret of victory lay within the people themselves, not in the material resources they might command. This was the familiar tocsin, ringing out the appeal to the people to give their lives for Japan.

On July 1 the government warned the people of Japan that the fall of Okinawa would bring those increased air assaults. This would mean B-24s and other aircraft would now be able to reach the home islands, and the B-29s would become less important.

All the more reason, then, for General LeMay to continue and even to intensify his fire bombing while he might. Kure was the target on the night of July 1, 1945.

Some eighty B-29s were used. They also bombed five other cities. The next day they were back, against another six cities. So many places, so many bombers, it was hard for the Japanese to keep track. On July 3 and 4, Himeji, Takumatsu, Tokushima, Kochi—places most Americans had never heard of—were now being destroyed as part of General LeMay's campaign to burn up Japan. In addition, P-51s and P-47s were coming in from Okinawa already. The pressure grew and grew.

Even small towns were being burned. On July 6, five towns around Chiba were burned. On July 12, about 150 B-29s hit Utsunomiya, Tsurumi, and Koriyama. These were pretty small pickings, but LeMay was determined. Again it was firebombs.

LeMay was competing now with the air force planes operating out of Okinawa and with Admiral Halsey's Third Fleet, which on July 15 continued its attacks on the Japanese homeland with a naval shelling of Muroran on Hokkaido, as well as with carrier attacks.

In mid-July, LeMay's bombers moved in on the Yokosuka Naval District, hitting such small places as Numazu, Hiratsuka, Odawara, Chigasaki, and Tsujido, which would not have been worth the effort if General LeMay had not made his vow. Most of these places had virtually no military significance. It was again a matter of bombing the people out of their houses.

The government now revealed that many thousands of Tokyo people were living in air-raid shelters in the burned-out areas of the city. They had returned to the burned out buildings and somehow patched them up enough or dug under them to provide shelter. It was a very intelligent approach. Even General LeMay was not likely to send bombers against totally destroyed sections of the Japanese cities.

The government took cognizance of this situation in late July, in discussions of what was to be done about the growing number of "sheds" that were springing up in Tokyo. The defense authorities claimed that these jerry-built structures created new air-raid dangers. But the people would not move out.

And it was not just in Tokyo. The success of LeMay's policy was attested to by the citizens of Shizuoka, a small city, where 20 percent of the people were now living in shacks, having been bombed out by the B-29s. Another 20 percent were living in the houses of relatives. Twenty-five percent had fled to other parts of Japan. Thirty-five percent had moved to farms and villages nearby. About 1,200 people were still living in air-raid shelters because they had no other place to go. The same sort of figures held for town after town. The situation of Japan was a tribute to the success of General LeMay's perspicacity: if higher authority would just let him alone, he would indeed burn up Japan.

. But as far as defense was concerned, something else was happening. The aircraft and other defense factories were moving underground, so that the enemy air attacks were ever less effective against Japan's ability to continue to wage war. Since the focus of the defense was going to be almost entirely on suicide attack, this boded ill for the survival of the first waves of attackers. The figures of possible employment and casualties went up in the Allied headquarters. Admiral Nimitz, in particular, knew very well that the Japanese aircraft industry was still powerful and posed a great threat for the invasion effort. Some officers were talking now about Allied casualties of a million men in the coming assault on Japan.

Then, near the end of July, General Spaatz handed General LeMay a letter from the War Department, authorizing the use of a new device, called an atomic bomb. Obviously, it was generally agreed that the device was so inhuman that it demanded special attention. A special organization of B-29s had been flown to Tinian Island, and on August 6, 1945, one of those aircraft carried out a mission against Hiroshima with a single atomic bomb. The result was the immediate death of 86,000 people.

The Japanese were called upon to surrender, but the Japanese military demurred. They could live with the atomic bomb, they said, just as they had learned to live with the firebombing. Then came the bombing of Nagasaki with another atomic bomb, and another 26,000 people died.

This bombing, plus the entry into the war of the Soviet Union, was too much. Emperor Hirohito took matters into his own hands and insisted on the surrender of Japan. Marquis Kido, one of his advisors, summed it all up when he said that the firebombings had been completely dreadful. But then the Americans had showed that they could kill almost as many people using just one aircraft with just one bomb, and that was the final straw.

General Curtis LeMay did not agree with that verdict. He always believed that the dropping of the atomic bombs was unnecessary and redundant. He had done the job, he said, with his firebombings of Japan. Indeed he had. The total number of people killed by the atomic bombs was 112,000 people. The total number of people killed by other bombing, most of it the B-29 bombing, was well over 200,000 people, and, considering what little is known of the total deaths in the Tokyo fire raid of March 10–11, 1945, may have been as high as 300,000 people. Besides this, the number of wounded, burned out, and otherwise afflicted people from the fire raids goes into the millions.

Ironically, the Japanese and General LeMay agree on one point, that the fire raids against Japan were the single most important factor in wrecking Japanese home morale and ruining the lives of civilians, most of them women and children.

More irony: General LeMay's service was great to the United States in terms of saving American lives by shortening the war, but it scarcely could be deemed a service to the people of Japan. Yet in 1964 General LeMay, who had become Chief of Staff of the United States Air Force, was decorated with the First Class Order of the Grand Cordon of the Rising Sun, the highest decoration that can be given by the Japanese government to a foreigner. To be sure, LeMay's decoration was symbolic; all of the American chiefs of staff got automatic decorations from America's staunch new ally, Japan. But in the case of "Devil LeMay," as the general had come to be known in Japan, many Japanese citizens believed and still believe an exception might have been made.

LeMay always believed that he had won the war against Japan with his firebombing, and many Japanese will agree with that. Katsumoto Saotome, who became the most prominent Japanese historian of the firebombings, says that after the Tokyo fire raid, the Japanese government ought to have surrendered, seeing the handwriting on the wall. That was, of course, asking too much of the Japanese militarists, who were determined never to say die, even if it meant sacrificing every Japanese man, woman, and child.

The firebombs did their awful job very well. By the end of the war, the Japanese people were completely worn out. As Takako Iga, one of those wounded and forever disfigured by the firebombing of Osaka, put it, "When we heard the Emperor's words, speaking of the surrender of Japan, we could only thank God. It meant that from that point on we could go to bed at night and be sure we would be alive when morning came."

That was the legacy of General LeMay.

One further irony remains. Once the war was ended, and the shock and horror of the Hiroshima and Nagasaki raids began to permeate the consciousness of the people of the world, all sorts of help came to the survivors of the atomic bombs. The Japanese government made provision for their assistance as well. But as for the survivors, ten times as many, of the firebombings of Japan, there was no help or any international attention. There was nothing romantic about the devastation of their lives. They just happened to be in the wrong place at the wrong time when General LeMay's B-29s came along.

Acknowledgments

I AM INDEBTED TO ORUGA HOITO FOR ALSO STANDING AND waiting during the weeks I spent in Japan on research for this book, as well as for research assistance at Maxwell Air Force Base in the historical files of the 20th Air Force, and for reading and editing the manuscript. Various people at the Albert F. Simpson Historical Research Center at the Air University there were also helpful, including Lynn O. Gamma, P. Bickerstaff, and Major Lester Sliter.

In Tokyo, I am particularly grateful to Seiichi Soeda of the Japan Press Center for many weeks of work in arranging interviews with survivors of the firebombings in Tokyo, Nagoya, Kobe, and Osaka. His assistance was superb.

I am indebted to Katsumoto Saotome, survivor of the Tokyo firebombing and the most prominent historian of the Japan firebombings of 1945; Masatake Obata, another survivor, who is devoting his life to the establishment of a Tokyo Air Raid Memorial Museum; Chisako Sugiyama of Nagoya; Dr. Hitoshi Koyama of Osaka, another historian of the firebombings; Shigeharu Kobayashi; Takako Iga; Masahisa Kimimoto; Kimiko Mikitani; Kumiko Yokoyama of Tokyo; Hideo Kanai of Tokyo; Mitsuro Kanai of Tokyo; Takeijiro Ueba of Tokyo; Satoko Sano of Tokyo; Niwa Koshiba of Tokyo; Kinosuke Wakabayashi of Tokyo; Katushiko Sakai, correspondent for *Chunichi Shimbun* in New York; Yukio Higuchi of Chuko Broadcasting Corp, Nagoya; Tsuneo

Acknowledgments

Misawa of Tokyo; Yoko Asakawa, interpreter, of Tokyo; Takashi Kaise of Tokyo; Masaki Yokozawa of Tokyo; Tetsuro Inoue of Tokyo; Yuzo Osawa of *Chunichi Shimbun*, Nagoya; Eiko Aoki of Tokyo; Kozo Adachi, director, Curatorial Division, Nagoya City Museum; and to various authorities of Kobe city, the firebombing museum, and the public library. Also, I am thankful to the Buddhist priest Satoshimi Goto of Kobe's Tanoshi Senji (Eternal Happiness Temple) for his hospitality. My interpreter and translator, Hiroko Hattori, did far more for me than could be expected, particularly after I returned from Japan. She answered a myriad of questions about proper names, and matters dealing with the Japan of the war years. In this she enlisted many of her friends and I am grateful to them all.

Hoito Edoin
November 1986

Bibliographical Note

I used the following materials:

Coffey, Thomas M. *Iron Eagle: The Turbulent Life of General Curtis LeMay*. New York: Crown, 1986.

Hoyt, Edwin P. *Japan's War*. New York: McGraw-Hill, 1986.

Records, XXI Bomber Command, 20th Air Force, 1945.

Japan Times, 1945

Mainichi Shimbun, 1945

Asahi Shimbun, 1945

Kobe kushu taiken ki (Account of the Kobe Air Raids), by Fusa Tsudori

Tokyo dai kushu kyugo taichu no kiroku (Great Tokyo Air Raid's Rescue Leader's Records), by Kubota Shigeru.

Osaka dai kushu (Osaka Great Air Raids), by Koyama Hitoshi

Nagoya dai kushu taiken suru au (An Account of the Great Nagoya Air Raids), by the editors of *Chunichi Shimbun*

Seitachi no ki (The Story of My Life), by Sano Satoko

Sono bi o seki tsudzukete (The Day Life Continued), by Koya Aoki

Tokyo dai kushu (The Great Tokyo Air Raids), by Saotome Katsumoto

Nagoya dai kushu ten (Nagoya Great Air Raid Display), by the editors of *Chunichi Shimbun*

Tokyo ga moeta bi (The Day They Burned Tokyo), by Saotome Katsumoto

Nagoya shiro (Nagoya Castle), by Yamada Akiei

And many pamphlets, documents, clippings, and records furnished by Japan's National Liaison Committee for Citizens Wounded by Air

Bibliographical Note

Raids; the Kobe Group to Record Air Raids; the Air Raids Reference Room of the Nagoya Municipal Museum; the Osaka Shakai Fukushi Kaikan; Kobe Central City Library; and the Japan Foreign Press Center.

Index

Aircraft industry, 33, 34, 205, 211
Aircraft production, 19–20, 21
Air-raid defense, 6, 25, 26–30, 48, 58–59, 109, 123, 129–30, 157, 167–68; criticism of, 125; Nagoya, 173–74, 179; Osaka, 133–34, 137; press reports, 194–95; see also Antiaircraft defense
Air Raid General Defense Headquarters, 26
Air-raid shelters, 2, 29–30, 49, 51, 52, 187, 197–98; homeless living in, 236, 237; lack of, 118, 127
Air-sea rescue efforts (U.S.), 116, 153, 164, 174
Akiyama, Kuni, 47
Aleutians, 48
Allies, 4, 18, 24
Ando, General, 30
Anshan, Manchuria, 12
Antiaircraft defense, 6, 15, 39, 46, 110–11, 116, 130, 133–34, 173, 176; lack of, 157; navy in, 31
Aomori, 230, 231
Arnold, H. H., 34, 172, 182, 185, 229
Atomic bomb, 230, 237–38, 239
Attu Island, 48
Axis, 3–4

B-29 bombers (Super fortresses), 10–22, 182; attacks on Japanese cities, 1–3, 4, 5, 9, 14–16, 19, 20, 27, 31, 34, 36–39; crew morale, 39; effectiveness of bombing raids, 4, 14, 15, 17, 18, 21, 34, 114–15, 237, 239; fighter support, 37, 110–11, 174, 196; flying without guns, gunners, 41, 43, 81, 146, 152–53;

B-29 bombers (Super fortresses) (con't) losses, 4, 5, 11, 12, 14, 15, 16–17, 20, 21, 109, 133, 145, 147, 164, 183, 213–14; numbers of, in raids, 46, 58, 78, 109, 159, 164, 175, 179, 199, 201, 203, 206; production of, 6; used to lay mines, 184–85; see also Firebombing raids
Bangkok, 11
Berlin, 18, 156
"Blind bombing," 16, 35, 56, 159
Burma, 4, 24, 97

Cairo Conference, 10
Caroline Islands, 13
Chiang Kai-shek, 10
Chichi Jima, 46, 133
Chikushi, Jiro, 47
China, 7, 18, 24; bases in, 10, 11, 13, 17
Chujo, Takisei, 208–10
Chungking, 50
Churchill, Winston, 10
Civil defense, 27–30, 112–14, 118; responsibility for, 48, 51, 92, 113–14, 130; Tokyo, 48–52, 186–90, 197, 227–28
Civilian casualties, 18, 148, 238; atomic bomb, 237; Kobe raid, 162, 163; Nagoya, 114–15, 117, 175, 179, 180, 181, 204; Osaka, 146–47; Tokyo, 78, 100–1, 102–3, 106, 200, 201
Civilians: American attacks on, 17–18, 22, 100, 120, 234, 239

Dai Nippon Mothers' Association, 8
Domei (news agency), 154–57, 194–95
Doolittle, James, 14–15, 47, 112, 129, 229

Index

Dresden, 18
Dutch East Indies, 7
Dutch New Guinea, 24

European Theater, 177
Evacuation of cities, 8, 118, 121, 138, 158, 166, 189–90, 201

Fighter planes (Japanese), 14, 15, 20, 26, 133, 134, 152–53, 165, 174, 176–77, 194–95; lack of, 230–31
Fire storm(s), 117, 121, 152; Tokyo, 69, 73–74, 77, 83, 84, 88, 91, 110, 186, 201
Firebombing raids, 17–18, 218, 226–32, 234, 234–37, 238–39; American justification for, 114; bomb mix, 2, 114, 154, 195, 199, 202, 206–7, 215–16, 231; Kobe, 37, 40, 150–63, 168–69, 173, 174, 203–14, 218–25, 226; Nagoya, 37, 40, 112–18, 120–21, 128, 135, 137, 146, 147, 151–52, 172–81, 186, 203–4, 215; Osaka, 37, 40, 131–49, 151–52, 153, 158, 206, 207–14, 215, 218, 226; results of, 95–108, 109–10, 116–18, 119–28, 150, 158, 165, 169, 171, 172, 175–76, 177, 179, 180–81, 182–83, 201–2, 216, 236–37; tactics, techniques, 36–39, 109, 110, 116, 137–38, 147, 155–56, 173, 178, 195–97, 215–25, 230–31; Tokyo, 37–38, 40, 41–46, 47, 58–76, 77–94, 95–108, 109–10, 117–18, 120–21, 122–24, 125–26, 127, 128, 135, 137, 146, 147, 150, 152, 158, 195–202, 206, 215–16, 217, 226, 228–29, 234, 238
Firefighting, 113–14, 173, 195–96, 197, 206, 207, 231; futility of, 140–41; responsibility for, 219; Tokyo, 72, 77, 92, 122–23, 199–200, 201; women of Tokyo, 227–28
Food supplies, 7, 69–70, 216–17
Formosa, 13
Fujimoto, Kenji, 196
Fukuoka, 168, 226

Germany, 3–4, 18, 47, 48; collapse of, 205, 229
Goto, Satoshi, 163
Great Japan Air Defense Association, 30
Grew, Joseph, 53
Guadalcanal, 47
Guam, 13, 19, 20, 38, 42, 55, 132, 153, 159, 165, 174, 205

Halsey, William F., 112, 205–6, 226, 230, 236
Hamburg, Germany, 18, 156
Hammatsu, 51–52, 81, 82, 218
Hankow, China, 18
Hansell, Haywood S., 13
Hanshin, 218
Harada, Kumakichi, 234–35
Harino, Masuko, 67–68, 84–86
Hashimoto, Seizo, 68, 86
Hayashi, Matsuo, 74
Hayauchi, Captain, 55
Hideyoshi, Kaneko, 74–75, 93–94
Higashikuni, Naruhiko, 16, 50
High-altitude precision bombing, 21, 22; effectiveness of, 34, 35, 36, 114–15
Hiratsuka, Saki, 65–66, 84, 187
Hirohito, emperor of Japan, 2, 5, 24–25, 107–8, 125–26, 127, 165–66, 184, 196; "Imperial Rescript," 233; and surrender of Japan, 237–38
Hirose, Osamu, 196
Hiroshima, 2; atomic bomb, 163, 237, 239
Hokkaido, 130, 134
Homeless, 78, 106, 146, 147, 162, 234
Homma, Masaharu, 32–33
Honda, Takashi, 19
Honshu, 13, 97, 134, 185

Iga, Takako, 239
Iguchi, Sadao, 169–70
Ikuma, Takeo, 218–25
Imajiyo, Kinoseko, 134–37, 149
Imperial General Headquarters (IGH), 12, 16–17, 32, 126, 169, 194, 196, 207, 226, 235; on bombings, 1, 2, 25, 116, 147, 158, 183; propaganda, 3, 4–5, 7, 15, 147–48
Imperial General Staff, 129–30
Imperial Japanese Navy and Combined Fleet, 24
Imperial Palace, 21, 95, 107, 200, 206, 216
Imperial Rescript(s), 2, 233
Imperial Rule Assistance Association, 107
Imperial Way, 188, 190
Incendiary bombs, 22, 35–39, 41, 59–60, 64, 77–94, 110, 111, 115, 133; lack of, 154, 173, 176, 186; new, 230–32; see also Magnesium bombs
India, 10, 11, 17, 21
Indochina, 7
Industry: cottage (feeder), 8–9, 22, 42, 69, 123, 132, 184; dispersal of, 123, 189, 197

Index

Ishiuchi, Kiku, 52

Italy, 4

Iwo Jima, 4, 13–14, 17, 20, 37, 45, 97, 115, 155, 196; base, 38, 110–11, 164–65, 177, 208; fall of, 21, 54, 55, 189, 207–8

Japan: belief could not be invaded, 30, 50, 56–57, 134, 137, 237; Cabinet, 121, 124, 166; defenses, 23–33, 46, 110–11 (see also Air-raid defense); Diet, 24, 106, 107; Foreign Office, 123; home islands (Hondo), 134; Home Ministry, 26, 27, 28, 30, 51, 118, 119–20, 123, 124–25, 126, 130, 148, 166, 180, 195, 217, 219, 232; Inner Empire, 134, 183; preparations for invasion of, 127–18, 233–34, 237; Privy Council, 23; sacred territory, 134; Supreme Council for the Direction of the War, 24, 26; surrender, 238

Japanese air force, 1–2, 5, 7, 11, 12; see also Kamikaze pilots; Ramming attacks

Japanese Army, 130, 314, 190, 196

Japanese government, 7, 166, 190; and air raids, 226–27; Cabinet Ministers' council for relief of air-raid victims, 167–68; decorations to U.S. chiefs of staff, 238; and defense of industry, 197–98; information bureau, 117; keeping results of raids from people, 157–58, 168–69, 194; press policy, 120, 168–69; see also Militarist government

Japanese navy, 31

Japanese people: apathy, 158, 182–83; effect of firebombing raids on, 117–118, 182–83, 184, 196, 238; knowledge that war was lost, 7, 50, 93, 108, 118, 183, 188; morale, 2, 32, 48, 49, 57, 123, 124–25, 126, 127, 158, 165, 180, 229; war-weariness, 148; will to fight, 16, 17, 20, 24, 39, 41, 52–53, 121–22, 183, 189, 233–34, 235

Kagawa, Toyohiko, 229

Kagoshima, 218, 229

Kakehi, Mitsuaki, 227–29, 235

Kamikaze attacks, 170, 203, 205

Kamikaze pilots, 31, 171, 183, 185, 190, 193; see also "Wild eagles" (suicide pilots)

Kanto Plain, 2, 3, 25, 51, 58–59, 196

Kawabe, Lt. Gen., 50

Kawasaki, 201–2

Kido, Marquis, 23, 238

Kikusui attacks, 205

King, Ernest J., 185

Kobe, 121, 130, 178; aftermath of raid on, 164–71; see also Firebombing raids, Kobe

Kochi City, 2, 236

Kodama, Hideo, 188

Koiso, Kuniaki, 24, 107, 126, 165, 189; fall of government of, 196

Koizumi, Shinzo, 235

Korea, 24, 134

Koriyama, 236

Koshiba, Aiyawa, 61, 62, 79–81

Koshiba, Ichibei, 61

Koshiba, Miwa, 60–62, 79–81

Koshiba, Yae, 61

Koyama, Hitoshi, 136

Kubota, Shigenori, 95–104

Kurai, Toshizo, 196

Kure, 203, 235

Kuribayashi, Lt. Gen., 55

Kurusu, Ryo, 1–2

Kurusu, Saburo, 1

Kushimoto, 133, 250

Kyushu Island, 11, 97, 130, 134, 185, 190, 193, 203

LeMay, Curtis, 12, 19, 34, 69, 81, 109, 121, 123, 128, 135, 148, 156, 164, 177, 190, 206, 211; decorated by Japanese government, 238; demoted, 230; firebombing strategy, 17–18, 20–21, 22, 26, 35–36, 37, 43, 110–11, 119, 128, 131–32, 147, 150, 152–53, 154, 172–73, 174, 177, 182, 184, 185, 186, 196, 199, 201, 202, 203, 204, 205, 216, 218, 229–30, 235, 236, 237, 238

Leyte Island, 4, 13, 16, 19

Lockwood, Charles, 7

London, 18, 48

Luzon Island, 55

Magnesium bombs, 154, 160, 199, 206, 215, 220

Mainichi Shimbun, 51–52, 81, 82, 125, 168

Manchuria (Manchuko), 24, 31, 130

Mariana Islands, 11, 12–13, 26, 55; base, 13, 21, 35, 36, 37, 50, 115, 128, 155, 177, 199, 204, 207, 230, U.S. capture of, 5, 6

Marshall, George C., 185

Marshall Islands, 55

Index

Matsumura, Shutsu, 54–55
Medical supplies: lack of, 91, 96–97, 103, 104, 144, 224
Mikitani, Kimiko, 159–62
Militarist government (*Gunbatsu*), 148, 233–34
Militarists, 23, 30, 108, 122, 148, 239
Mitsubishi factories, 17, 18, 19, 20, 112, 114–15, 117, 179, 180, 197, 204, 215
Mobilization, total, 53–54, 114, 169
Moral strength, 190, 235
Moro, Kenji, 74, 93
Mukden, 17, 18
Muroran, 236
Musashino aircraft factory, 14, 16, 20, 21, 34
Mussolini, Benito, 3–4

Nagano, Adm., 50
Nagasaki, 154; atomic bomb, 163, 237, 239
Nagata Death Band, 55
Nagazumi, Torahiko, 126
Nagoya, 3, 17, 18, 19, 20, 121, 130; see also Firebombing raids, Nagoya
Nakamura, Shizue, 162
National Labor Mobilization Ordinance, 53–54
Night fighters: Japanese, 26, 37, 58, 59, 157; U.S., 12–13
Nimitz, Chester, 19, 20, 21, 190, 204, 205, 237; B-29 use, 177, 184–85, 203
Nishio, Toshizo, 126
Norstad, Lauris, 12
Numazu, 205, 236

Obata, Masatake, 69–72, 88–91
Obata, Mrs., 70, 89–90
Odachi, Shigeo, 189–90
O'Donnell, Emmett, 14
Ogata, Junichi, 19, 196
Ohnishi, Takejiro, 170–71
Oita, 204, 205
Okada, Adm., 23
Okayama, 2, 13
Okinawa, 193, 196, 205, 236; fall of, 235; invasion of, 37, 185, 190
Okuzaki, 204
Omura, 11, 229
Ono, Kimie, 63–65, 82–84
Ono, Toraji, 104
Osaka, 121, 129–31, 150, 168, 178; see also Firebombing raids, Osaka
Oshima, Sanjiro, 138, 139–45, 147, 148
Oshima, Shinichi, 138–45, 147

Oshima, Shiyo, 138, 140, 142, 144, 147, 148
Oshima, Takako, 138–45, 147

Pacific Theater, 10
Pearl Harbor, 171, 205
Philippines, 4, 13, 17, 19, 24, 32, 97, 170, 183
Powers, Thomas, 88
Propaganda (Japanese), 3, 6, 25, 92, 117, 127–28, 147–48, 170
Propaganda leaflet campaign (U.S.), 53, 125, 126, 130–31, 148, 166, 231–32
Press (Japanese), 7, 17, 18–19, 47, 48, 117, 125–26, 155–57, 166–67, 193–95; coverage of firebombing raids, 120–21, 157–58; government policy regarding, 120, 168–69
Psychological warfare (U.S.), 16, 156, 165, 197, 230

Radar: bombing by (U.S.), 34, 159, 164; Japanese, 58, 134
Radio Tokyo, 106, 116, 121–22, 148, 177–79, 187
Ramming attacks (*taiatari*), 15, 16–17, 19, 31, 116, 133, 196
Refugee centers, 126
Refugees, 118, 119–20, 187
Roosevelt, Franklin D., 10
Ryukyus, 134

Saipan Island, 11–12, 13, 16, 17, 38, 42, 44; base, 132, 159, 165, 174; battle for, 183; fall of, 7, 15, 23, 24, 50, 55
Sakai, Tatsu, 75, 94
Sakamoto, Chiyoko, 68–69, 86–88
Samamoto, Masawi, 25–26
Sano, Satoko, 62–63, 81–82
Saotome, Katsumoto, 72–73, 91–93, 191–93, 238–39
Sasebo, 11
Sensue, Yoshi, 210, 211, 212–13
Shibayama, Kenshiro, 189
Shikoku, 2, 134, 234
Shimada, Toshio, 24
Shimizu, Goro, 32
Shirama, 133
Shizuoka, 203, 236–37
Shunsaku, Rear Adm., 234
Singapore, 21
Solomons, 55
Soviet Union, 4, 237
Spaatz, Carl, 229, 230, 237
Strategic bombing, 20, 22, 182; see also Firebombing raids

Index

Students: mobilization of, 187–88

Sugiyama, Field Marshal, 107, 177, 180

Suicide attacks, 3, 20, 237; see also Kamikaze attacks; Ramming attacks

Suicide pilots, 25–26, 31–32, 145; see also Kamikaze pilots; "Wild eagles" (suicide pilots)

Suzuki, Kantaro, 196

Taiwan, 134, 185

Takumatsu, 236

Takushima, 218, 236

Tatsukawa, 203, 218, 226

Teisaki, Hiroko, 153–54

"Thought control police," 48, 124, 148, 180

Tinian, 11, 13, 16, 17, 38, 42, 44, 55, 132, 159, 165, 174, 203, 237

Tobata, 11

Tojo, Hideki, 6, 30, 32, 50, 190

Tojo government, 23–24, 118

Tokudaiji, Sansatsu, 126

Tokyo, 167, 168, 232–34, 236; antiaircraft guns, 130; bombing raids, 1–2, 3, 5, 9, 14–16, 21, 27, 31, 35–36 (see also Firebombing raids, Tokyo); civil defense, 27–30, 48–52, 186–90; defense ordinance, 166–67

Tolischus, Otto, 184

Total warfare concept, 18, 123

Toyobashi, 226

Tsu, 230–32

Tsumano, Toyo, 104

Tsurumi, 236

Twining, Nathan, 229

Ueba, Aichi, 60

Ueba, Takeiro, 60, 78–79

Ueba, Ueko, 60

Ueba, Umeko, 60

Uji Yamada, 133

Umehara, Saburo, 5

Unconditional surrender: demand for, 4, 183, 184

United States: Joint Chiefs of Staff, 10, 18, 128, 184, 185, 197, 202; Office of War Information, 231; preparation for invasion of Japan, 205–6, 229, 230, 237

U.S. Army Air Force, 13–14

U.S. Army Air Forces Headquarters, 34

U.S. Navy, 170–71, 177, 185; carrier task force, 1; kamikaze attacks on, 203, 205; Pacific Fleet, 7, 20; Third Fleet, 236

Ushijima, Mitsuru, 235

Utsunomiya, 236

Volunteer Corps: Nagoya, 114; Toklo, 98, 233

Volunteer Students' Brigade, 191

Wakabayashi, Kinosuke, 73–74, 93

War effort (Japan), 7, 10, 11, 42, 53–54, 112, 114; effect of U.S. bombing on, 4, 123, 237; weaknesses in, 234–35

War work: home industries in, 8–9, 22, 42, 69, 123, 132, 184

"Wild eagles" (suicide pilots), 16–17, 18–19, 145, 183, 195, 196, 207–8; see also Kamikaze pilots

Winds, 11, 35, 39, 58–59, 109, 117, 123, 152, 176, 218

Wooden structures, 49, 113, 151, 154, 201

Yamamoto, Katsuko, 104–5

Yamaoka, Koji, 210–13, 215

Yawata, 12

Yokkaichi, 229, 231

Yokohama, 16, 121, 205, 206, 234

Yokozawa, Chiyoko, 76

Yokozawa, Maasaki, 76

Yoshie, Koiko, 75–76, 94

Yoshizawa, Heikichi, 5

Yoshizumi, Masao, 190